# Inhaltsverzeichnis

\* Hierbei handelt es sich um eine offizielle Musteraufgabe des Ministeriums für Kultus, Jugend und Sport Baden-Württemberg.

| Übungsaufgabe Kommunikationsprüfung

| Original-Prüfungsaufgaben

**Hörverstehen 2023** .................................. **www.stark-verlag.de/mystark**

Sobald die Original-Prüfungsaufgaben 2023 freigegeben sind, können Sie über die Plattform MyStark darauf zugreifen (Zugangscode vgl. Umschlaginnenseite).

Sollten nach Erscheinen dieses Bandes noch wichtige Änderungen in der Abiturprüfung 2024 vom Kultusministerium bekannt gegeben werden, finden Sie aktuelle Informationen dazu ebenfalls auf der Plattform MyStark.

2024

# Abitur

Original-Prüfungsaufgaben
mit Lösungen

Gymnasium Baden-Württemberg

## Englisch LF

**STARK**

## Audio-Dateien

 Hörverstehen Übungsaufgabe 1
Hörverstehen Übungsaufgabe 2
Hörverstehen Übungsaufgabe 3
Hörverstehen Übungsaufgabe 4
Hörverstehen Übungsaufgabe 5
Abiturprüfung 2021
Abiturprüfung 2022
Abiturprüfung 2023

Auf die Audio-Dateien können Sie ebenfalls über die Plattform MyStark zugreifen.

## Autorinnen und Autoren

Hinweise und Tipps: Andrea Bailer, Sonja Corleis, Dr. Dirk Großklaus, Rainer Jacob, Elena Nowitzki
Lösungen Übungsaufgaben 1 bis 3 (Hörverstehen): Dr. Andrea Pelmter
Übungsaufgabe 1 (Textaufgabe): Andrea Bailer, Elena Nowitzki
Übungsaufgabe 2 (Textaufgabe): Rainer Jacob
Übungsaufgabe 4 (Hörverstehen): Paul Jenkinson
Übungsaufgabe 5 (Hörverstehen): Constantin Rieske
Lösungen offizielle Musteraufgaben: Dr. Dirk Großklaus, Henning Christiansen
Übungsaufgaben Kommunikationsprüfung: Clemens Arnold/Redaktion
Lösungen Abiturprüfungsaufgaben (Hörverstehen): Dorothée Just
Lösungen Abiturprüfungsaufgaben (Textaufgaben): Dr. Dirk Großklaus

# Vorwort

Liebe Schülerin, lieber Schüler,

bald werden Sie Ihre Abiturprüfung im Leistungsfach Englisch ablegen. Wir begleiten Sie auf Ihrem Weg zu einem guten Abschluss und helfen Ihnen, sich mit den Anforderungen des Abiturs in Baden-Württemberg vertraut zu machen.

In diesem Band finden Sie verschiedene Möglichkeiten, sich vorzubereiten:

- Im Kapitel „**Hinweise und Tipps zum Abitur**" sind wichtige Fakten zum Abitur im Leistungsfach Englisch zusammengefasst. Außerdem finden Sie hier wertvolle Tipps zu den **Prüfungs- und Aufgabenformen** sowie eine **Liste von Operatoren**.
- Mit den **abiturähnlichen Übungsaufgaben** können Sie für die Prüfung trainieren. Alle Sets bestehen – genau wie Ihre Prüfung auch – aus einem **Hörverstehensteil** und einer **Textaufgabe**. Bei drei der fünf Textaufgaben handelt es sich um die offiziellen, vom Ministerium gestellten **Musteraufgaben**. Sie können sich hier also einen Eindruck von den im Abitur möglichen Aufgabenformaten verschaffen. Zugriff auf die dazugehörigen Audio-Dateien erhalten Sie über die Plattform „MyStark". Die Textaufgaben sind, genau wie Ihre Abituraufgaben, auch entweder auf das **Schwerpunktthema** „The Ambiguity of Belonging" oder auf weitere Themen des Oberstufenlehrplans abgestimmt. Auf das Schwerpunktthema sowie auf weitere abiturrelevante Inhalte können Sie sich optimal mit unserem „**AbiturSkript – Englisch – Baden-Württemberg**" (Bestell-Nr.: 8546S2) vorbereiten.
- Die **Übungsaufgabe zur Kommunikationsprüfung** führt Ihnen mögliche Fragestellungen und Arbeitsstrategien im mündlichen Teil Ihres Abiturs vor.
- Den **Original-Prüfungen 2021 und 2022** liegen zwar zum Teil noch andere Aufgabenformate zugrunde, dennoch können Sie sich auch mit diesen auf mögliche Themenschwerpunkte Ihrer eigenen Prüfung vorbereiten. Die **Original-Aufgaben zum Hörverstehen** (2021/2022 im Buch, 2023 auf MyStark) entsprechen exakt den Aufgabenformaten, die Sie in Ihrer Prüfung erwarten.
- Zu jeder Aufgabe haben unsere Autorinnen und Autoren vollständig auf Englisch ausformulierte **Lösungen** und **Bearbeitungshinweise** erstellt.

Viel Erfolg bei Ihrer Abiturprüfung!

# Hinweise zu den digitalen Zusätzen

Auf alle digitalen Zusätze können Sie online über die Plattform **MyStark** zugreifen. Ihren persönlichen Zugangscode finden Sie auf der Umschlaginnenseite, vorne im Buch.

## PDF der Original-Prüfungsaufgaben 2023

Um Ihnen die Prüfung 2023 schnellstmöglich zur Verfügung stellen zu können, bringen wir sie in digitaler Form heraus.
Sobald die Original-Prüfungsaufgaben 2023 freigegeben sind, können Sie über die Plattform MyStark darauf zugreifen.

## Lernvideos

Textaufgaben sind Teil vieler Prüfungen und Klausuren – und machen oft einen Großteil der Prüfungsleistung aus. Mithilfe der **Lernvideos zum richtigen Umgang mit Textaufgaben** können Sie sich optimal auf die Anforderungen in diesem Bereich vorbereiten. Am Beispiel von zwei Texten mit je drei Aufgabenstellungen wird gezeigt, wie man an Textaufgaben herangeht und sie erfolgreich löst.

**Die Lernvideos beinhalten:**

- **Schritt-für-Schritt-Anleitungen** zum richtigen Vorgehen anhand exemplarischer Aufgabenstellungen
- **Sachtext** und **literarischer Text** als Grundlage
- nützliche Hinweise zu **häufigen Operatoren** und **Zieltextsorten**

## MP3-Dateien

Über die Plattform **MyStark** können Sie sich außerdem die Hörverstehens-texte der Übungsaufgaben sowie der Abiturprüfungen 2021 bis 2023 anhören.

## Interaktives Training

Im **Online-Training „Basic Language Skills"** erhalten Sie Zugriff auf zahlreiche **interaktive Aufgaben** zu Grundlagen wie **Hörverstehen, Leseverstehen** und **Sprachverwendung im Kontext**. Dies sind ganz wichtige „Basics", die Sie für eine gute Sprachbeherrschung brauchen.

**Das interaktive Training bietet Ihnen:**

* **„Listening"** – authentische Audiodateien mit vielfältigen Aufgaben, die Ihr Hörverstehen testen
* **„Reading"** – abwechslungsreiche Lesetexte und dazugehörige Aufgaben
* **„English in Use"** mit gemischten Aufgaben rund um den Gebrauch der englischen Sprache
* Alle Aufgaben können Sie direkt am PC oder Tablet bearbeiten und erhalten sofort eine Rückmeldung zu Ihren Antworten.

## Web-App „MindCards"

Mit der Web-App **„MindCards"** können Sie am Smartphone Vokabeln lernen. Auf diesen interaktiven Karteikarten finden Sie hilfreiche Wendungen, die Sie beim Schreiben von Texten oder im mündlichen Sprachgebrauch einsetzen können.
Scannen Sie einfach die QR-Codes oder verwenden Sie folgende Links, um zu den „MindCards" zu gelangen:
https://www.stark-verlag.de/mindcards/writing-2
https://www.stark-verlag.de/mindcards/speaking-2

Writing

Speaking

# Stichwortverzeichnis Textaufgaben

HINWEISE UND TIPPS

# Hinweise und Tipps zum Abitur

## Allgemeine Hinweise und Tipps zum Abitur

Die schriftliche Abiturprüfung im Leistungsfach Englisch wird durch eine Kommunikationsprüfung ergänzt.
Die Aufgaben in diesem Buch beziehen sich hauptsächlich auf die schriftliche Abiturprüfung. Außerdem können Sie sich mithilfe einer Übungsaufgabe auf die Kommunikationsprüfung vorbereiten.

## Die schriftliche Abiturprüfung

Die schriftliche Abiturprüfung im Leistungsfach Englisch umfasst einen **Hörverstehensteil** sowie den **Prüfungsteil Schreiben**. Für letzteren wählen Sie aus zwei Texten (literarischer Text oder Sachtext, mit oder ohne Bezug zum Schwerpunktthema) einen aus und bearbeiten den dazugehörigen Aufgabenapparat. Dieser besteht jeweils aus einer **Leseverständnisaufgabe**, einer **Textanalyseaufgabe** und einer *Composition*, wobei Sie für letztere zwischen einer persönlichen Stellungnahme und einer kreativen, gestaltenden Aufgabe wählen können.

### Bearbeitungszeit und erlaubte Hilfsmittel

Die schriftliche Prüfung im Fach Englisch dauert 255 Minuten, wovon 30 Minuten auf den Hörverstehensteil entfallen. In den restlichen 225 Minuten ist auch die Zeit eingerechnet, die Sie benötigen, um sich während der Prüfung zwischen alternativen Texten und Aufgaben zu entscheiden.
Als Hilfsmittel stehen Ihnen ein einsprachiges und ein zweisprachiges **Wörterbuch** sowie ein Nachschlagewerk zur deutschen Rechtschreibung zur Verfügung.

I

## Prüfungsinhalte und Ablauf

### Prüfungsteil Hörverstehen

Ihre Prüfung beginnt mit dem Hörverstehensteil. Hier werden Ihnen mehrere authentische Hörtexte in der Fremdsprache vorgespielt, zu denen Sie nach jeweils zweimaligem Anhören **geschlossene und halboffene Fragestellungen** beantworten müssen (vgl. hierzu die möglichen Aufgabenformate auf S. VIII/IX). Ein Einzeltext sollte fünf Minuten nicht überschreiten und meistens wird Ihre Prüfung aus drei bis vier voneinander unabhängigen Hörtexten bestehen. Die Texte stammen aus verschiedenen thematischen Bereichen, wie beispielsweise Politik, Zeitgeschichte, Kultur oder Lebenswelt von Jugendlichen und können Reden, Radiobeiträge, Diskussionen, Gespräche oder Interviews sein. Ein Bezug zum Schwerpunktthema muss nicht gegeben sein. Die authentischen Aufnahmen können Herausforderungen aufweisen, die das Hörverstehen erschweren (z. B. Hintergrundgeräusche, wechselndes Sprechtempo, von der Standardsprache abweichende Varietäten). Nach 30 Minuten ist der Hörverstehensteil der Prüfung beendet und die dazugehörigen Aufgaben werden eingesammelt, sodass Sie sich nun voll und ganz auf den zweiten Prüfungsteil, die Textaufgabe, konzentrieren können.

### Prüfungsteil Schreiben allgemein

Für diesen Prüfungsteil dürfen Sie entweder einen literarischen Text oder einen Sachtext, jeweils mit dazugehöriger Aufgabenstellung, zur Bearbeitung auswählen. Beide Texte werden eine Länge von maximal 1 000 Wörtern aufweisen. Einer der zur Wahl stehenden Texte bezieht sich auf das **Schwerpunktthema**. Das geltende Schwerpunktthema lautet „**The Ambiguity of Belonging**". Der dazugehörige Pflichtkanon umfasst Tom Franklins Roman *Crooked Letter, Crooked Letter* sowie Clint Eastwoods Film *Gran Torino*. Der zweite Prüfungstext wird weitere **landeskundliche Themengebiete** behandeln. Da Sie vorher nicht wissen, welcher der beiden Texte und welche Aufgabenstellungen Ihnen besser liegen, sollten Sie sich darauf einstellen, dass Sie für die Prüfung gute Kenntnisse in beiden Bereichen benötigen. Für die inhaltliche Vorbereitung empfehlen wir das „AbiturSkript Englisch Baden-Württemberg" (Bestellnr. 8546S2). Darin finden Sie umfassende Informationen zu *Crooked Letter, Crooked Letter* und *Gran Torino* sowie zu weiteren prüfungsrelevanten Aspekten des Schwerpunktthemas und anderer landeskundlicher Bereiche.

### Prüfungsteil Schreiben – Teilaufgabe Leseverstehen

In der ersten Aufgabe zum Text wird geprüft, ob Sie dessen Inhalt verstanden haben. Im Abschnitt „Prüfungs- und Aufgabenformen" können Sie genauer nachlesen, was Sie in diesem Prüfungsteil erwartet und wie Sie sich darauf vorbereiten können.

### Prüfungsteil Schreiben – Teilaufgabe Analyse

Die zweite Aufgabe im Prüfungsteil Schreiben bezieht sich ebenfalls auf den Text, den Sie bereits in der Leseverstehensaufgabe bearbeitet haben. Sie sollen nun aber nicht mehr nur zusammenfassen, was im Text gesagt wird, sondern die dargestellten Inhalte bzw. die Aussageabsicht des Textes im Detail analysieren. Hier geht es also um sprachliche Mittel, den Aufbau des Textes o. Ä. Eventuell wird Ihnen zusätzlich zum Ausgangstext auch noch weiteres Material, wie z. B. ein Foto oder eine Statistik, zur Verfügung gestellt, welches Sie dann zum Text in Bezug setzen müssen. Detaillierte Informationen dazu, wie Sie eine Analyseaufgabe am besten bearbeiten, finden Sie im Abschnitt „Prüfungs- und Aufgabenformen".

### Prüfungsteil Schreiben – Persönliche Stellungnahme bzw. gestaltende Schreibaufgabe

Für die dritte Teilaufgabe im Prüfungsteil Schreiben können Sie zwischen zwei Aufgaben wählen. Eine der Aufgaben bezieht sich normalerweise auf den Text, aus dem Sie einzelne Aspekte in Ihrer Lösung aufgreifen und mit Ihrem Hintergrundwissen zum Schwerpunktthema bzw. zu weiteren landeskundlichen Themen weiter ausführen sollen. Auch die zweite Wahlaufgabe lehnt sich thematisch an den Text an.

Für die erste Wahlaufgabe müssen Sie in der Regel einen eher sachlichen Kommentar verfassen und zu einer umstrittenen These Stellung nehmen. Für die zweite Wahlaufgabe wird häufig ein situativer Rahmen geschaffen. Sie müssen dann beispielsweise einen Brief, einen Tagebucheintrag, einen Artikel oder eine Rede formulieren.

Auch hierzu finden Sie weitere Bearbeitungs- und Vorbereitungshinweise im Abschnitt „Prüfungs- und Aufgabenformen".

Achtung: Bearbeiten Sie in eigenem Interesse wirklich nur eine der beiden Aufgaben aus diesem Prüfungsteil. Sollten beide Aufgaben bearbeitet sein, wird nur eine davon bewertet, in der Regel die erste.

### Leistungsbewertung

Der **Hörverstehensteil** fließt mit **20 %**, die **Textaufgabe** mit **55 %** in Ihre Gesamtnote ein (die restlichen 25 % entfallen auf die Kommunikationsprüfung). Je nach Anzahl der Aufgaben im Hörverstehensteil können Sie in diesem Teil Ihrer Prüfung unterschiedlich viele Bewertungseinheiten erreichen. Diese werden anschließend prozentual auf die Notenskala von 0 bis 15 Punkten umgerechnet. In der **Textaufgabe** werden Inhalt und Sprache einzeln bewertet. Inhaltlich können Sie auf jede der drei Teilaufgaben maximal 15 Punkte bekommen. Ihre Gesamtleistung im inhaltlichen Bereich wird dann durch eine vorgegebene Gewichtung der einzelnen Fragen zueinander bestimmt. So kann eine Textverständnisaufgabe beispielsweise zu 25 % in Ihre Gesamtpunktzahl einfließen, während die Analyseaufgabe 40 % und die Stellungnahme bzw. gestaltende Aufgabe 35 % Ihrer Punktzahl ausmacht. Die sprachliche Leistung wird für alle drei Textaufgaben gemeinsam bepunktet. In Ihre letztliche Gesamtpunktzahl für die Textaufgabe fließt Ihre sprachliche Bewertung zu 60 % ein, die inhaltliche zu 40 %.

Insgesamt werden bei der Textaufgabe u. a. die folgenden Aspekte beurteilt:

- Werden die gestellten Aufgaben umfassend beantwortet?
- Werden die Regeln für die jeweilige Textsorte erfüllt?
- Ist der Text logisch und übersichtlich strukturiert?
  Werden *connectives* (Konjunktionen und verknüpfende Wendungen) verwendet?
- Ist die Wortwahl stilistisch angemessen? Wie umfangreich ist der Wortschatz?
- Ist die Syntax grammatikalisch richtig und abwechslungsreich?
- Beherrscht der Prüfling die Grundregeln der englischen Grammatik?
- Werden die orthografischen Regeln befolgt?

## Die Kommunikationsprüfung

In einer globalisierten Welt nimmt nicht nur die Bedeutung der englischen Sprache als Schriftsprache zu, es wird auch zunehmend wichtiger, dass man mündlich in der Lage ist, in der Fremdsprache zu kommunizieren. Um die Bedeutung des mündlichen Sprachgebrauchs zu würdigen, müssen Sie neben der schriftlichen Prüfung auch eine Kommunikationsprüfung ablegen.

### Bearbeitungszeit und erlaubte Hilfsmittel

Zunächst haben Sie 15 Minuten Vorbereitungszeit. Der zeitliche Rahmen der eigentlichen Prüfung hängt von der Anzahl der Prüflinge ab. Die Einzelprüfung dauert etwa 15 Minuten, die Tandemprüfung mindestens 20 Minuten.

Als Hilfsmittel liegen Ihnen ein **ein-** und ein **zweisprachiges Wörterbuch** vor. Verwenden Sie diese aber nur dann, wenn Ihnen inhaltliche Aspekte des Materials oder der Aufgabenstellung, die Sie als wichtig einschätzen, unklar sind. Sie haben für die Vorbereitung nur begrenzt Zeit! Nutzen Sie diese, um sich hilfreiche **Notizen** zu Aspekten zu machen, die Sie in der Prüfung verwenden können. Die Notizen sollten stichpunktartig und kurz gefasst sein. Sie dienen Ihnen lediglich als Hilfe für eine inhaltliche Gliederung Ihres Vortrags/des Dialogs. Um sich sprachlich auf das einzustellen, was Sie gerne sagen möchten, können Sie einzelne Aspekte bereits im Kopf formulieren. Da Sie in der Prüfung frei sprechen müssen, ist es nicht sinnvoll, alles genau aufzuschreiben.

### Prüfungsinhalte und Ablauf

Die Kommunikationsprüfung wird als **Einzel-** oder **Tandemprüfung** abgehalten. Ob Sie lieber alleine oder mit einem Partner oder einer Partnerin geprüft werden wollen, ist Ihre Entscheidung.

**Thematisch** orientiert sich die Prüfung an den Inhalten, die laut Bildungsplan im Unterricht behandelt werden müssen. Auch das Schwerpunktthema kann Bestandteil der Prüfung sein. Ähnlich wie bei der schriftlichen Prüfung wird Ihnen als Impuls jedoch kein Ausschnitt aus der im Rahmen des Schwerpunktthemas behandelten Lektüre oder aus dem behandelten Film vorgegeben, sondern lediglich Material, das thematisch Bezug darauf nimmt. Besprechen Sie mit Ihrem Lehrer bzw. Ihrer Lehrerin, auf welche Themen Sie sich gezielt vorbereiten können.

In der **fünfzehnminütigen Vorbereitungszeit** werden Ihnen **Impulse in englischer Sprache** vorgelegt. Es kann sich bei den Impulsen um schriftlich ausgeführte Texte oder bildliche Impulse (Grafiken, Diagramme, Karikaturen, Bilder ...) handeln, es kann Ihnen aber auch ein Hörtext oder eine kurze Filmsequenz gezeigt werden. Erkundigen Sie sich vor der Prüfung, auf welche Art von Materialien Sie sich einstellen müssen. Gemeinsam mit dem Impuls erhalten Sie Aufgaben und evtl. Hinweise für den monologischen und dialogischen Teil der Prüfung. Der zusätzliche Einsatz von deutschsprachigen Texten in der Prüfung im Rahmen einer Mediationsübung ist möglich.

Unabhängig davon, ob Sie sich für eine Einzel- oder eine Tandemprüfung entschieden haben, gliedert sich die Prüfung in zwei Abschnitte: das monologische und das dialogische Sprechen. Am Anfang der Prüfung steht das **monologische Sprechen** (etwa 5 Minuten pro Teilnehmer\*in). Hier tragen Sie die Ergebnisse, die Sie zu Ihrem Material gesammelt haben, möglichst zusammenhängend vor. Falls Sie doch einmal ins Stocken geraten, lassen Sie sich nicht verunsichern. Versuchen Sie auf die Hilfestellung, die Ihre Lehrkraft Ihnen gibt, einzugehen und zu Ihrem Vortrag zurückzukommen. In der Tandemprüfung sehen Sie jetzt bereits das Material Ihres Tandempartners bzw. Ihrer Tandempartnerin. Es ist wichtig, dass Sie genau zuhören, da das monologische Sprechen in das dialogische Sprechen übergeht und Sie hier wichtige Aspekte, die Ihr Gegenüber genannt hat, aufgreifen können.

Der zweite Teil der Prüfung ist dem **dialogischen Sprechen** gewidmet. Bei der Einzelprüfung erfolgt das Gespräch mit der Lehrkraft, bei der Tandemprüfung mit dem Tandempartner bzw. der Tandempartnerin. Achten Sie im dialogischen Teil der Prüfung (etwa 10 Minuten) auf ausgewogene Redeanteile. Ist Ihre Tandempartnerin sehr wortkarg, dann fragen Sie sie gezielt nach ihrer Meinung oder nach Aspekten, die sie in ihrem Vortrag genannt hat. Lässt Ihr Diskussionspartner Sie nicht zu Wort kommen, dürfen Sie ihn durchaus (höflich!) unterbrechen. Auch eine geschickte Gesprächsführung fließt in die Beurteilung mit ein. Wenn das Gespräch ins Stocken gerät oder sich von der Aufgabenstellung wegbewegt, kann Ihre Lehrkraft helfend eingreifen.

Auch zur Kommunikationsprüfung finden Sie noch weitere hilfreiche Tipps und Vorbereitungshinweise im Abschnitt „Prüfungs- und Aufgabenformen".

## Leistungsbewertung

Die schriftliche Prüfung und die Kommunikationsprüfung fließen im Verhältnis 3:1 in Ihre Abiturnote ein. Die Kommunikationsprüfung macht nämlich 25 % Ihrer Gesamtnote aus, die restlichen 75 % entfallen auf Hörverstehen und Textaufgabe.

Die Beurteilung der **Kommunikationsprüfung** ist in drei Teilbereiche gegliedert: Aufgabenerfüllung und Inhalt, Strategie und interaktive Gesprächsfähigkeit sowie sprachliche Leistung. Auch hier gilt die Notenskala von 0 bis 15 Punkten für die Bewertung. Wenn Sie im Bereich der Sprache viele Fehler machen, können Sie dies zum Teil durch eine gute inhaltliche Argumentation und geschickte Gesprächsführung ausgleichen und umgekehrt. Wird einer der drei Teilbereiche mit der Note „ungenügend" bewertet, können Sie insgesamt maximal 3 Punkte erreichen.

# Prüfungs- und Aufgabenformen

Im folgenden Kapitel finden Sie zu den Prüfungs- und Aufgabenformen, die Ihnen in Ihrem Abitur begegnen können, wichtige Informationen. Diese sollen Ihnen die Vorbereitung auf diese Aufgabenformen erleichtern und Ihnen Strategien für deren Bearbeitung an die Hand geben.

## Kommunikationsprüfung

### Wichtige Fakten

| | |
|---|---|
| **Art der Prüfung:** | Ergänzung zur schriftlichen Abiturprüfung |
| **Zeitpunkt:** | Prüfungszeitpunkt von der Schule festgelegt, kann vor oder nach der schriftlichen Abiturprüfung sein |
| **Prüfungsaufbau:** | Vorbereitungszeit und Prüfungsgespräch (bestehend aus monologischem und dialogischem Teil) |

### Tipps zur Vorgehensweise

Während der 15-minütigen **Vorbereitungszeit**, die Sie in einem separaten Raum verbringen, sollten Sie sich mit dem Material und den Aufgaben auseinandersetzen, die Sie erhalten haben. Nutzen Sie diese Zeit, um

- das Material zu verstehen. Unabhängig davon, ob es sich um einen kurzen Text, ein Bild, einen Cartoon, eine Statistik o. Ä. handelt, sollten Sie versuchen, es in größere **Themenzusammenhänge** einzuordnen. Das hilft Ihnen, Ihr Vorwissen zu aktivieren und in Ihrem Monolog vorbereitet bzw. im Dialog spontan darauf zurückzugreifen.

- **sinnvolle** Notizen zu machen. Die Aufgabenstellungen leiten Sie, weil sie Ihnen genau vorgeben, welche Aspekte Sie behandeln sollten. Fassen Sie sich allerdings kurz und verwenden Sie lieber übersichtliche Strukturierungen wie Tabellen, Mindmaps oder Stichpunkte, anstatt einen Fließtext für Ihren Vortrag zu erstellen. Abgesehen davon, dass die 15 Minuten nicht ausreichen werden, um sämtliche Punkte, die Sie behandeln wollen, ausführlich niederzuschreiben, wird es nicht als positiv bewertet, wenn Sie einen komplett ausgearbeiteten Text nur ablesen. Stattdessen sollen Sie möglichst frei sprechen und spontan auf Nachfragen Ihrer Lehrkraft oder Ihres Mitprüflings reagieren können.

Für Ihren etwa 5-minütigen monologischen Vortrag sollten Sie die folgenden Punkte beachten:

- Sprechen Sie **strukturiert** und gehen Sie genau auf die Aufgabenstellung(en) ein. Hierbei helfen Ihnen Ihre vorher erstellten Notizen sowie an passenden Stellen eingesetzte sogenannte *connectives*, die Ihre Aussagen gliedern und Ihrem Publikum das Zuhören erleichtern.

- Achten Sie darauf, **Blickkontakt** mit Ihrem Publikum herzustellen und nicht an Ihren Notizen zu „kleben". Auch die **Körpersprache** kann ein entscheidender Faktor sein: Dass Sie aufgeregt sind, ist in einer Prüfungssituation ganz natürlich, aber denken Sie daran, dass Sie gut vorbereitet sind, und treten Sie deshalb möglichst selbstbewusst, freundlich und offen auf.

In einer Tandemprüfung hören Sie anschließend bzw. vor Ihrem eigenen Vortrag den 5-minütigen Monolog Ihres Partners bzw. Ihrer Partnerin. Dabei sollten Sie

- **aufmerksam zuhören** und sich Notizen machen.

- in Ihren **Notizen** besonders relevante Stellen markieren, auf die Sie später im Dialog eingehen wollen.

Während des 10-minütigen Dialogs, den Sie mit Ihrer Lehrkraft oder Ihrem Mitprüfling führen, ist es wichtig, dass Sie

- auf Ihre\*n Gesprächspartner\*in eingehen. Es geht nicht nur darum, dass Sie möglichst viele zu Ihrer Aufgabenstellung passende Inhalte nennen, sondern vor allem darum, dass Ihre **Gesprächsführung** geschickt und ausgewogen ist.

- möglichst **gelassen und höflich** bleiben, auch wenn Sie zu geäußerten Thesen eine andere Meinung haben. Sie dürfen ruhig die eine oder andere umgangssprachliche Wendung einfließen lassen, schließlich soll es sich um ein „natürliches" Gespräch handeln. Dennoch sollten Sie insgesamt formales und vor allem korrektes Englisch verwenden.

### Hilfreiche Wendungen

In Ihrem monologischen Vortrag können Sie die folgenden Textbausteine anwenden:
- *I would like to speak about …*
- *To start with, I'll …*
- *Firstly, …, secondly, …, thirdly, …, finally, …*
- *Last but not least, …*
- *We must also take into account …*
- *The next point to be considered …*
- *Another argument we shouldn't forget is that …*
- *In conclusion, …*

Für den Dialog bieten sich die folgenden Ausdrücke an, um auf Ihre\*n Gesprächspartner\*in einzugehen und Ihre Meinung auszudrücken:
- *Have I understood you correctly …?*
- *As you/I said before, …*
- *Could you please explain that in a bit more detail?*
- *I agree with you on the point that …*
- *I'm sorry to disagree, but I think …*
- *What is your opinion on …?*
- *Maybe a compromise would be to say that …*

## Vorbereitung auf diesen Prüfungsteil

Auf den mündlichen Teil der Abiturprüfung können Sie sich in **sprachlicher** und **inhaltlicher** Hinsicht vorbereiten. Zudem sollten Sie auch **methodische/strategische** Aspekte wie das Halten eines Monologs und das spontane Gespräch mit einem Partner bzw. einer Partnerin trainieren. In jedem Fall hilft alles, was Ihnen die Scheu nimmt, in der Fremdsprache zu reden. Nutzen Sie die Unterrichtszeit, indem Sie sich häufig beteiligen. Aber suchen Sie auch in Ihrer Freizeit Möglichkeiten, **auf Englisch zu kommunizieren**. Auch wenn Sie keine internationalen Kontakte haben, können Sie in Ihrem Freundeskreis beispielsweise einen Tag festlegen, an dem Sie sich nur auf Englisch unterhalten. Sobald festgelegt wurde, mit wem Sie die Prüfung gemeinsam ablegen werden, bietet sich eine gemeinsame Vorbereitungszeit an, in der Sie die Prüfungssituation simulieren. Für die sprachliche Vorbereitung hilft es außerdem, sich einige **Floskeln und Formulierungen**, beispielsweise zur Bildbeschreibung und zur Reaktion auf Aussagen Ihres Gegenübers (Zustimmen, Ablehnen etc.) zurechtzulegen. Hier können Sie auch die „**MindCards**" (vgl. „Hinweise zu den digitalen Zusätzen") nutzen, interaktive Vokabelkärtchen mit vielen hilfreichen Wendungen, die Sie in einem Prüfungsgespräch gebrauchen können. Inhaltlich sollten Sie sich mit dem Schwerpunktthema und den Pflichtwerken gut auskennen und sich über aktuelle und im Unterricht besprochene landeskundliche Themen auf dem Laufenden halten.

## Hörverstehen

### Wichtige Fakten

| Prüfungsteil: | erster Teil Ihrer schriftlichen Abiturprüfung |
|---|---|
| Prüfungsablauf: | mehrere maximal fünfminütige Hörverstehenstexte, die je zweimal angehört werden und zu denen geschlossene und halboffene Fragen beantwortet werden müssen |

### Mögliche Aufgabenformate

1. *multiple choice questions*

   Bei Multiple-Choice-Aufgaben müssen Sie häufig einen gegebenen Satzanfang vollenden, indem Sie aus mehreren Möglichkeiten die zum Hörtext passende auswählen. Ihnen wird üblicherweise vorgegeben, ob es nur eine richtige Lösung gibt oder ob Sie alle zutreffenden Antworten ankreuzen sollen.

2. *true or false?*

   Hier sollen Sie auswählen, ob ein vorgegebener Satz richtig oder falsch ist. Es ist dabei sehr wichtig, die Aussagen und den Text genau zu vergleichen. Oft sind es geringfügige Details, die eine auf den ersten Blick als richtig erscheinende Aussage im Text doch widerlegen.

3. *complete the sentence/fill in the gap(s)/short answer questions*
Hierbei handelt es sich um halboffene Fragestellungen. Sie müssen Sätze mit Informationen aus dem Hörtext vervollständigen, einen Lückentext ergänzen oder kurze Fragen zum Text beantworten. Da es nicht darum geht, Ihre produktiven Schreibfähigkeiten zu testen, sondern bloßes Verstehen abgefragt werden soll, müssen Sie normalerweise nur wenige Wörter schreiben und sprachliche Fehler werden nur gewertet, wenn sie sinnentstellend sein sollten.

4. *put in the correct order*
Sie müssen angeben, in welcher Reihenfolge bestimmte Informationen im Text aufeinanderfolgen.

5. *matching*
Zuordnungsaufgaben können recht vielfältig sein. Zum Beispiel kann es Ihre Aufgabe sein, Satzanfänge den richtigen Satzenden, Meinungen oder Charaktereigenschaften den vorkommenden Personen oder Überschriften den passenden Textabschnitten zuzuordnen.

## Tipps zur Vorgehensweise

Da die Zeit während des Hörens sehr knapp ist und das Zuhören Ihre volle Konzentration erfordert, ist es essenziell, sich die Aufgaben vorher sehr genau durchzulesen, das Thema zu erfassen und sich so eventuelle Antwortmöglichkeiten schon vorher zu überlegen. Hilfreich kann es auch sein, **Signalwörter** in den Aufgaben zu markieren. So wissen Sie am ehesten, welche Abschnitte des Hörtextes für welche Aufgaben relevant sind. Wichtig ist dennoch, sich nicht vorschnell auf scheinbar eindeutige Lösungen festzulegen und vor allem beim zweiten Hören sehr genau zuzuhören, da oft Details darüber entscheiden, ob eine Antwort richtig oder falsch bzw. welche von mehreren Antwortmöglichkeiten die richtige ist.

Insgesamt sollten Sie also alle **Phasen der Hörverstehensprüfung** sinnvoll nutzen: die **Einlesephase** zur Vorbereitung, **das erste Hören und Bearbeiten**, um den Text generell zu verstehen und um die Aufgaben, die Ihnen leichtfallen, bereits zu erledigen, **das zweite Hören und Bearbeiten** dann zum Überprüfen Ihrer Lösungen bzw. um noch einmal gezielt auf Stellen zu achten, die Sie vorher noch nicht verstanden haben. Wichtig ist, dass Sie während des Hörens nicht zu lange bei einer Aufgabe verharren und somit riskieren, auch die folgenden Lösungen zu verpassen. Das **Wörterbuch** sollten Sie nur in der Einlesephase einsetzen, wenn Sie Aufgabenstellungen nicht verstehen. Während des Hörens müssen Sie nicht jedes einzelne Wort kennen und können konzentrierter arbeiten, wenn Sie sich nicht durch Wörterbucharbeit ablenken lassen.

## Vorbereitung auf diesen Prüfungsteil

Langfristig gesehen gibt es viele Möglichkeiten, sich auf die Hörverstehensprüfung **vorzubereiten**. Als schwierig empfinden viele Schüler*innen das Verstehen von *native speakers*, die in natürlicher Sprechgeschwindigkeit, oftmals mit regionalen Akzenten oder untermalt von ablenkenden Hintergrundgeräuschen sprechen. Deshalb sollten Sie sich an solche Hörsituationen gewöhnen, indem Sie sich Filme im englischen Originalton ansehen oder die zahlreichen Podcasts, die das Internet bietet, nutzen.

# Leseverstehen

## Wichtige Fakten

| Prüfungsteil: | Teilaufgabe 1 (Schreiben) |
| --- | --- |
| erwartete Leistung: | übersichtliche Darstellung der wichtigsten (bzw. durch die Aufgabenstellung eingegrenzter) Inhaltselemente eines Textes in eigenen Worten |

## Tipps zur Vorgehensweise

- Lesen Sie sich zunächst einmal den Text in seiner **Gesamtheit** durch. So verschaffen Sie sich schon einmal einen **groben Überblick** über seinen Inhalt und verstehen die grundsätzlichen Zusammenhänge. Sie sollten hier nicht in Panik geraten, wenn Sie nicht jedes einzelne Wort verstehen. Wichtig ist, dass Sie nach der Lektüre zusammenfassen könnten, worum es im Text geht, welche Personen im Text vorkommen, welche Meinungen die handelnden Charaktere und der Verfasser oder die Verfasserin des Textes vertreten usw.

- Anschließend sollten Sie die **Arbeitsanweisung** sehr genau lesen. Zum einen verrät Ihnen der Operator (vgl. Abschnitt „Liste ausgewählter Operatoren"), was von Ihnen erwartet wird. Zum anderen wird vielleicht auch eingeschränkt, auf welche Textteile Sie gesondert achten sollen.

- Der nächste Schritt ist die **Arbeit mit dem Text**. Suchen Sie die Stellen, die für Ihre Beantwortung relevant sind, und nutzen Sie verschiedene Methoden des *highlighting*, z. B. Unterstreichungen in unterschiedlichen Farben, Randnotizen o. Ä., um Aspekte, die Sie in Ihrer Antwort erwähnen wollen, hervorzuheben. Da bestimmte Punkte, wie Beispiele oder Wiederholungen im Ausgangstext, in Ihrer Zusammenfassung normalerweise nicht vorkommen sollten, können Sie derartige Stellen auch einklammern oder durchstreichen. Sie sollten jedoch leserlich bleiben, da Sie sie für die zweite Aufgabe, die Analyseaufgabe, möglicherweise verwenden wollen.

- Nach der Textarbeit sollten Sie Ihren **Schreibprozess vorbereiten**. Auch wenn Ihre Arbeitszeit begrenzt ist, ist es hilfreich, vorab eine kurze **Gliederung** Ihrer Antwort zu skizzieren. Vermeiden Sie es jedoch, eine Vorschrift Ihres Textes anzufertigen, die Sie dann noch einmal abschreiben müssen. Ein gutes stichpunktartiges Konzept sollte ausreichen, um in Ihrer Antwort beim Thema zu bleiben und einzelne Argumente sinnvoll zu verknüpfen.

- Achten Sie beim Schreiben darauf, diese **Verknüpfungen** auch sprachlich deutlich zu machen. Besondere Bedeutung kommt dabei den sogenannten *connectives* zu (vgl. die folgenden hilfreichen Wendungen oder auch die „**MindCards**" auf MyStark).

- Planen Sie mindestens einen Korrekturdurchgang ein. Ihren fertigen Text sollten Sie sowohl auf sprachliche Richtigkeit als auch auf inhaltliche Geschlossenheit und Logik überprüfen.

X

## Hilfreiche Wendungen

### Allgemeine Aussagen zum Text:
- *The text refers to/contains information about ...*
- *The speaker/journalist/author says/maintains/points out/makes it clear that/ wants to make people aware of ...*
- *She/He argues/proves/attacks/criticises/condemns ...*
- *She/He praises/applauds ...*
- *She/He makes fun of/ridicules ...*
- *She/He gives/makes/delivers a speech on/about ...*

### Satzverknüpfungen nach Aussageabsicht *(connectives, linking words)*:

| Aussageabsicht | Satzverknüpfung |
|---|---|
| • einen Gedanken hinzufügen: | *in addition, furthermore, also, besides, in the same way* |
| • das Gegenteil ausdrücken: | *yet, however, on the other hand, on the contrary, in contrast* |
| • einen Vergleich anstellen: | *similarly, in the same way, likewise, compared to/with ..., in comparison to/with ...* |
| • eine Folgerung ausdrücken: | *consequently, therefore, as a result, hence* |
| • etw. einräumen: | *although, though, even if, after all, in any case, in spite of* |
| • eine zeitliche Verbindung knüpfen: | *after, before, while, eventually, recently, lately, at last, in the end, in the past, when, as soon as* |
| • eine Begründung anführen: | *therefore, that is why, for this reason, because, since* |
| • eine Bedingung ausdrücken: | *if, unless, provided that, in case that* |
| • ein Beispiel anführen: | *for example, for instance, in other words* |
| • die Reihenfolge anzeigen: | *first, second, next, finally, in the end* |
| • einen Gedanken neu formulieren: | *in other words, that means, that is, that is to say* |
| • einen Gedankengang abschließen: | *in conclusion, in brief, in short, on the whole* |

### Vorbereitung auf diesen Prüfungsteil

Die **Lesekompetenz** verbessert sich mit jedem Text, den man liest. Suchen Sie sich einfach Texte, die Sie interessieren – im Internet, im Buchhandel oder in Zeitungen. Achten Sie beim Lesen darauf, dass Sie den Gesamtzusammenhang verstehen. Nicht jedes Wort ist für das Textverständnis entscheidend. Sie können zu Übungszwecken auch versuchen, die Texte, die Sie finden, für andere möglichst knapp und präzise mündlich **zusammenzufassen**. Als Richtschnur sollte immer gelten, dass auch jemand, der den Text nicht selbst gelesen hat, weiß, wovon dieser handelt, ohne aber Detailinformationen aufzählen zu können.

Zur **sprachlichen Vorbereitung** hilft Ihnen die nochmalige Beschäftigung mit dem Schwerpunktthema sowie anderen in der Oberstufe behandelten Bereichen. Da auch

Ihre Prüfungstexte Bezug zu einem oder mehreren der oben genannten Themen aufweisen werden, hilft Ihnen ein breit gefächerter Wortschatz, Alternativformulierungen zu finden und die Worte aus dem Text nicht eins zu eins wiederholen zu müssen. Auch Ihren sogenannten „**Funktionswortschatz**" sollten Sie themenunabhängig immer weiter ausbauen. Dazu gehören übliche Satzanfänge ebenso wie typische *connectives*, um logische Bezüge darzustellen (vgl. die hilfreichen Wendungen oben sowie weitere nützliche Formulierungen auf den digitalen „MindCards").

## Textanalyse

### Wichtige Fakten

| Prüfungsteil: | Teilaufgabe 2 (Schreiben) |
|---|---|
| Kurzdefinition „Analyse": | <u>Was</u> wird gesagt? – (**Inhalt**)<br><u>Wie</u> wird es gesagt? – (**Form/Sprache**)<br><u>Warum</u> wird es so gesagt? – (**Funktion**) |

### Tipps zur Vorgehensweise

Da es sich auch hier um eine Textaufgabe handelt, sollten grundsätzlich ähnliche Arbeitsschritte wie bei der Leseverstehensaufgabe (s. S. X) gelten. Das heißt, auch hier müssen Sie

- den Text in seiner **Gesamtheit** erfassen,
- die **Aufgabenstellung** genau lesen,
- **mit dem Text arbeiten** und wichtige Stellen für Ihre Lösung herausfiltern,
- Ihren **Schreibprozess planen**,
- geschickte **Formulierungen** verwenden
- und am Schluss alles noch einmal **Korrektur lesen**.

Die **Arbeit mit dem Text** wird hier besonders ausführlich ausfallen, da Sie für alle Ihre Überlegungen und Deutungsvorschläge Textbelege finden müssen.

### Hilfreiche Wendungen

- *To illustrate/show/prove their point that ..., the author uses/employs ...*
- *This message is stressed by the use of ...*
- *He/She corroborates/supports his/her message by ...*
- *This stylistic device implies/alludes to the fact that ...*
- *The reader can directly share the protagonist's/the author's view that ....*
- *Proof/Evidence of this can be found in lines ...*

### Vorbereitung auf diesen Prüfungsteil

Auch die Vorbereitung auf die Textanalyseaufgabe lässt sich vor allem **sprachlich** grob mit der auf eine Textverständnisaufgabe vergleichen. Für die Textanalyse brauchen Sie außerdem, je nachdem, ob es sich bei dem zu analysierenden Text um einen fiktionalen oder um einen Sachtext handelt, ein gewisses **literarisches und methodisches Grundwissen oder Rüstzeug**. Im Folgenden wiederholen wir zunächst wichtige Elemente, die man an einem literarischen Text analysieren kann. Anschließend geht es um die Analyse von Sprache und Form, die bei beiden Textsorten (literarischen sowie Sachtexten) gefragt sein kann.

1. **Interpretation eines fiktionalen Textes**

   Wenn Sie einen Ausschnitt aus einem fiktionalen Text interpretieren, sollten Sie über einige grundlegende Elemente, wie etwa erzählerische Mittel, Bescheid wissen. Zu den Aspekten, die es zu untersuchen gilt, da sie für eine Interpretation ergiebig sein können, gehören vor allem die Erzählsituation, die Behandlung der Zeit und die Charakterisierung einzelner Figuren.

   **Erzählsituation:** Für die Interpretation eines literarischen Textes ist die Analyse der Erzählsituation (auch Erzählperspektive oder Erzählhaltung genannt) wichtig, da durch den Blickwinkel der Erzählfigur und deren Einstellung bestimmte Effekte erzielt werden. Unter Erzählsituation *(point of view)* versteht man das Verhältnis zwischen Erzähler und erzähltem Geschehen. Der Erzähler *(narrator)* darf nicht mit dem Autor/der Autorin *(author)*, dem Verfasser/der Verfasserin der Geschichte, gleichgesetzt oder verwechselt werden. Manchmal ist die Erzählinstanz als eigenständige Person klar zu erkennen, bleibt jedoch oft ungenannt. Bei der Interpretation eines fiktionalen Textes müssen Sie also der Frage nachgehen: Wer erzählt das Geschehen? Welche Haltung nimmt der Erzähler zu den Ereignissen ein? Im Prinzip unterscheidet man drei grundlegende Erzählsituationen:

   a) **Auktoriale Erzählsituation** *(omniscient narrator)*: Die Erzählinstanz vermittelt zwischen Autor*in und Leser*in. Sie steht außerhalb der Ereignisse, bewahrt Distanz zum Geschehen, kommentiert es zuweilen und wendet sich evtl. auch direkt an die Leserschaft. Manchmal entsteht auch der Eindruck einer objektiven Vermittlung der Vorgänge, die für sich selbst sprechen und aus denen man sich bei der Lektüre eine eigene Meinung bilden soll. Man nennt dies berichtende Darstellung.

   b) **Personale Erzählsituation** *(third-person narrator)*: Hier fehlt die Vermittlung zwischen Autor*in und Leser*in, das Geschehen wird aus der Perspektive einer Figur in der Geschichte in der 3. Person erzählt. Beim Lesen erhält man den Eindruck, man verfolge das Geschehen unmittelbar und befände sich auf dem Schauplatz des Geschehens – wie im Theater. Man spricht daher auch von dramatischer oder szenischer Darstellung. Eine Mischung zwischen auktorialer und personaler Erzählsituation wird als *third-person-omniscient* bezeichnet.

   c) **Ich-Erzählsituation** *(first-person narrator)*: Diese Erzählperspektive ist vergleichbar mit der personalen: Die Story wird aus der Perspektive einer Figur – hier in der 1. Person – vermittelt. Dabei unterscheidet man noch genauer zwischen „I as witness", d. h., der Erzähler beobachtet das Geschehen und steht am Rande der Ereignisse, und „I as protagonist", d. h., erzählt wird von der Hauptfigur und man erlebt die Ereignisse aus deren Sicht.

**Die Behandlung der Zeit:** Man unterscheidet zwischen erzählter Zeit und Erzählzeit. Die erzählte Zeit *(acting time)* ist die Zeit, über die sich das Geschehen erstreckt. Als Erzählzeit *(narrating time)* bezeichnet man die Zeit, die zur Lektüre benötigt wird. Aus dem Verhältnis zwischen Erzählzeit und erzählter Zeit lassen sich Rückschlüsse auf die Erzählweise *(mode of presentation)* ziehen. Zur Verdeutlichung: In dem Satz „*Five months passed in that way*" ist die erzählte Zeit fünf Monate und die Erzählzeit beträgt nur ein, zwei Sekunden. Die erzählte Zeit ist also größer als die Erzählzeit, d. h., in der Geschichte vergeht mehr Zeit, als zur Lektüre benötigt wird. Man nennt dies Zeitraffung *(compression)*. Der Erzähler überspringt einen größeren Zeitraum, da er für seinen Bericht unwichtig ist. Wird ein Ereignis so ausführlich geschildert, dass man als Leser*in den Eindruck gewinnt, man nehme direkt daran teil, spricht man erzähltechnisch von Zeitdeckung *(correspondence)*, d. h., die erzählte Zeit entspricht ungefähr der Erzählzeit, die Lektüre nimmt genauso viel Zeit in Anspruch wie das geschilderte Geschehen. Mit dieser Technik erhält die Erzählung eine dramatische Wirkung. Seltener kommt auch die Zeitdehnung *(expansion)* vor, bei der die Erzählzeit länger ist als die erzählte Zeit.

**Charakterisierung:** Unter Charakterisierung versteht man die Art und Weise, wie eine Figur gezeichnet und ihre Eigenschaften verdeutlicht werden. Bei der indirekten Charakterisierung *(implicit/indirect characterisation)* offenbart die Figur ihren Charakter durch ihre äußere Erscheinung, Kleidung, Gesten und Handlungen selbst. Direkte Charakterisierungen werden vom Erzähler oder von handelnden Personen unmittelbar über eine Person geäußert *("He was a mean and horrible man.")*. Die folgende Tabelle und die dazugehörigen Hinweise können bei der Erstellung einer Charakterisierung helfen:

**Writing a Character Analysis**
Remember:
- collect all factual information
- move from the outward appearance to the character's inner nature

| Name of character | |
|---|---|
| **Outward appearance** <br> • physique <br> • clothes <br> • movement, gestures <br> • tone of voice, use of language <br> • behaviour, manners | |
| **Inner nature** <br> • motives and drives, attitudes <br> • feelings and emotions | |
| **Relationship to other characters** | |
| **Function in the story** | |

## 2. Analyse von Sprache und Form

Es kann ebenfalls Ihre Aufgabe sein, formale, stilistische Elemente *(stylistic devices)* der Textvorlage zu erarbeiten, da es nicht nur darauf ankommt, was gesagt wird (Inhalt), sondern ebenfalls darauf, wie (Form) und warum (Funktion) es so ausgedrückt wird. Diese Textanalyse kann sowohl an fiktionalen als auch an nicht fiktionalen Texten durchgeführt werden. Entsprechend lauten die Arbeitsanweisungen z. B.: *Describe how the author creates the atmosphere in the excerpt,* oder *Analyse the rhetorical devices, taking into account the situation in which the speech is delivered.* In der Aufgabe müssen Sie den Zusammenhang zwischen Form und Inhalt in Bezug auf die Funktion klären.

Sie können je nach Aufgabenstellung und Text u. a. die folgenden Punkte in Ihre Analyse einbeziehen:

- **Wortwahl:** Stilebene, Register, „positive"/„negative" Wortfelder, etc.
- **Aufbau** und **Struktur**
- Gebrauch von **Pronomina**, um Personengruppen einzubeziehen bzw. auszuschließen, etc.
- **Quellen, Autoritäten, Zahlen** (sog. *facts and figures*)
- *tone:* Welche Grundhaltung wird im Text zum Ausdruck gebracht? Steht der Verfasser/die Verfasserin einem Thema ironisch, kritisch, emotional oder neutral gegenüber?
- **Stilmittel** *(Figures of Speech)* (vgl. Tabelle auf der Folgeseite)

Wichtig ist bei einer sprachlichen Analyse, dass Sie alle Auffälligkeiten, die Sie im Text finden, stets in größere Zusammenhänge einordnen oder eine bestimmte Aussageabsicht mit ihnen verknüpfen. Niemals sollten Sie beispielsweise Stilmittel einfach nur auflisten, sondern immer die Fragestellungen „**Was** wird gesagt?", „**Wie** wird es gesagt?" und „**Warum** wurde diese Art der Darstellung gewählt?" verknüpfen.

## Figures of Speech (Redefiguren)

| Bezeichnung (englisch) | Bezeichnung (deutsch) | Erklärung | Beispiel |
|---|---|---|---|
| *Alliteration* | Alliteration, Stabreim | Mehrere Wörter beginnen mit dem gleichen Laut. | *[...] face the fire at freedom's front.* (Ronald Reagan) |
| *Antithesis* | Antithese | Gegenüberstellung gegensätzlicher Begriffe und Gedanken | *To err is human, to forgive divine.* (Alexander Pope) |
| *Ellipsis* | Ellipse | Auslassung eines Wortes oder Satzteils | *Mastercard accepted.* |
| *Euphemism* | Euphemismus | Beschönigung; Unangenehmes mit angenehmen Worten sagen | *early retirement = unemployment* |
| *Hyperbole, Exaggeration* | Hyperbel | Übertreibung | *He nearly died laughing.* |
| *Irony* | Ironie | Man sagt das Gegenteil von dem, was man meint. | *You broke that window really well!* |
| *Metaphor* | Metapher | Wort in übertragener Bedeutung; Bild, Vergleich (ohne „as" oder „like") | *All the world's a stage.* (Shakespeare, *As You Like It*) |
| *Parallelism* | Parallelismus | gleichartiger Satzbau | *What a day may bring, a day may take away.* |
| *Paradox* | Paradox | scheinbar falsche Aussage | *Fair is foul and foul is fair.* (Shakespeare, *Macbeth*) |
| *Personification* | Personifikation | Vermenschlichung, Verkörperung (in Gestalt einer Person) | *The day has eyes, the night has ears.* |
| *Pun* | Wortspiel | Der witzige Effekt beruht auf der Doppeldeutigkeit des gebrauchten Wortes. | *We shot two bucks, but that was all the money we had.* (*buck* = 1. Bock; 2. Dollar) |
| *Repetition* | Wiederholung | mehrmaliges Aufführen desselben Wortes / Ausdrucks zur Verstärkung einer Aussage | *Tomorrow and tomorrow and tomorrow.* (Shakespeare, *Macbeth*) |
| *Rhetorical question* | Rhetorische Frage | Scheinfrage, auf die keine Antwort erwartet wird | *How is it that a country that prides itself on its economic success could have so many very poor people?* |
| *Simile (Comparison)* | Vergleich | Form des Bildes; direkter Vergleich (mit Vergleichswort) | *My love is like a red, red rose.* (Robert Burns) |

# Analyse eines Cartoons oder Bildes

## Wichtige Fakten

| | |
|---|---|
| **Prüfungsteil:** | Schreiben: kann als Zusatzmaterial zu Teilaufgabe 2 (Analyse) oder als eigenständige Aufgabe in Teilaufgabe 3 vorkommen |
| **Erscheinungs-formen:** | politische Karikaturen (meist aktuelles politisches Thema), Karikaturen, die allgemeinmenschliche Schwächen aufs Korn nehmen; gestellte Fotografien, Schnappschüsse, Standbilder aus Filmen |

## Tipps zur Vorgehensweise

- Halten Sie bei der Analyse eines visuellen Impulses zunächst fest, was auf dem Bild zu sehen ist (Situation, Personen) und was geschieht (Aktion), also was diese Personen tun. Verwenden Sie wie bei einer Inhaltsangabe das Präsens in der einfachen Form *(The cartoon shows two people ...)* und in der Verlaufsform *(The men are working on ...)*. Versuchen Sie, sich bei der Beschreibung des Cartoons oder Bildes kurz zu fassen und auf die Aspekte zu konzentrieren, die für die Botschaft (vgl. nächster Schritt) wichtig sind.

- Der Beschreibung folgt die Interpretation. Dabei sollten Sie versuchen, etwa vorhandene Bilder und Symbole (die Taube steht z. B. für den Frieden) zu entschlüsseln und die dargestellte Situation auf ein politisches oder gesellschaftliches Thema zu beziehen. Wichtige Fingerzeige für die Aufschlüsselung der Botschaft sind in diesem Zusammenhang natürlich auch eine eventuell vorhandene Bildunterschrift *(caption)* oder Aussagen der Personen in den Sprechblasen *(bubbles)*.
  Vor allem bei Fotografien spielt zusätzlich zum Inhalt des Bildes auch die Perspektive eine Rolle für die Analyse. Ist man nah am Geschehen oder weit entfernt? Wird das Motiv von unten, also aus Froschperspektive *(= low-angle shot, worm's-eye view)*, oder von oben (Vogelperspektive = *high-angle shot, bird's-eye view*) gezeigt? Überlegen Sie sich, welche Rolle die Perspektive für die Wirkung des Bildes spielt.

- Je nach Aufgabenstellung und Prüfungsteil kann es verlangt sein, dass Sie den Cartoon oder das Bild zum Prüfungstext bzw. zum Schwerpunktthema (oder einem anderen Themenkomplex) in Bezug setzen. Wird das gleiche Thema behandelt oder geht es nur um thematisch verwandte Bereiche? Stellt der Cartoon das Thema von der gleichen Position aus dar wie der Text oder bietet er eine gegensätzliche Sichtweise? Gibt es direkte inhaltliche Anknüpfungspunkte, die sich für einen Vergleich eignen? Ihre Aufgabe kann andererseits aber auch sein, persönlich zum im Cartoon oder Bild behandelten Thema Stellung zu nehmen, also darzustellen, warum Sie mit der von Ihnen erarbeiteten Botschaft des Cartoons übereinstimmen oder nicht.

Die folgende Tabelle kann Ihnen bei der Erstellung Ihrer Analyse helfen:

| | |
|---|---|
| **Title/caption of cartoon** | |
| **Description** <br> • Scene <br> • People (presented in a positive or negative light) <br> • Objects <br> • Action | |
| **Interpretation/meaning** <br> • Decipher symbols, icons and labels <br> • Relate the cartoon to a political or social situation <br> • Identify the cartoonist's point of view <br> • Explain the message | |
| **Personal view** <br> • Your own experience <br> • Do you agree or disagree with the cartoonist? | |
| **Comparison** <br> • Does the cartoon display the same topic as the text/ <br> *Gran Torino/Crooked Letter, Crooked Letter*? <br> • Does it have the same perspective? If not, which <br> attitude is more convincing in your opinion? | |

## Hilfreiche Wendungen

- *The cartoon shows …/In the cartoon, there is/are …*
- *In the background …/In the foreground …/In the centre of the cartoon …*
- *On the left …/In the top right-hand corner there is/are …/The left half shows …*
- *The facial expression shows that …*
- *The cartoon has a/no caption …*
- *The caption reads …*
- *The cartoonist/artist illustrates …/wants to express the fact that …*
- *The cartoonist/artist makes clear/criticises/emphasises …*
- *The cartoon is a reference to …/refers/alludes to …/is a criticism of …*
- *The message of the cartoon is …/The cartoon might suggest that …*
- *It is an interesting, multi-layered cartoon …/It shows an exaggerated view of …*
- *To get across this message, the cartoonist …*

Auch für die Analyse eines Cartoons oder Bildes können Sie mit den „**MindCards**" (vgl. „Hinweise zu den digitalen Zusätzen") einige nützliche Wendungen wiederholen.

## Vorbereitung auf diesen Prüfungsteil

Neben der sprachlichen Vorbereitung können Sie sich vor allem auf politische Karikaturen am besten vorbereiten, indem Sie sich über aktuelle Ereignisse auf dem Laufenden halten. Machen Sie es sich beispielsweise zur Gewohnheit, regelmäßig englischsprachige Nachrichten zu lesen, was im Internet sehr einfach möglich ist. So bleiben Sie nicht nur auf dem neuesten Stand, was die politische Lage betrifft, sondern erweitern gleichzeitig Ihren Wortschatz und Ihre Lesefähigkeiten.

## Analyse von Statistiken

### Wichtige Fakten

| | |
|---|---|
| **Prüfungsteil:** | Schreiben: kann als Zusatzmaterial zu Teilaufgabe 2 (Analyse) oder als eigenständige Aufgabe in Teilaufgabe 3 vorkommen |
| **Mögliche Diagrammarten:** | *bar chart/graph, flow chart, line graph, pie chart, organisation(al) chart, table* (s. unten) |

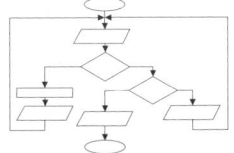

*bar chart/graph* (Balken-, Säulendiagramm)   *flow chart* (Flussdiagramm)

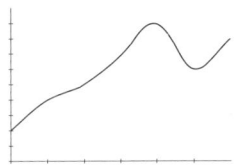

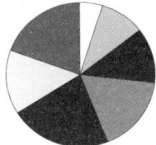

*line graph* (Kurvendiagramm)   *pie chart* (Kreisdiagramm, Kuchendiagramm)

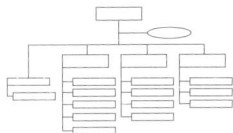

*organisation(al) chart* (Organigramm)   *table* (Tabelle)

**Tipps zur Vorgehensweise**

- Benennen Sie zunächst das Thema des Schaubilds. Häufig wird dieses bereits in einer Bildunterschrift genannt, lässt sich also einfach ablesen.
- Bei der näheren Beschreibung der dargestellten Informationen sollten Sie darauf achten, Wesentliches von Unwesentlichem zu unterscheiden. Nicht jeder einzelne Wert ist wichtig. Stattdessen sollten Sie größere Trends oder besonders auffällige Erscheinungen thematisieren.
- Ähnlich wie bei einer Cartoon- oder Bildbeschreibung reicht es nicht aus, die dargestellten Fakten aufzuzählen. Sie sollten sie immer in größere Zusammenhänge einordnen, interpretieren, ihre Ursachen und Folgen aufzeigen, etc.
- Je nach Aufgabenstellung und Prüfungsteil müssen Sie Ihre Ergebnisse eventuell mit Informationen aus dem Lesetext vergleichen oder einen Bezug zwischen Ihren Ergebnissen und dem Schwerpunktthema bzw. einem anderen Themenkomplex herstellen. Finden Sie Anknüpfungspunkte und denken Sie daran, nicht nur Gemeinsamkeiten, sondern falls vorhanden auch Unterschiede aufzuzeigen. Wenn die Analyse der Statistik als eigenständige Aufgabe gestellt wird, kann auch Ihre eigene Meinung zu gezeigten Entwicklungen oder eine Art Fazit gefragt sein. Positionieren Sie sich zu der dargestellten Situation: Stufen Sie diese als kritisch oder bedenklich ein? Sollte eine Entwicklung Ihrer Meinung nach noch weitergehen? Haben Sie Vorschläge, wie man einen Zustand verbessern oder unterstützen könnte?

**Hilfreiche Wendungen**

**Allgemeine Aussagen zu Statistiken:**
- *The pie chart shows/compares …*
- *As can be seen from the line graph …*
- *The bar graph demonstrates …*
- *This table gives information about …*
- *Its most significant feature is …*
- *The figures in the table show that …*
- *The figures prove that …/This implies that …*
- *The statistics suggest that …*
- *The diagram makes it clear that …*
- *There is evidence that …*

**Beschreibung des Kurvenverlaufs:**

**Zunahme**

| | |
|---|---|
| • *to rise/go up/increase by … to …* | *Temperatures rose by 2 to 2.5 degrees.* |
| • *to rise/go up/increase from … to …* | *Profits went up from 20 % to 25 %.* |
| • *an increase/a rise of …* | *There was an increase/a rise of 5 %.* |

**Abnahme**

| | |
|---|---|
| • *to drop/go down/decrease/fall by … to …* | *Expenses dropped by $55,000 to $320,000.* |

- *to drop/go down/decrease/fall from …*    *Interest rates decreased from 18 % to*
  *to …*    *16 %.*
- *a drop/decrease/fall of …*    *There was a drop/decrease/fall of*
    *2 %.*
- *a drop/decrease/fall in …*    *The company experienced a drop/de-*
    *crease/fall in sales …*

### Qualitative Veränderung

- *slightly/steadily/dramatically/sharply*    *Temperatures have fallen slightly.*
- *continually* (stetig)/*gradually*    *Prices have gone up continually.*
  (allmählich)
- *significantly* (deutlich)/*insignificantly*    *Growth is expected to rise insignifi-*
  (unbedeutend)/*negligibly* (geringfügig)    *cantly.*

Beachten Sie auch hier die „**MindCards**" (s. „Hinweise zu den digitalen Zusätzen").

---

## Persönliche Stellungnahme

### Wichtige Fakten

| Prüfungsteil: | Auswahlmöglichkeit in Teilaufgabe 3 (Schreiben) |
| --- | --- |
| **Mögliche Operatoren:** | eigene Meinung zu einem Thema sachlich darstellen *(comment)*, Für und Wider eines Themas diskutieren *(discuss)*, unterschiedliche Aspekte eines Themas beleuchten *(assess, explain, …)* |

### Häufige Diskussionsgrundlagen

- Zitate/Sprichwörter (Beispiel: *"Nobody can give you freedom. Nobody can give you equality or justice or anything. If you're a man, you take it."* Malcolm X, 1965 – *Comment on the issue of equality with reference to the quotation.*)
- Aspekte des Schwerpunktthemas aus dem Pflichtkanon (Beispiel: *Explain the role of Carl Ott's rifle in the novel* Crooked Letter, Crooked Letter *and its influence on Larry and Silas's relationship.*)
- Verbindung von allgemeinen Problemstellungen mit Aspekten des Pflichtkanons (Beispiel: *In Gran Torino, the older Hmong speak their native language, the younger generation speaks both English and Hmong. – Comment on the importance of language for the integration of immigrants.*)

### Tipps zur Vorgehensweise

- Bei einer solchen Aufgabenstellung ist die **Konzeptarbeit** besonders wichtig. Grundsätzlich sollten Sie Ihren Aufsatz immer nach dem dreigliedrigen Schema Einleitung, Hauptteil, Schluss aufbauen (vgl. S. XXII für weitere Details).
- Teilaufgabe 3 passt thematisch in der Regel zum **Text** (und ggf. zum Schwerpunktthema). Sie können in Ihrem Brainstorming also auch Gedanken aus dem Text weiterführen bzw. passende Aspekte des Pflichtkanons sammeln.

- Achten Sie beim Verfassen Ihrer Lösung darauf, klare, überschaubare Sätze zu formulieren und Ihre Einzelgedanken sinnvoll und logisch miteinander zu verknüpfen (vgl. *connectives* auf Seite XI, die folgenden hilfreichen Wendungen sowie die entsprechenden Teilbereiche der „**MindCards**").
- Planen Sie genügend Zeit ein, um Ihren Text am Schluss noch einmal **Korrektur lesen** zu können.

## Typischer Aufbau eines sachlich-argumentativen Textes

- **Einleitung** *(introduction)*: Hinführung zum Thema; Problem aufgreifen; Interesse des Lesers wecken (Zitat, provokative Aussage, persönliche Erfahrung)
- **Hauptteil** *(body, main part)*: neuer Absatz für einen neuen Gedanken/ein neues Argument; Argumentationsschema (These, Begründung, Beispiel, Schlussfolgerung) beachten (selbstverständlich müssen nicht alle Bausteine bei jedem Argument genannt werden); Sätze sinnvoll verbinden
- **Schluss** *(conclusion)*: kurze zusammenfassende, wertende Aussage; wenn möglich: Bezug zur Einleitung herstellen

## Hilfreiche Wendungen:

| Aussageabsicht | Formulierung |
|---|---|
| • Argumente ordnen: | *First of all/To begin with, I would like to …* <br> *Another (significant) reason/advantage/ consequence is …* <br> *This brings us to the question of whether …* <br> *In addition/Moreover/Besides/Furthermore, you cannot deny that …* <br> *It is worth stating at this point that …* <br> *But above all …* |
| • eigene Meinung ausdrücken: | *It seems to me …/It has been my experience …/I've had a similar experience/In my experience/As far as I can see …/The way I see it …* <br> *I am afraid the author is wrong in saying/ claiming …* <br> *I maintain that …/I am convinced that …/ In my opinion/To my mind, you can say/ accept that …* <br> *My main argument/My point is that …* <br> *Surely/Obviously/Doubtlessly, it is wrong to say that …* <br> *The author is terribly/greatly mistaken in his conception of …* <br> *Unfortunately/Regrettably, he fails to see that …* |

- auf die Gegenmeinung eingehen: *All the same/Nevertheless, it is wrong to say that ...*
  *Contrary to public belief/the popular idea/ notion ...*
  *Despite all those arguments, we still face the problem that ...*
  *In contrast to/As opposed to/Unlike the writer, I think ...*
  *It is true that ... but it is definitely wrong to say that ...*
  *We must not forget, however, that ...*

- logische Folgerung ziehen: *All this shows that it is unwise to assume that ...*
  *From all this follows that ...*
  *So/Therefore/That is why we cannot assume that ...*

- Schluss formulieren: *All in all, I therefore reject the view that ...*
  *In sum/In brief, I cannot accept the suggestion that ...*
  *To conclude/In conclusion/As a result, you can safely say that ...*
  *To sum up, I am seriously opposed to the writer's position that ...*
  *Weighing the pros and cons, one comes to the conclusion that ...*

## Gestaltende Schreibaufgabe

### Wichtige Fakten

| Prüfungsteil: | Auswahlmöglichkeit in Teilaufgabe 3 (Schreiben) |
|---|---|
| Häufig erwartete Zieltextformate: | Artikel, Rede, E-Mail, Blogeintrag, Brief/Leserbrief, innerer Monolog |

### Mögliche Aufgabenstellungen

Im Wesentlichen können die Aufgabenstellungen entweder textnah oder themenbezogen sein. Auch hier ist bei einem der beiden Auswahltexte eine (zusätzliche) Anknüpfung an das Schwerpunktthema vorgesehen.

- **textnahe Aufgaben:** Hier sollen Sie Aspekte des Textes in kreativer Form, beispielsweise in einem Leserbrief oder Blogeintrag, kommentieren. Es kann aber auch eine Weiterführung oder Umgestaltung gefordert sein, z. B. indem Sie aus der Sicht einer bestimmten Person die Ereignisse rekapitulieren, weiterführen oder anderweitig durchdenken sollen.

- **themenbezogene Aufgaben:** Hier wird das Thema des Textes in einen größeren Kontext eingeordnet, mit dem Sie sich kreativ auseinandersetzen sollen. Dabei kann z. B. ein Artikel, eine Rede oder ein Blogeintrag zu einer bestimmten Fragestellung verlangt sein.

- **Schwerpunktthemenbezug:** Bei einem der beiden Textvorschläge werden die Teilaufgaben 3 in der Form über den Text hinausgehen, dass sie Kenntnisse aus *Crooked Letter, Crooked Letter* oder *Gran Torino* abfragen. Die oben genannten Aufgabenbeispiele können dann z. B. die Perspektive einer Figur aus Roman oder Film miteinbeziehen oder Roman bzw. Film zur Diskussionsgrundlage machen (Beispiel: *You are taking part in an international school project called* The American Dream in Film. *Write an article for the project website, commenting on whether social mobility as presented in* Gran Torino *is something worth striving for.*)

## Tipps zur Vorgehensweise

Für die Vielfalt der kreativen Aufgabenformen müssen unterschiedlichste Anforderungen beachtet werden. Als Grundregel sollen jedoch die folgenden gelten:

- **Perspektive:** Aus welcher Perspektive schreiben Sie Ihren Text? Bei einem fiktiven Tagebucheintrag oder inneren Monolog müssen Sie stets im Hinterkopf behalten, was Sie über die Person wissen, aus deren Sicht Sie schreiben. Hat das Auswirkungen auf die Ausdrucksweise oder den Schreibstil?

- **Formale Elemente:** Eine Rede beginnt beispielsweise immer mit einer Begrüßung und hat den Auftrag, ein Publikum zu fesseln, was sich auch in der rhetorischen Gestaltung widerspiegeln sollte. Ein Artikel sollte eine Überschrift sowie einen klaren, in Absätze gegliederten Aufbau haben. Auch für Briefe gibt es ganz bestimmte formale Vorgaben, die am Beispiel eines Leserbriefes hier aufgelistet sind:

| | |
|---|---|
| *Date:* | *15 May 20xx* |
| *Salutation:* | *Sir/Madam,* |
| ***Body of letter:*** | |
| *Reference:* | *I am writing to you following your recent article "(title)", written by (author) and published on (date) in (source) …* |
| | *With reference to your article on …, I would like to point out that …* |
| | *I would like to congratulate you on …* |
| | *Thank you very much for the article concerning …, which was really an eye-opener.* |

| | |
|---|---|
| *Your opinion:* | *In my opinion, his arguments are highly prejudiced and somewhat ignorant of the real situation in our society today.*<br>*The article ... on the problem of ... seems to present an unrealistic and excessively negative picture of ...*<br>*The concern you have shown in your article ... is highly commendable. However, ...*<br>*I must strongly protest against the claim that ...* |
| *Arguments:* | *It would, in my opinion, be wrong to ...*<br>*I can see no reason why ...*<br>*There is no proof whatsoever that ...*<br>*It is simply not true that ...*<br>*On the one hand, ..., on the other hand, ...*<br>*It is true that ... but ...* |
| *Rounding off:* | *To put it all in a nutshell, I have the impression that ...*<br>*All in all, ...*<br>*Therefore I conclude that/I would say/think ...*<br>*As a result, .../Consequently, ...* |
| *Closing formula: (optional)* | *Regards,/Best regards,/Yours faithfully, ...* |
| *Signature:* | *Full name (possible: hometown)* (ggf. fiktional) |

- **Sprachebene/Register:** Auch hier ist einerseits zu beachten, aus welcher (fiktiven) Perspektive Sie schreiben. Wenn Sie beispielsweise die Rolle einer Figur aus dem Text oder dem Lektürekanon einnehmen, wird es positiv vermerkt, wenn Sie deren Sprachstil soweit möglich imitieren. Andererseits ist auch das Zielpublikum wichtig für die Wahl der richtigen Sprachebene: E-Mails an gleichaltrige, gute Bekannte oder Blogeinträge können in einem freundschaftlichen und eher informellen Ton gehalten sein, während eine Ausarbeitung oder ein Referat für die Schule oder für ein mehr oder weniger wissenschaftliches Projekt formeller klingen sollten.

# Liste ausgewählter Operatoren

Die folgenden Erläuterungen zu einzelnen Arbeitsanweisungen sollen Ihnen einen Einblick vermitteln, wie die Aufgabenstellung zu verstehen ist und welche Leistung von Ihnen erwartet wird. Ganz genau und endgültig kann dies jedoch nicht festgelegt werden, da es immer darauf ankommt, in welchem Kontext eine Arbeitsanweisung gestellt wird. Mit ein und demselben Operator lassen sich unterschiedlich komplexe Aufgaben formulieren. Sie müssen also die Aufgabe genau lesen. In Klammern hinter den Operatoren steht, in welcher Teilaufgabe die jeweilige Arbeitsanweisung am häufigsten zu erwarten ist, was aber nicht als ausschließliche Angabe verstanden werden soll.

1. **analyse** (TA 2): Beschreiben und erklären Sie etwas genau, indem Sie die Grundbestandteile, nämlich Inhalt und Form, untersuchen und dann ihre Funktion klären. Sie untersuchen also, was gesagt wird (Inhalt), wie es gesagt wird (Form) und warum etwas auf eine bestimmte Weise ausgedrückt wird (Funktion). Das Verständnis des Ganzen soll durch die Zergliederung in seine Einzelteile ermöglicht werden.

   Beispiel: *Analyse the opening paragraph of the short story.*

   Wenn Sie einen Textanfang analysieren sollen, müssen Sie beschreiben, wovon die Passage handelt, wie der Autor/die Autorin sie gestaltet hat und warum.

   Dem Beginn eines Textes kommt immer eine besondere Bedeutung zu. Die wichtigsten Funktionen sind Hinführung zum Thema bzw. zur Geschichte und Motivation, d. h. die Leser*innen anzuregen, weiterzulesen.

   - Anfang eines Sachtextes: In Pressetexten wird häufig versucht, die Aufmerksamkeit der Leserschaft zu gewinnen, indem Texte wie Geschichten aufgebaut werden: *„The president sat in the Oval Office when the phone rang and the director of the CIA ..."* Ein Sachtext kann auch mit der Erwähnung eines aktuellen Ereignisses oder der Klärung eines zentralen Begriffes einsetzen: *„When scientists talk of biodegradable products, they mean ..."*
   - Anfang eines literarischen Textes: Der Anfang eines Romans oder einer Kurzgeschichte soll ebenfalls dazu dienen, zum Weiterlesen einzuladen: *"I once saw a bloke try to kill himself."* (Alan Sillitoe, "On Saturday Afternoon"). Durch diesen ersten Satz der Kurzgeschichte wird auch die Erzählperspektive *(point of view)* festgelegt: Ich-Erzählung *(first-person narration)*. Häufig geht es auch darum, am Beginn den Schauplatz der Handlung darzustellen, eine Person einzuführen oder eine bestimmte Atmosphäre zu schaffen. Letztere Funktion ist eng mit der sprachlichen Gestaltung verbunden. Schauen Sie sich die Wortwahl genau an (im Besonderen die Adjektive).

2. **characterise** (TA 2): Beschreiben und analysieren Sie eine Person.

   Beispiel: *Characterise the protagonist of the story.*

   Wenn man eine Figur charakterisieren will, beginnt man zunächst mit der Beschreibung des Äußeren, d. h. mit Gestalt, Kleidung, Alter, Familienstand, Herkunft, sozialer Stellung etc. Untersuchen Sie dann, ob die Person vom Autor/von der Autorin oder von anderen Personen bzw. aus deren Sicht beschrieben wird (direkte Charakterisierung) oder ob ihre Eigenschaften durch ihr Verhalten anderen gegenüber gezeigt werden (indirekte Charakterisierung).

3. **comment** (TA 3): Äußern Sie eine begründete persönliche Meinung zu einem bestimmten Thema, Problem oder Standpunkt.

   Beispiel: *Comment on the government's assessment of the economic crisis.*

   Erwartet wird Ihre persönliche Meinung, ob die Regierung die Wirtschaftskrise richtig oder falsch eingeschätzt hat. Voraussetzung für eine gute Lösung sind Sachkenntnis und die Fähigkeit, eine Meinung überzeugend zu vertreten. Es geht weniger darum, das Problem noch einmal von mehreren Seiten zu beleuchten – das wäre eine Erörterung –, sondern Sie sollen zeigen, dass Sie argumentieren können. Halten Sie in einem Einleitungssatz noch einmal kurz das Thema/Problem fest und leiten Sie dann zu Ihrer Meinung über. Folgen Sie dem dreistufigen Aufbau einer guten Argumentation:
   - Behauptung/These *(In my view the government's way of dealing with the crisis is rather weak/ineffective/convincing ...)*
   - Begründung *(because ...)*
   - Beleg/Beispiel *(As we can see from ...)*

   Schließen Sie Ihre Beweisführung mit einer Schlussfolgerung, einem Fazit, ab: *Therefore I think/would say .../As a result, .../Consequently, ...*

   Eine gute Note ist nicht davon abhängig, ob Sie – in diesem Beispiel – das Vorgehen der Regierung positiv oder negativ bewerten oder ob Sie – in einem anderen Fall – für oder gegen eine Maßnahme sind. Sie lösen die Aufgabe gut, wenn Ihre Argumentationskette inhaltlich und sprachlich überzeugt.

4. **compare** (TA 2 oder 3): Stellen Sie Ähnlichkeiten und Unterschiede zwischen zwei oder mehreren Dingen dar und ziehen Sie Schlüsse daraus.

   Beispiel: *In the novel* Crooked Letter, Crooked Letter *Silas and Larry have the same father, Carl Ott. Compare how they have been influenced by him when growing up.*

   In dieser Aufgabenstellung geht es darum, Gemeinsamkeiten und Unterschiede zwischen den beiden Romancharakteren auszumachen. Anschließend sollten Sie eine Schlussfolgerung ziehen. Als gemeinsamer Ausgangspunkt lässt sich hier beispielsweise die eher negative Beeinflussung durch Carl Ott anführen. Während sich dieser Einfluss in Larrys Leben aber eher durch die dominante Präsenz und Unterdrückung durch seinen Vater äußert, ist Silas' Leben durch die Abwesenheit einer Vaterfigur geprägt. Larry ist ein sehr unsicherer Junge, der mit allen Mitteln versucht, seinen Vater zufriedenzustellen, damit aber immer wieder scheitert. In Silas dagegen verstärkt das Aufwachsen mit einer alleinerziehenden, sozial benachteiligten Mutter den Eindruck, vom Leben ungerecht behandelt worden zu sein und sich somit auch bestimmte Handlungen oder Versäumnisse erlauben zu dürfen, gerade gegenüber Larry, von dem er sich einredet, er habe es viel besser als er. Ein Fazit könnte also sein, dass Carl Ott beide Jungen stark beeinflusst, den einen aber durch seine An-, den anderen durch seine Abwesenheit, und sich dieser Einfluss somit auch bei beiden jeweils vollkommen unterschiedlich äußert.

5. **contrast** (TA 2 oder 3): Stellen Sie Informationen, Sachverhalte, Argumente, Urteile etc. einander beschreibend gegenüber.

Beispiel: *Contrast the attitudes of different EU member states towards the euro.*

Hier handelt es sich um eine Aufgabenstellung, die eine ähnliche Vorgehensweise wie beim Operator *compare* verlangt, jedoch sollen Sie sich auf die Unterschiede konzentrieren. Dazu müssen Sie in unserem Beispiel wissen bzw. dem Text entnehmen, welche Auffassungen die einzelnen EU-Länder in Bezug auf die Euro-Währung haben. Aufzeigen sollen Sie dann auffällige Unterschiede in den Vorstellungen der einzelnen Regierungen. Die Aufgabenstellung wird sich in der Regel nur auf Themenbereiche beziehen, bei denen Sie klare Unterschiede herausarbeiten können.

6. **criticise** (TA 3): Drücken Sie Ihre Kritik am Verhalten oder an der Einstellung einer Person aus oder beurteilen Sie die Vor- oder Nachteile eines Verhaltens, einer Entscheidung usw.

Beispiel: *Criticise the government's decision to do away with military service.*

Mit dieser Anweisung werden Sie aufgefordert, zu einem Sachverhalt Stellung zu nehmen. Anders als bei einer Erörterung (siehe Arbeitsanweisung *discuss*) wägen Sie ein Problem nicht neutral ab, sondern kritisieren etwas und bringen klar Ihre Meinung zum Ausdruck. Hier gehen Sie allerdings wie bei der Erörterung vor: Sie stellen Ihre persönliche These auf, die Sie durch eine sinnvolle Begründung und ein anschauliches Beispiel belegen. Es ist oft ratsam, auf gegnerische Argumente einzugehen, d. h. an sie anzuknüpfen, um dann eine abweichende Auffassung vorzubringen und die der Gegenseite als irrig darzustellen. Begründete Kritik ist stets berechtigt, sie hat nichts mit Besserwisserei zu tun. Frei nach G. E. Lessing gilt: „Wer etwas kritisiert, muss es nicht unbedingt besser können."

7. **describe** (TA 1): Beschreiben Sie in eigenen Worten eine bestimmte im Text dargestellte Entwicklung, Sachlage, Person, etc.

Beispiel: *Describe the protagonist's relationship to his brother.*

Wichtig ist, dass Sie sich bei dieser Aufgabenstellung auf Aspekte beschränken, die im Text genannt werden. Normalerweise sind hier keine Interpretationen oder Deutungen gefragt, sondern ein bloßes Herausfiltern der passenden Informationen aus dem Text.

8. **discuss** (TA 3): Beleuchten Sie ein Problem von allen Seiten, indem Sie Argumente ausführen – belegt durch Details, Beispiele, weitere Informationen – und sinnvoll ordnen.

Beispiel: *Discuss attempts to legalise certain soft drugs.*

Diese Aufgabenstellung ist vergleichbar mit einer Erörterung. Sie sollen ein Problem, hier die Freigabe von sogenannten weichen Drogen, zunächst identifizieren und dann erörtern, d. h. Argumente pro <u>und</u> kontra erfassen und die zugehörigen Begründungen darstellen. Beachten Sie, dass sich hier fast immer zwei verschiedene Arten von Problemen ableiten lassen: Sachprobleme *(What are soft drugs? – What kinds of genetic tests are used in medical research?)* und Wertprobleme *(Is it right to legalise soft drugs? – Should insurance companies be allowed to make use of genetic test information?).* Bei der Erörterung eines Sachproblems sollten Sie auf relativ gesicherte und nachweisbare Tatsachen zurückgreifen (Statistiken, allgemeine Lebenserfahrung): *There is statistic evidence that the legalisation of drugs ...* Vermeiden Sie es allerdings, sich Prozentzahlen auszudenken, wenn Sie sich auf Statistiken beziehen. Werturteile sind schwieriger zu begründen, da man hier unterschiedliche Einstellungen vertreten kann. Es liegt in der Natur der Sache, dass persönliche Meinungen umstritten sind: *I am of the opinion that the government ought to be stricter ...* Wichtig ist, dass Ihre Argumentation logisch ist und einleuchtet.

9. **evaluate** (auch: **assess**) (TA 3): Geben Sie ein Werturteil ab, stellen Sie eine negative oder positive Behauptung nach sorgfältiger Abwägung auf. Dabei sollen Sie Ihre Antwort durch Belege, beispielsweise Fakten und Zahlen, absichern.

   Beispiel: *Evaluate the efficiency of former British Prime Minister David Cameron's "Remain" campaign (anti-Brexit).*

   Hier handelt es sich um die Bearbeitung eines Wertproblems: *In my view Cameron's campaign has not done enough to check the spread of anti-European sentiments.* Erwartet wird, dass Ihr Urteil begründet ist. Besonders geeignete – weil kaum widerlegbare – Argumente für eine These sind u. a. nachprüfbare Tatsachen, Statistiken und verallgemeinerte Erfahrungen: *There is statistical evidence that UKIP steadily gained support after the party's foundation in the 1990s.* Es ist unausweichlich, dass Ihre Einschätzung nicht von jedermann geteilt wird. Werturteile, persönliche Meinungen und Gefühle sind immer umstritten, da man bei (fast) allen Problemen verschiedener Auffassung sein kann. Wenn Sie z. B. die Meinung äußern *I think there should not have been a referendum at all,* kann es gut sein, dass Sie mit dieser Aussage auf Widerspruch stoßen werden. Deshalb ist es wichtig, dass Sie sich treffende Begründungen für Ihre Argumentation zurechtlegen, damit man Ihre Einschätzung, wenn schon nicht übernehmen, so doch zumindest nachvollziehen kann.

10. **explain** (TA 2): Erläutern Sie etwas, machen Sie etwas verständlich. Mit dieser Aufgabe kann das Verständnis einer Textstelle bzw. des gesamten Textes überprüft werden. Sie geht über eine reine inhaltliche Zusammenfassung hinaus.

    Beispiel: *Explain the author Susan Porterey's stance towards the relationship between the USA and Great Britain.*

    Mit einer solchen Aufgabenstellung wird meist eine Analyseaufgabe eingeleitet. Hier sollen Sie also einerseits eine inhaltliche Frage beantworten („Wie schätzt die Autorin die amerikanisch-britische Beziehung ein?"). Andererseits sollen Sie Ihre Aussagen auch begründen, also Textstellen anführen, an denen ihre Haltung zum Ausdruck gebracht wird. Sehr häufig müssen Sie zur Beantwortung einer solchen Fragestellung zwischen den Zeilen lesen: Es könnte also sein, dass nicht wortwörtlich im Text steht, ob Susan Porterey den Stand der amerikanisch-britischen Beziehungen als gut oder schlecht beurteilt. Stattdessen macht sie das vielleicht eher indirekt, zum Beispiel durch bestimmte sprachliche Mittel, deutlich.

11. **interpret** (TA 2): Untersuchen Sie etwas ausführlich, um die Aussage, die der Verfasser/die Verfasserin treffen möchte, deutlich zu machen. Ähnlich wie bei den Operatoren „analyse" und „explain" kommt es nicht nur darauf an, was im Text gesagt wird, sondern vor allem auch darauf, wie etwas sprachlich ausgedrückt wird und warum eine bestimmte Darstellungsart gewählt wurde.

Beispiel: *Interpret the poem .../short story ...*

Diese Aufgabenstellung ist recht global, weil keine weiteren Hilfsfragen gestellt werden. Daher müssen Sie wissen, was bei einer literarischen Interpretation zu tun ist, nämlich den inhaltlichen Aufbau, die sprachlichen Gestaltungsmittel und den Zusammenhang zwischen beidem herauszuarbeiten. So gehen Sie dabei vor: Nach sorgfältigem, mehrmaligem Lesen halten Sie fest, wovon das Gedicht/die Kurzgeschichte handelt. Versuchen Sie, die Absicht des Verfassers/der Verfasserin als Arbeitshypothese zu formulieren. Danach klären Sie den Aufbau des literarischen Textes und untersuchen die sprachlichen Mittel, die verwendet werden. Beschreiben Sie die Wirkung von Gestaltungselementen. Überprüfen Sie Ihre Arbeitshypothese auf ihre Richtigkeit – vielleicht müssen Sie Ihren ersten Eindruck revidieren. Sie sollten daran denken, dass es hier keine richtige oder falsche Lösung gibt. Ihre Arbeit wird danach beurteilt, ob Ihre Auslegung stimmig ist. Das bedeutet, Ihre Interpretation muss nachvollziehbar und einleuchtend sein. Das erreichen Sie, indem Sie immer wieder überprüfen, ob Ihre Deutungen durch den Text gesichert sind.

12. **justify** (TA 3): Sagen Sie, warum eine Meinung, ein Standpunkt oder eine Maßnahme richtig oder angemessen ist. Eine Rechtfertigung ist in der Regel positiv. Heben Sie die Vorteile eines Standpunkts gegenüber seinen Nachteilen hervor.

Beispiel: *Justify the steps taken against drug addiction.*

Bei dieser Arbeitsanweisung sind Sie nicht mehr frei, Ihre persönliche Meinung zu äußern und zu begründen, sondern sollen eine Rolle übernehmen. In diesem Beispiel sollen Sie Maßnahmen gegen Drogensucht verteidigen. Diese Aufgabe ist eine Art rhetorische Übung, bei welcher der Schwerpunkt auf der Technik des Argumentierens liegt. Dabei soll Ihre eigene Meinung ganz bewusst zur Seite geschoben werden. Es kommt bei solchen Rhetorikübungen darauf an, das (fiktive) Publikum zu überzeugen. Wenn Sie eine Aufgabe mit dem Operator *justify* bearbeiten, können Sie wie bei einer linearen Erörterung vorgehen. Sie suchen Argumente, führen sie mit einem Beleg und einem Beispiel aus und ordnen sie dann in steigernder Form an, d. h., Sie gehen von einem weniger wichtigen zum wichtigsten Argument für oder gegen eine Maßnahme oder einen Vorschlag.

13. **outline** (TA 1): Sie sollen eine Inhaltsangabe verfassen. Dabei gehen Sie vor wie bei *summarise.*

Beispiel: *Outline the pros and cons of genetic engineering us described in the newspaper article.*

Häufig werden Sie nicht den gesamten Text zusammenfassen müssen. Stattdessen wird erwartet, dass Sie bestimmte Aspekte (*„the pros and cons of genetic engineering"*) aus dem Text herausarbeiten und in Ihren eigenen Worten wiedergeben.

XXX

14. **summarise/sum up** (TA 1): Fassen Sie die Hauptgedanken eines Textes in knapper Form ohne Veranschaulichungen und Beispiele zusammen.

Beispiel: *Summarise the author's arguments against abortion.*

Die Aufgabe verlangt, dass Sie einen Text oder eine Argumentation knapp und sinnvoll zusammenfassen. Hier wird zweierlei überprüft: Ihr Textverständnis und Ihre Sprachfertigkeit. Zunächst müssen Sie die wichtigsten Aussagen aus der Vorlage herausfiltern und sie danach mit eigenen Worten knapp wiedergeben. Wichtigste Voraussetzung für eine erfolgreiche Lösung dieser Aufgabe ist, dass Sie das Original gut verstanden haben. Lesen Sie deshalb den Text mehrmals sehr sorgfältig und kennzeichnen Sie die Stellen, die Ihnen wichtig erscheinen. Gehen Sie den Text Abschnitt für Abschnitt durch und verfolgen Sie den Gedankengang. Unterscheiden Sie dabei zwischen Haupt- und Nebengedanken. Identifizieren Sie dann Wiederholungen, Belege und Beispiele, die die Argumentation untermauern. Das sind die Teile der Vorlage, auf die Sie in Ihrer Zusammenfassung verzichten werden. Es ist eine bewährte Methode, nach dem sorgfältigen Durcharbeiten des Textes jeden einzelnen Abschnitt knapp – vielleicht mit einem Satz – zusammenzufassen. Achten Sie bei Ihrer Lösung darauf, dass Sie keine neuen Gedanken oder neuen Beispiele einführen und dass Sie keine eigenen Wertungen abgeben. Was die Formulierung betrifft: Zeigen Sie, dass Sie über einen guten Wortschatz verfügen. Lösen Sie sich sprachlich von der Vorlage, indem Sie, sofern es sich nicht um Fachbegriffe handelt, den ursprünglichen Text durch Synonyme und Umschreibungen wiedergeben. Verfassen Sie Ihre Zusammenfassung im Präsens.

Dieses Buch soll Ihnen die Möglichkeit geben, sich optimal auf die schriftliche Abiturprüfung vorzubereiten. Anhand der **abiturähnlichen Übungsaufgaben** können Sie die Kompetenz des **Hörverstehens** trainieren sowie verschiedene, für Ihre Prüfung zu erwartende Aufgabenformate einüben. Auch im Bereich **Schreiben** sind sowohl die **offiziellen Musteraufgaben** als auch die abiturähnlichen Übungsaufgaben so aufgebaut, wie Sie sie in Ihrer eigenen Prüfung erwarten können. Es wurde hier außerdem bewusst eine Mischung aus fiktionalen und nicht-fiktionalen Texten mit und ohne Schwerpunktthemenbezug abgedruckt, damit Sie alle möglichen Schreibaufgaben kennenlernen können.

Zusätzlich enthält dieses Buch eine **Übungsaufgabe zur Kommunikationsprüfung**. Damit können Sie sich auf den mündlichen Teil Ihrer schriftlichen Abiturprüfung vorbereiten.

Bei den **Prüfungsaufgaben 2021 und 2022** handelt es sich um Original-Abituraufgaben. Beide enthalten ebenfalls **Hörverstehensaufgaben**, wie sie Ihnen in Ihrer Prüfung begegnen könnten. Die Textaufgaben waren bis 2023 noch anders aufgebaut. Dennoch können Ihnen die Vorlagen eine realistische Vorstellung von Länge und Schwierigkeit von Abiturtexten vermitteln. Anhand der Musterlösungen zu den vormaligen Prüfungsteilen *Analysis* und *Composition* können Sie außerdem wichtige Aspekte des Lektürekanons wiederholen. Der Prüfungsteil *Reading Comprehension* wurde in den Original-Prüfungen weggelassen, da er in Ihrem Abitur ganz anders aussehen wird als die früheren Fragestellungen. Den Prüfungsteil **Hörverstehen von 2023** finden Sie online auf MyStark.

Alle Aufgaben sind mit **Musterlösungen** versehen. Oft ist es hilfreich, diese nach der eigenen Bearbeitung durchzulesen. Hierbei können Sie nicht nur abgleichen, ob Sie die inhaltlichen Punkte der Fragestellung abgedeckt haben, Sie können auch sehen, wie man die Lösung sinnvoll gliedern kann und wie sich Aspekte sprachlich gelungen ausdrücken lassen. Selbstverständlich müssen Sie nicht genau das schreiben, was in der Musterlösung genannt wird. Lassen Sie sich nicht verunsichern. Auch mit einer geringeren Anzahl an Aspekten, die Sie sinnvoll strukturiert haben, oder einfacheren, aber korrekten Formulierungen können Sie eine sehr gute Leistung erreichen. Nutzen Sie die Musterlösungen als Anregungen für Ihre Vokabel- oder Konzeptarbeit. Zusätzlich dienen Ihnen die der Lösung vorangestellten **Tipps** als Hilfe für die Bearbeitung. Greifen Sie darauf zurück, falls Sie einmal nicht vorankommen oder um Ihre Lösung zu überprüfen.

ÜBUNGSAUFGABEN

**HÖRVERSTEHEN**

### Task 1: BBC News

You will hear several items from the BBC radio news. Choose from the list (A–H) which description applies to which news item (1–7). For each item there is only one correct answer. Put the letters (A–H) into the correct box. There is one more description than you need.

| | Description |
|---|---|
| A | Assault on institutions causing many casualties |
| B | Country's attempt to stop a push for independence |
| C | Critical voices facing legal action |
| D | Government officials sentenced for wrongdoing |
| E | Historic town about to be retaken |
| F | Inhabitants escaping from embattled city |
| G | Rebel attack prevented by UN peace keepers |
| H | Two conflicting parties accused of human rights violations |

| News item | 1 | 2 | 3 | 4 | 5 | 6 | 7 |
|---|---|---|---|---|---|---|---|
| Description A–H | | | | | | | |

Listen to a radio report. While listening, tick (✓) the correct answer (a, b, c or d). There is only one correct answer.

1 Sande Hashimoto remembers that Japanese Americans were ...
   a ☐ relieved to be taken to a location close by.
   b ☐ reluctant to leave their neighborhood.
   c ☐ separated from family members by the military.
   d ☐ trying to find buyers for their possessions.

2 When the Hashimotos came back, they ...
   a ☐ hired African Americans to work in their shop.
   b ☐ ran the same shop as before.
   c ☐ were happy to see their customers return.
   d ☐ worked in an African American shop.

3 Little Tokyo experienced ...
   a ☐ a cultural decline.
   b ☐ a demographic change.
   c ☐ an economic downturn.
   d ☐ an improved housing situation.

4 When Sande Hashimoto came back, she ...
   a ☐ became friends with the new neighbors.
   b ☐ had a hard time making friends.
   c ☐ met some of her old friends again.
   d ☐ was discriminated against.

5 Adrian Florido says that Blacks from the South came to Los Angeles ...
   a ☐ because of the availability of cheap housing.
   b ☐ because of the dynamic Black community.
   c ☐ to escape discrimination.
   d ☐ to find employment.

6 Historian Martha Nakagawa claims that ...
   a ☐ African Americans went to court to remain in their homes.
   b ☐ Blacks ultimately profited from the Japanese Americans' return.
   c ☐ landlords favored Japanese Americans over African Americans.
   d ☐ whites helped African Americans to find new housing.

2

**7** Martha Nakagawa's view of the Japanese American community seems …

a ☐ critical.

b ☐ indifferent.

c ☐ prejudiced.

d ☐ factual.

**8** Today's visitors are reminded of the Bronzeville era by a …

a ☐ bronze statue in Little Tokyo.

b ☐ Charley Parker painting.

c ☐ phrase engraved in the pavement.

d ☐ small historical marker.

## Task 3: Young People's Literature

Listen to an interview with Gene Luen Yang and Jacqueline Woodson. While listening, answer the questions. You need not write complete sentences.

**1** What do the writers Gene Luen Yang and Jacqueline Woodson have in common?

_____

**2** Which rewards of his position did Yang enjoy? *(Name one.)*

_____

**3** What did Jon Scieszka, who held the position first, try to achieve?

_____

**4** What does Yang mean when he refers to "diversity of format"?

_____

**5** Which two examples of "underserved people" does Woodson give?

• _____     • _____

**6** What effects do labels like "struggling reader" have according to Woodson?

_____

**7** What does Woodson say about the ideal effect of reading a book?

_____

**8** What tone is evoked by the repeated reference to a helicopter?

_____

*Bei den für Set 1 abgedruckten Aufgaben zum Hörverstehen handelt es sich um die Original-Aufgaben des Hörverstehensteils der zentral gestellten Kursarbeit 2019 in Rheinland-Pfalz.*

| Text | Chimamanda Ngozi Adichie: *Americanah* |

*Americanah is a novel by the Nigerian author Chimamanda Ngozi Adichie. It tells the story of a young Nigerian woman, Ifemelu, who emigrates to the United States to attend university. The novel traces Ifemelu's life in both countries; she is a blogger who writes about her experiences as a non-American Black woman in the United States. Both Curt and Blaine are American men Ifemelu has a relationship with in the course of the novel. Curt is a White man and well-off; he helps Ifemelu to get a green card. Blaine is African American and admires Barack Obama. A substantial part of the novel is told in flashbacks.*

1  […] Some years later, at a dinner party in Manhattan, a day after Barack Obama became the Democratic Party's candidate for President of the United States, surrounded by guests, all fervent Obama supporters who were dewy-eyed with wine and victory, a balding white man said, "Obama will end racism in this country", and a large-hipped,
5  stylish poet from Haiti agreed, nodding, her Afro bigger than Ifemelu's, and said she had dated a white man for three years in California and race was never an issue for them.
"That's a lie," Ifemelu said to her.
"What?" the woman asked, as though she could not have heard properly.
10  "It's a lie," Ifemelu repeated.
The woman's eyes bulged. "You're telling me what my own experience was?"
Even though Ifemelu by then understood that people like the woman said what they said to keep others comfortable, and to show they appreciated How Far We Have Come; even though she was by then happily ensconced in a circle of Blaine's friends, one of
15  whom was the woman's new boyfriend, and even though she should have left it alone, she did not. She could not. The words had, once again, overtaken her; they overpowered her throat, and tumbled out.
"The only reason you say that race was not an issue is because you wish it was not. We all wish it was not. But it's a lie. I came from a country where race was not an
20  issue; I did not think of myself as black and I only became black when I came to America. When you are black in America and you fall in love with a white person, race doesn't matter when you're alone together because it's just you and your love. But the minute you step outside, race matters. But we don't talk about it.
We don't even tell our white partners the small things that piss us off and the things
25  we wish they understood better, because we're worried they will say we're overreacting, or we're being too sensitive. And we don't want them to say, Look how far we've come, just forty years ago it would have been illegal for us to even be a couple blah blah blah, because you know what we're thinking when they say that? We're thinking why the fuck should it ever have been illegal anyway? But we don't say any of this
30  stuff. We let it pile up inside our heads and when we come to nice liberal dinners like this, we say that race doesn't matter because that's what we're supposed to say, to keep our nice liberal friends comfortable. It's true. I speak from experience."

4

The host, a Frenchwoman, glanced at her American husband, a slyly pleased smile on her face; the most unforgettable dinner parties happened when guests said unex-
35 pected, and potentially offensive, things.

The poet shook her head and said to the host, "I'd love to take some of that wonder-ful dip home if you have any left," and looked at the others as though she could not believe they were actually listening to Ifemelu. But they were, all of them hushed, their eyes on Ifemelu as though she was about to give up a salacious secret that would both
40 titillate and implicate them. Ifemelu had been drinking too much white wine; from time to time she had a swimming sensation in her head, and she would later send apology e-mails to the host and the poet. But everyone was watching her, even Blaine, whose expression she could not, for once, read clearly. And so she began to talk about Curt.

It was not that they avoided race, she and Curt. They talked about it in the slippery
45 way that admitted nothing and engaged nothing and ended with the word "crazy", like a curious nugget to be examined and then put aside. Or as jokes that left her with a small and numb discomfort that she never admitted to him. And it was not that Curt pretended that being black and being white were the same in America; he knew they were not. It was, instead, that she did not understand how he grasped one thing but was
50 completely tone-deaf about another similar thing, how he could easily make one im-aginative leap, but be crippled in the face of another. [...]

At [his cousin Ashleigh's wedding] reception, he kept his fingers meshed with hers. Young females in tiny dresses, their breaths and bellies sucked in, trooped across to say hello to him and to flirt, asking if he remembered them, Ashleigh's friend from
55 high school, Ashleigh's roommate in college. When Curt said, "This is my girlfriend, Ifemelu", they looked at her with surprise, a surprise that some of them shielded and some of them did not, and in their expressions was the question "Why her?" It amused Ifemelu. She had seen that look before, on the faces of white women, strangers on the street, who would see her hand clasped in Curt's and instantly cloud their faces with
60 that look. The look of people confronting a great tribal loss. It was not merely because Curt was white, it was the kind of white he was, the untamed golden hair and handsome face, the athlete's body, the sunny charm and the smell, around him, of money. If he were fat, older, poor, plain, eccentric, or dreadlocked, then it would be less remarkable, and the guardians of the tribe would be mollified. And it did not help that although she
65 might be a pretty black girl, she was not the kind of black that they could, with an effort, imagine him with: she was not light-skinned, she was not biracial. At that party, as Curt held on to her hand, kissed her often, introduced her to everyone, her amuse-ment curdled into exhaustion. The looks had begun to pierce her skin. She was tired even of Curt's protection, tired of needing protection. [...]                    *987 words*

**1** Summarise Ifemelu's reasons for disagreeing with the Haitian poet. (20 %)

**2** Analyse the means and strategies the author uses to present Ifemelu's attitude as convincing. Also take into account the narrative perspective. (40 %)

**3** Choose *one* of the following tasks: (40 %)

**3.1** "Obama will end racism in this country." (l. 4)

Discuss whether this hope has become a reality in the United States.

**or**

**3.2** Interpret the cartoon and comment on its message.

© *Joseph Rank / cartoonstock.com*

**Information**

"The New Colossus" is a sonnet by Emma Lazarus. It was cast onto a bronze plaque and can be found inside the Statue of Liberty.

The original version of the second stanza of the poem is as follows:

"Give me your tired, your poor,
Your huddled masses yearning to breathe free,
The wretched refuse of your teeming shore.
Send these, the homeless, tempest-tossed to me,
I lift my lamp beside the golden door!"

**HÖRVERSTEHEN**

| **Transcript 1** **BBC News** |

BBC News with Debbie Russ.

**1** A United Nations investigation into the battle for Aleppo last year has concluded that the Syrian air force was responsible for an attack on a UN Aid aid convoy in which 14 people died. It also accuses Syrian forces of deploying chemical weapons. Rebels are also said to have committed war crimes by using civilians as human shields and indiscriminately shelling neighbourhoods under government control.

**2** The Iraqi government says that over the past ten days, 26,000 civilians have fled Mosul as the army continues its offensive to recapture the city from the Islamic State group. Iraqi forces are currently trying to drive militants out of the western half of the city.

**3** A Chinese Foreign Ministry spokesman says Beijing is willing to work with the international community to fight Uighur Islamist militants who want to establish a separate state in the western Chinese province of Xinjiang. The comments followed the release of a video purportedly by the Islamic State group showing Uighur fighters training and issuing threats against China.

**4** Syrian government forces fighting Islamic State militants have reportedly advanced into the edge of Palmyra, the desert city that's home to world-famous ancient ruins. The militants first captured Palmyra in 2015 and deliberately destroyed some of its 2000-year-old monuments and towers.

**5** Two suicide attacks in different parts of the Afghan capital Kabul have left at least 16 people dead and more than 50 wounded. One targeted a military training college, the other was aimed at the National Intelligence headquarters.

**6** Six journalists working for opposition newspapers are expected to appear in court in Ivory Coast. They are charged with spreading false information following a mutiny last week by soldiers demanding bonus payments.

**7** Myanmar's police court has found three senior officers guilty of negligence after insurgents attacked three border control posts on their watch. The officers will serve between two and three years in prison.

BBC News.

*BBC WorldService, BBC News Summary, 2017/03/01, https://www.bbc.co.uk/programmes/p04tnn56*

Identify key words in the descriptions and then listen for similar key words in the news items. However, be careful to focus on the content rather than waiting for exact repetitions. The listening text and the tasks may often use synonymous expressions.

1 News item **1** tells us "that the Syrian air force was <u>responsible for an attack on a UN Aid aid convoy</u> in which 14 people died" (ll. 3/4). Furthermore, "Syrian forces [are accused] of <u>deploying chemical weapons</u>" (l. 4) and "[r]ebels are also said to have <u>committed war crimes</u>" (ll. 4/5). In other words, two different factions, namely the Syrian forces as well as the rebels, are "accused of human rights violations" (description **H**). Don't be misled by the quite prominent mention of the UN (cf. ll. 2/3). Although the UN also comes up in description **G**, peace keepers who have prevented an attack are not mentioned in the news item.

2 News item **2** deals with "<u>26,000 civilians</u> [who] <u>have fled Mosul</u> as the army continues its <u>offensive to recapture the city</u> from the Islamic State group" (ll. 7–9). "To flee" is a synonym of "to escape", so description **F** fits.

3 The most important information news item **3** provides is that people "who want to establish a <u>separate state</u> in the western Chinese province of Xinjiang" (ll. 12/13) are fought by the Chinese government. In other words, China is trying "to stop a push for independence" (description **B**).

4 According to news item **4**, "Palmyra, the desert city that's home to <u>world-famous ancient ruins</u>" (l. 17), in other words a "[h]istoric town", is close to be "retaken" (description **E**) by "Syrian government forces" (l. 16).

5 News item **5** explains that "[t]wo suicide attacks in different parts of the Afghan capital Kabul have left at least <u>16 people dead</u> and <u>more than 50 wounded</u>" (ll. 20/21). In other words, it deals with "many casualties" (description **A**). The targets were "<u>a military training college</u> [as well as] <u>the National Intelligence headquarters</u>" (ll. 21/22), so the key word "institutions" from description **A** also fits.

6 "Six journalists working for <u>opposition newspapers</u> are expected to appear <u>in court</u> in Ivory Coast." (ll. 23/24) This statement from news item **6** fits the key words "[c]ritical voices" as well as "legal action" from description **C**.

7 "Myanmar's police court has found <u>three senior officers guilty</u> of negligence" (l. 26). Police officers are "[g]overnment officials", so description **D** fits.

| News item | 1 | 2 | 3 | 4 | 5 | 6 | 7 |
|---|---|---|---|---|---|---|---|
| Description A–H | H | F | B | E | A | C | D |

**A Los Angeles Neigborhood**

1 **Lourdes Garcia-Navarro** *(host)*: Seventy-five years ago today, President Franklin D. Roosevelt signed an executive order that forced 120,000 Japanese and Japanese Americans into World War II internment camps. Adrian Florido of NPR's Code Switch team has the story of a woman, Sande Hashimoto, who recalls what hap-
5 pened to her and what happened to her neighborhood.

**Adrian Florido** *(byline)*: Hashimoto and her family lived in LA's Little Tokyo. She remembers her parents and neighbors rushing to sell off their belongings, and she remembers the day they packed their bags.

**Sande Hashimoto:** And there were soldiers with rifles. And they told us all to, you know,
10 get on the train, so we did.

**Florido:** The train took them 200 miles away to the Manzanar internment camp. They lived there for more than three years. When they were released, the family moved back home, reopened their dry cleaning business. But Little Tokyo had changed.

**Hashimoto:** It was all black. You know, all our customers was [*sic*] black.

15 **Florido:** Where there used to be Japanese restaurants and shops, the businesses were now African American. The apartments the Japanese families left behind now housed black workers. Little Tokyo even had a new name, Bronzeville. Hashimoto made her first black friend, a little girl who lived nearby.

**Hashimoto:** And sometimes I would go over to her place, her mother would be braiding
20 her hair. And then as soon as she finished braiding her hair, then she says, "I'll braid yours, too". So I said, "OK".

**Florido:** One day, her friend moved away. And gradually, the other black residents in the neighborhood did too.

**Hashimoto:** The black people were there. And then all of a sudden, the Japanese Ameri-
25 can – they were all coming out of camp – and one by one, it was Little Tokyo again. I thought maybe I was dreaming these stories where they were there and they were gone.

**Florido:** But it wasn't a dream. It is a little-known bit of LA history. Historian Christopher Jimenez y West met me in Little Tokyo. He says after the Japanese were
30 interned, building owners had a lot of vacant property to fill. And this coincided with the arrival of many Southern blacks who came to LA for wartime jobs.

**Christopher Jimenez y West:** You're coming with very little resources, and so you're looking for the least expensive place to stay.

**Florido:** But in segregated LA, only about 5 percent of residential areas were open to
35 blacks, including Little Tokyo. So black workers crowded in.

**Jimenez y West:** They just got stuffed in like sardines into the community.

**Florido:** The neighborhood's population nearly quadrupled. This brought problems like overcrowding and communicable disease. Still, the community was vibrant – bars, barbecue joints, jazz clubs opened where you could see Charlie Parker perform.

40 *(SOUNDBITE OF MUSIC)*

**Florido:** But just as quickly as it sprang up, after the war, Bronzeville disappeared. Martha Nakagawa is a local historian.

**Martha Nakagawa:** Japanese Americans slowly came back, and the white building-owners preferred to have them come back, so sometimes they would not renew the
45 leases of the African American businesses. Or the Japanese Americans would come back and buy the leases out. And so that's how, slowly, the transition happened.

**Florido:** She says this transition created both tension and efforts at solidarity. In a couple of cases, Japanese organizations sued black business owners to get property back. Other Japanese folks worked to help displaced black residents find new places
50 to live. Today, few physical reminders of the Bronzeville era remain. There used to be a mural with Charlie Parker, but it's been painted over. But if you're walking in Little Tokyo and you look down, you'll see a timeline etched into the sidewalk. The words, 1942 – Little Tokyo becomes Bronzeville, are inscribed in gold. Adrian Florido, NPR News, Los Angeles.

55 *(SOUNDBITE OF GLEN PORTER'S "TRANSIENT")*

---

**TIPP**

---

Have a close look at the sentence beginnings and all the possible sentence endings and identify their key words, so that you know what to listen for. Afterwards, you should be able to identify relevant passages in the audio text by listening for these key words. However, the listening text may also use synonyms of the key words. Therefore, focusing on the content is more helpful than waiting for an exact repetition of the words used in the tasks. The tasks usually follow the chronology of the text, so it might also help to bear that in mind when trying to focus on a specific task. Furthermore, you might sometimes feel insecure as to whether there really is only one correct sentence ending, so it can be important to exclude wrong answers. The following text passages will help you find the correct answers:

1 "She remembers her parents and neighbors <u>rushing to sell off their belongings</u>" (ll. 6/7)

2 "When they were released, the family moved back home, <u>reopened</u> their dry cleaning business." (ll. 12/13)

3 "<u>But Little Tokyo had changed</u>. It was all black. You know, all our customers was [*sic*] black. Where there used to be Japanese restaurants and shops, the businesses were now African American." (ll. 13–16) When looking at all the sentence endings for **3**, you will notice that **a** and **c** both include a negative assessment of the situation while **d** describes "an improved [...] situation". Flori-

do and Hashimoto, however, neutrally describe the changes without evaluating them.

4 "Hashimoto made her first black friend, a little girl who lived nearby." (ll. 17/18)

5 The reason why "Blacks from the South" came to LA is mentioned in lines 30 and 31: "And this coincided with the arrival of many Southern blacks who came to LA for wartime jobs." Here you have to be very exact because both "cheap housing" (option a) and "discrimination" (option c) are also mentioned: The African Americans who came were "looking for the least expensive place to stay" (l. 33), but there were not many cheap housing options available because of segregation (cf. ll. 34/35). In other words, they might have wanted to escape discrimination and find cheap housing, but they could not do so in LA.

6 "Japanese Americans slowly came back, and the white building-owners preferred to have them come back, so sometimes they would not renew the leases of the African American businesses." (ll. 43–45)

7 Nakagawa's view of the Japanese American community is factual: she does not use any adjectives, adverbs or phrases which might reveal a critical or prejudiced attitude. In addition to that, she mentions positive as well as negative outcomes of the transitions mentioned (cf. ll. 47–50). While you might be tempted to choose b "indifferent", that would imply that she is not interested in the Japanese American community, which is clearly not true.

8 "Today, few physical reminders of the Bronzeville era remain. There used to be a mural with Charlie Parker, but it's been painted over. But if you're walking in Little Tokyo and you look down, you'll see a timeline etched into the sidewalk. The words, 1942 – Little Tokyo becomes Bronzeville, are inscribed in gold." (ll. 50–53)

1 Sande Hashimoto remembers that Japanese Americans were …

   d ☑ trying to find buyers for their possessions.

2 When the Hashimotos came back, they …

   b ☑ ran the same shop as before.

3 Little Tokyo experienced …

   b ☑ a demographic change.

4 When Sande Hashimoto came back, she …

   a ☑ became friends with the new neighbors.

5 Adrian Florido says that Blacks from the South came to Los Angeles …

   d ☑ to find employment.

6 Historian Martha Nakagawa claims that …

   c ☑ landlords favored Japanese Americans over African Americans.

**7** Martha Nakagawa's view of the Japanese American community seems …

**d** ✓ factual.

**8** Today's visitors are reminded of the Bronzeville era by a …

**c** ✓ phrase engraved in the pavement.


| Transcript 3 | Young People's Literature |

1 **Kelly McEvers** *(host)*: At the Library of Congress today, Gene Luen Yang officially ended his tenure as national ambassador for young people's literature and handed the baton to Jacqueline Woodson. She is the sixth children's book author to hold the position. And for the next two years, she will be encouraging children and teenagers
5 to read and to read more. NPR's Lynn Neary talked to the two writers about the job.

**Lynn Neary** *(byline)*: Gene Luen Yang admits that when he became ambassador two years ago, he was a little disappointed. He thought the job would come with a few more perks.

**Gene Luen Yang:** Yeah. I thought there would be a crown and maybe, like, a helicopter
10 of some kind, but none of that happened.

**Neary:** As she takes on the job, Jacqueline Woodson has no illusions about the perks. But if anything, she has higher expectations.

**Jacqueline Woodson:** My hope is that by that time I'm no longer national ambassador I'll have changed the world.

15 **Neary:** OK. So the national ambassador for young people's literature may not be the most powerful position in the nation's capital, but Yang says it has rewards of a different kind.

**Yang:** At a very fundamental level, I got to go to all these different places. I got to hear voices. You know, I got to hear the voices of kids.

20 **Neary:** Each ambassador gets to choose his or her own mission. For example, Jon Scieszka, who held the position first, was particularly interested in encouraging young boys to read. Yang, an award-winning graphic novelist, challenged kids to step out of their comfort zones and read about different kinds of people, unfamiliar topics or new types of books.

25 **Yang:** The nation is getting more diverse. And that is reflected in the material that draws the kids in. And I mean diversity in every sense of the word, not just cultural diversity, but also diversity of format. You know, I think kids today are more open to more different kinds of stories than kids in the past.

**Neary:** Yang is thrilled to be handing over the job to Jacqueline Woodson, winner of
30 numerous awards, including the National Book Award for her memoir, *Brown Girl Dreaming.*

**Woodson:** I get to decide my own vision in the end about the work I want to do, how I want to do it, what rooms I want to walk into, what people I feel have not had the

kind of access that they should have – mainly underserved people, people in rural
35  communities, incarcerated people – and really point my energies in those directions.

**Neary:** Woodson says she'd love to get rid of labels like struggling reader or advanced
reader and encourage young people to concentrate more on how a book makes them
feel or think.

**Woodson:** Labeling is not the best way to get young people to deeply engage in reading.
40  I mean, at the end of the day, you take the qualifier away and they're a reader.
Childhood, young adulthood is fluid. And it's very easy to get labeled very young
and have to carry something through your childhood and into your adulthood that
is not necessarily who you are.

**Neary:** Woodson has come up with her own mathematical equation to spark conversa-
45  tion about literature.

**Woodson:** Reading equals hope times change. So of course it's that play on words, but
it's also the fact that we come to books looking for the hope in them. And when we
close a book, we're a different person than when we first opened that book. And
reading begins a conversation. And my hope is that we can start having these con-
50  versations that literature triggers around the country.

**Neary:** Woodson sees the job ahead of her as a continuum of the work that her predecessors have started. Looking back on his own tenure, Gene Luen Yang says the
national conversation Woodson hopes for is already underway.

**Yang:** I think that human storytelling is this long conversation about what it means to
55  exist, what it means to live, how to live a good life. And I think being ambassador
has just reinforced the importance of that conversation in my mind.

**Neary:** Like her predecessors, Jacqueline Woodson will be traveling all over the country to meet with young people. No helicopters or private planes will be involved.
Lynn Neary, NPR News, Washington.

60  *(SOUNDBITE OF JACK WILKINS'S "RED CLAY")*

**TIPP**

The following text passages show you where to look for the correct answers. As
always, reading the questions carefully before the first listening round will help
you to identify these relevant passages.

1  "Gene Luen Yang officially ended his tenure as national ambassador for young
people's literature and handed the baton to Jacqueline Woodson." (ll. 1–3);
"NPR's Lynn Neary talked to the two writers about the job." (l. 5)

2  "At a very fundamental level, I got to go to all these different places. I got to
hear voices. You know, I got to hear the voices of kids." (ll. 18/19)

**3** "For example, Jon Scieszka, who held the position first, was particularly interested in <u>encouraging young boys to read</u>." (ll. 20–22)

**4** "Yang, an award-winning <u>graphic novelist</u>, challenged kids to step out of their
comfort zones and read about different kinds of people, unfamiliar topics or
<u>new types of books</u>. The nation is getting more diverse. And that is reflected in
the material that draws the kids in. And I mean diversity in every sense of the
word, not just cultural diversity, but also diversity of format. You know, I think
kids today are more open to more <u>different kinds of stories</u> than kids in the
past." (ll. 22–28)

**5** "what people I feel have not had the kind of access that they should have –
mainly underserved people, <u>people in rural communities, incarcerated people</u>"
(ll. 33–35)

**6** "Woodson says she'd love to get rid of labels like struggling reader or advanced reader and encourage young people to <u>concentrate more on how a
book makes them feel or think</u>. Labeling is <u>not</u> the best way to get young people to <u>deeply engage in reading</u>. […] Childhood, young adulthood is fluid. And
it's very <u>easy to get labeled very young and have to carry something through
your childhood and into your adulthood that is not necessarily who you are</u>."
(ll. 36–43)

**7** "And when we close a book, <u>we're a different person</u> than when we first
opened that book. And <u>reading begins a conversation</u>." (ll. 47–49)

**8** In line 9, it already becomes quite obvious, especially in connection with the
assumption of there being a crown, that the expectation of getting a helicopter
when being a national ambassador for young people's literature is rather exaggerated and cannot be meant seriously. Thus, it can only be taken as fun.
Therefore, the tone evoked by the repeated reference to a helicopter (cf. ll. 9,
58) can be considered ironic, humorous, playful or mocking.

---

**1** What do the writers Gene Luen Yang and Jacqueline Woodson have in
common?
**ambassadors of young people's literature/writers**

**2** Which rewards of his position did Yang enjoy?
**going to different places/hearing voices of different kids/talking to kids**

**3** What did Jon Scieszka, who held the position first, try to achieve?
**encouraging young boys to read**

**4** What does Yang mean when he refers to "diversity of format"?
**new genres/new types of books/new kinds of stories/new text types/
graphic novels**

**5** Which two examples of "underserved people" does Woodson give?
- **people in rural communities**
- **incarcerated people**

**6** What effects do labels like "struggling reader" have according to Woodson?

**put people in a box/are difficult to shake off (although people themselves change)/might be discouraging/prevent people from really getting into reading/distract people from concentrating on how a book makes them feel or think**

**7** What does Woodson say about the ideal effect of reading a book?

**changing the reader/beginning a conversation**

**8** What tone is evoked by the repeated reference to a helicopter?

**ironic/humorous/playful/mocking**

---

 SCHREIBEN

**1** TIPP

Before you start outlining the reasons this task asks for, you should first of all establish the context by giving the basic facts about the excerpt and particularly by summarising the disagreement between the Haitian poet and Ifemelu. Then go through the text again and find out Ifemelu's opinion of the matter of contention. For a text comprehension task, you do not need to go beyond the text and interpret your findings. Furthermore, make sure you use your own words as far as possible and do not quote from the text.

The following points could be mentioned in your answer:

**Introduction**
- basic facts about the excerpt
- disagreement between Haitian poet and Ifemelu:
  - Haitian poet states that race was never an issue in her relationship with a White man (cf. ll. 5–7)
  - Ifemelu considers this a lie (cf. ll. 8–11)

**Main part: Ifemelu's reasons for disagreeing**
- exposure of the Haitian poet's "wishful thinking":
  - Haitian poet not wanting to make her White friends feel uncomfortable (cf. ll. 12/13, 31/32)
  - appreciation for what has already been achieved in terms of racial equality (cf. l. 13)
  - Haitian poet not wanting to acknowledge the fact that race matters (cf. ll. 18/19)
- Ifemelu's standpoint:
  - in a relationship between two people, race might not be an issue, but as soon as you leave your "bubble", the issue arises (cf. ll. 21–23)

- she could not even address the issue of microaggressions with her White partner because she was afraid of being accused of being too sensitive (cf. ll. 23–26)
- open disagreement instead of continually swallowing feelings of frustration:
  - slightly drunk, Ifemelu cannot hold back any longer (cf. ll. 15–17, 40/41)
  - memories of her own interracial relationship where she and Curt never really talked about her worries (cf. ll. 44–51) and Ifemelu bottled up her feelings of being judged as an inadequate girlfriend for Curt (cf. ll. 52–69)

In the excerpt from Chimamanda Ngozi Adichie's novel *Americanah*, which was published in 2013, the protagonist, Ifemelu, a young Nigerian woman living in the USA, attends a dinner party right after Barack Obama has been nominated as the Democratic presidential candidate. At the party Ifemelu has an argument with another Black woman, a poet from Haiti, who claims that she has never experienced race as problematic while dating a White American man. Ifemelu considers this a lie and contests it loudly.

Introduction

In Ifemelu's opinion, the Haitian poet denies the existence of interracial problems because she does not want to make her White friends feel uncomfortable and prefers to show appreciation for what has already been achieved in terms of racial equality. Ifemelu is convinced that what the poet says is wishful thinking rather than anything else: in her eyes, the Haitian poet does not want to acknowledge the fact that race still matters.

Ifemelu's reasons for disagreeing: exposure of the Haitian poet's "wishful thinking"

What Ifemelu concedes is that it is possible for race not to be an issue in a relationship between two people, but that as soon as you leave your "couple bubble" and interact with other people, the issue arises. Nevertheless, race can even become a challenge within a relationship because racism works on many levels, some of which are difficult for White people to grasp. Ifemelu feels that when together with a White man she could not address the issue of microaggressions because she was afraid of being accused of being oversensitive.

race an issue outside of "couple bubble" and even within

It becomes clear that it is Ifemelu's own experience that makes her disagree with the Haitian poet. She is tired of pretending that everything is all right when she herself has both felt society's indirect negative judgement of her and Curt's relationship and experienced their own inability to address the issue openly. In her slightly drunk state at the party, the feelings she has buried inside her to date can no longer stay hidden. *(319 words)*

feelings of frustration need to be expressed

**TIPP**

The assignment of this task already gives you the hypothesis you should work with in your analysis: The author wants the reader to take Ifemelu's perspective. Your job is to examine <u>how</u> this perspective is presented convincingly. You should therefore follow Ifemelu's portrayal throughout the excerpt. Focus on the general contents and structure of the excerpt as well as on striking stylistic devices that show Ifemelu as convincing. As required by the assignment, you should also add a paragraph on the narrative perspective of the excerpt. Please note that the sample below shows quite a number of means and strategies. Of course, you could also be successful with fewer points that you structure cohesively to create a convincing whole.

You could mention the following points:

**Introduction:** argument between Ifemelu and the Haitian poet

**Main part:** why the reader tends to sympathise with Ifemelu
- **narrative perspective:**
  - limited third-person narrator
  - Ifemelu's subjective point of view
- **description of society** as uncritical and naive:
  - "fervent" (l. 3), "dewy-eyed" (l. 3) Obama supporters
  - simplistic statement: "Obama will end racism in this country" (l. 4)
  - empty phrase (in capital letters): "How Far We Have Come" (l. 13)
- contrast: **Ifemelu's** almost brutal, yet clever, **honesty:**
  - repetition: "That's a lie" (l. 8), "It's a lie" (l. 10)
  - anaphora "even though" (ll. 12–15) → contrast between intellectual perspective and emotions
- Ifemelu's strong emotional involvement:
  - parallelism: "she did not. She could not" (l. 16)
  - hyperbole, tricolon, climax: "The words had [...] overtaken her; [...] overpowered her [...], and tumbled out." (ll. 16/17)
  - prolonged direct speech (cf. ll. 18–32)
  - use of pronouns: "I" (ll. 19/20, 32), "we" (ll. 23–31)
  - drastic language: "piss us off" (l. 24), "blah blah blah" (ll. 27/28), "why the fuck" (l. 29)
  - sarcasm: "nice liberal dinners" (l. 30), "our nice liberal friends" (l. 32)
- contrast to Haitian poet's weaker position: change of topic (cf. ll. 36/37) → shows that she cannot respond to Ifemelu's "speech" appropriately → sign of weakness
- **flashback** at the end of the excerpt shows Ifemelu's strong reaction as justified:
  - mixture of theoretical considerations (cf. ll. 44–51) and very direct participation in a discriminatory situation (cf. ll. 52–69)
  - anaphora "It was not that" (ll. 44, 47): showing covert racism

- comparison: "like a curious nugget to be examined and then put aside" (ll. 45/46)
- metaphorical language: "tone-deaf" (l. 50), "crippled" (l. 51)
- repetition: "surprise" (l. 56)
- sarcasm: "a great tribal loss" (l. 60), "the guardians of the tribe" (l. 64)
- figurative language: "The looks had begun to pierce her skin" (l. 68)
- repetition: "tired" (ll. 68/69)

**Conclusion:** insight into Ifemelu's emotions, personal experience and her well-expressed rational thoughts makes her viewpoint convincing

---

In the excerpt from *Americanah*, Ifemelu and a poet from Haiti clash over the question of whether race still matters in the USA. While the argument remains unresolved, the reader is nonetheless left with the feeling that Ifemelu is right in her negative view. This agreement with the protagonist is brought about by various means.

**Introduction**

Even though the text has a third-person narrator – a narrative perspective that is often associated with neutrality – the excerpt focuses on Ifemelu's thoughts and feelings. It is therefore her line of thought that the reader can most easily follow in the argument that unfolds.

**narrative perspective**

From the very beginning it becomes clear that Ifemelu is in the company of a rather uncritical crowd. The Obama supporters celebrating at the party are described as "fervent" (l. 3) and "dewy-eyed" (l. 3), suggesting that they are overenthusiastic and naive in their simplistic belief that "Obama will end racism in [the] country" (l. 4). Later on, the willingness of the party guests and society in general to overlook racist tendencies is expressed by the use of capital letters in the phrase "How Far We Have Come" (l. 13). This makes it look like an empty phrase that people use incessantly without critically examining its truthfulness.

**description of society** as uncritical and naive

In contrast to that, Ifemelu is almost brutally honest. She tells the Haitian poet bluntly that what the latter has said about interracial couples is "a lie" (ll. 8, 10), a statement she repeats without letting the other woman's questions (cf. ll. 9, 11) intimidate her. However, while Ifemelu's strong statements might suggest that her view is rash and unconsidered, this is not the case at all. On the contrary, the anaphorical use of the conjunction "even though" in lines 12 to 15 underlines Ifemelu's intellectual perspective. It shows that she has thought about her opponent's reasoning too and even understands it to a certain degree.

**contrast: Ifemelu's** brutal, yet clever, **honesty**

All the more striking is Ifemelu's inability to contain her emotions on the subject of racism. This is emphasised by the parallelism "she did not. She could not" in line 16 as well as by the hyperbole "[t]he

**Ifemelu's strong emotional involvement**

words had […] overtaken her; they overpowered her throat, and tumbled out" (ll. 16/17). It seems as if Ifemelu has an almost visceral reaction to the Haitian poet's statement – for her, staying silent is not an option.

The strength of Ifemelu's emotions becomes especially apparent in her prolonged direct speech from line 18 to line 32. The frequent use of the pronoun "I" (cf. ll. 19/20) makes it clear that she has a very personal interest in the topic of racism, which she even explicitly states at the end of her monologue (cf. l. 32). However, for Ifemelu, the problem is not limited to her individual experience, which she shows by repeatedly talking in the first-person plural (cf. ll. 23–31). Ifemelu is never aloof, but instead gets more and more agitated, which is exemplified by her use of drastic language and even swear words, such as "piss us off" (l. 24), "blah blah blah" (ll. 27/28) or "why the fuck" (l. 29). Her increasing bitterness and exasperation also become clear when she sarcastically refers to "nice liberal dinners" (l. 30) with "nice liberal friends" (l. 32), who do not want to hear the truth.

*prolonged direct speech: use of pronouns*

*drastic language and sarcasm*

Ifemelu's strong reaction is in stark contrast to that of the Haitian poet: the latter abruptly changes the topic (ll. 36/37) and tries to make Ifemelu's outrage appear ridiculous (cf. ll. 37/38). However, this only proves Ifemelu right in her opinion that racism tends to be intentionally overlooked.

*contrast to Haitian poet's weaker position*

Although the poet would like to present Ifemelu as overemotional and unreliable, the **flashback** at the end of the excerpt (cf. ll. 44–69) disproves that assumption. Both Ifemelu's theoretical considerations about herself and Curt (cf. ll. 44–51) and the direct glimpse of an event at which she clearly felt discriminated against (cf. ll. 52–69) stress that what Ifemelu accuses society of is backed up by her personal experience.

**flashback** *at the end of the excerpt*

The anaphora "it was not that" (ll. 44, 47) shows racism as something that is not always blatantly obvious. Ifemelu's argument is all the more convincing because she does not present it that way. Instead, her comparison of treating race "like a curious nugget to be examined and then put aside" (ll. 45/46) shows how she and Curt skirted around the topic in their relationship. That Curt is called both "tone-deaf" (l. 50) and "crippled" (l. 51) underlines the couple's – and especially the White partner's – inability to really get to the heart of the issue.

*anaphora, comparison and metaphorical language*

Ifemelu's experience at the reception then gives a direct example of the kind of implicit discrimination Ifemelu had to get used to in Curt's social circle. At his cousin's wedding some of the White guests look at the couple in a derogatory manner. Their "surprise" (l. 56) at Curt's and Ifemelu's relationship can be read as insulting,

*Ifemelu's experience with racism at the wedding reception*

19

and their reactions as "guardians of the tribe" (l. 64), as Ifemelu sarcastically terms them, even more so: their looks imply that the relationship is a waste and that a White, affluent American could easily find a "better" girlfriend than a Black woman from Nigeria. The reader empathises with Ifemelu, who is clearly hurt by this racist behaviour: we learn that "[t]he looks had begun to pierce her skin" (l. 68) and she is completely exhausted by always being looked down upon (cf. repetition of "tired", ll. 68/69).

All in all, the fact that the reader gets a very detailed insight into Ifemelu's thoughts and experiences enables them to take her side. In particular, the mixture of raw emotions with clearly thought-out rational arguments makes Ifemelu sound convincing. *(949 words)*

Conclusion

---

**3.1** **TIPP**

In this task, you are given a quote from the text, which you should contextualise in your answer. "Discuss" requires you to consider all sides of an issue, by providing relevant arguments and concrete examples. Your answer should contain four parts:
– an introduction
– arguments speaking for (against) the statement
– arguments speaking against (for) the statement
– a conclusion

**Introduction**
– context: first African American president
– election campaign raised high hopes (cf. e. g. given excerpt)

**Arguments for the statement**
– Obama as symbol of equality, leader of one of the most powerful countries in the world
– policies and acts aimed at ending discrimination
  • Affordable Care Act
  • overruling sentences (reducing the number of incarcerated Black Americans)
  • appointment of two Black attorneys general

**Arguments against the statement**
– facts and figures that still reveal inequality
  • African American men still six times more likely to be imprisoned
  • police violence against African Americans
  • largest number of high school dropouts and lower number of college graduates among African Americans
  • high level of poverty among African Americans
– Trump's policies
  • successful election campaign based on xenophobic agenda
  • border fence
  • revocation of DACA

Conclusion: statement is unrealistic
- too big a task for one person
- individual level / everyday racism cannot be controlled
- racism often subconscious

Barack Obama was the first African American to become president of the United States of America. After his first successful campaign, African Americans all over the country celebrated his presidency as a visible sign of true equality between the races, or – at least – as an important step towards this goal. However, did he actually achieve this tall order?

**Introduction**

On the one hand, Obama achieved a lot, not least at a symbolic level: the fact that a member of an ethnic minority could become the leader of one of the most powerful countries in the world inspired many US citizens who are members of minorities, and not only African Americans. Additionally, some of Obama's political decisions were aimed at ending discrimination. The Affordable Care Act, often referred to as Obamacare, for example, made the number of uninsured Black Americans diminish by a considerable amount. Furthermore, maybe in a bid to decrease the rate of Black incarceration, he commuted the sentences of hundreds of prisoners. Obama overruled more sentences than any of his predecessors. Moreover, he appointed two Black attorneys general, who revitalised the work of the justice department's civil rights division, which had not been a priority in the years before Obama took office.

**Arguments for the statement**

On the other hand, facts and figures continue to reveal a different picture: African American men are still much more likely to be incarcerated by the US judicial system than White Americans. Police violence towards African Americans hits the news almost every week. The educational system reveals a similar picture: African American teenagers are the largest group among high school dropouts. The share of college graduates is also much lower among African Americans than among Asian Americans or White Americans. This in turn leads to African Americans on average being less well-off than most of the other races in the United States.

**Arguments against the statement:** facts and figures that still reveal inequality

To compound these problems, African Americans are not the only group that has to deal with prejudice and distrust. Political measures like Obama's successor Trump's proposal for a border wall or his decision to revoke DACA, Obama's "dreamers" programme intended for the protection of illegal minors, showed that racism and prejudice were alive and kicking in the United States even after Obama's terms as president. The very fact of Trump's election success, despite or maybe even because of his xenophobic agenda, could be seen as a sign of an increase rather than a decrease in racism in the

**Trump's policies**

21

United States. While things may look slightly better with Biden's presidency, racism can surely not be called a thing of the past.

In conclusion, it is probably unrealistic to expect one man to end racism in all its different guises and at so many levels throughout society. Especially on an individual level, it possibly takes years and also educational and other reforms to achieve the aim of a more tolerant society. Only if everyone questions their own often subconscious mistrust and racial stereotypes can racist tendencies be combatted at large.

*Conclusion*

*(493 words)*

## 3.2  TIPP

The assignment comprises two parts: an interpretation of the cartoon and your comment on its message. In the first part, you should follow the procedure of analysing a cartoon, which means first describing the scene, the people and the action (remember to use the present progressive, e. g. "he is holding a gun in his hand"), and then explaining its message. In your comment, you should explain your own view on the cartoon's message. Of course, you can also include your background knowledge.

Possible key points are:

**Description of the cartoon**
- setting: New York, Liberty Island
- people: policeman on pedestal, African American in headlock
- text: cloud-shaped speech-bubble with changed version of "The New Colossus"

**Message of the cartoon**
- topic: racial profiling, injustice and inequality
- artist criticises the fact that African Americans are discriminated against by the police

**Comment**
- background: cases of African Americans who were shot by police, Black Lives Matter movement
- general problem: inequality in many areas of American society
- opinion: policy changes required

The cartoon "The New Colossus" by Joseph Rank deals with racial profiling in the United States. In the background there is the skyline of a city that is surrounded by water. The focus of attention is on a White policeman and an African American in the foreground. The policeman is standing on a pedestal and raising his right arm towards the sky. He is holding a gun in his right hand and has the African American in a headlock with his left hand. On the right-hand side

*Description of the cartoon*

there is a cloud in which you can read the second stanza of Emma Lazarus's poem "The New Colossus". However, some words have been altered: Instead of "I lift my lamp beside the golden door", the cartoonist wrote "And I'll take care of 'em for ya".

Since the policeman is standing on a pedestal and the cartoon is entitled "The New Colossus" – like Emma Lazarus's poem – it can be assumed that he has replaced the Statue of Liberty. Lady Liberty is a symbol of freedom and hope, especially for immigrants who come to the United States in search of a better life. Instead of holding a lamp guiding and welcoming immigrants, the policeman is holding a gun. This suggests that freedom and hope have been replaced by fear and threat. This is intensified by the fact that the policeman has the African American in a headlock. The original poem implies that the United States is open and caring towards immigrants from all over the world. In contrast, the line "And I'll take care of 'em for ya" uses a different connotation of the verb "take care": what it means is that the American state, represented by the police, does not treat all citizens impartially but discriminates against some citizens – especially African Americans by targeting them in police investigations. **Interpretation of the cartoon's elements**

The message of the cartoon is that from a country promising freedom, equality and hope to all, the United States has developed into a state in which racial profiling is a common occurrence. It thereby alludes to the fact that African Americans are very often the victims of excessive police violence. The Black Lives Matter movement, for instance, was founded in response to several cases where African Americans were shot by policemen, apparently without any reason at all, as they were often unarmed and did not pose any serious danger. **Message of the cartoon**

In my opinion, the cartoon depicts a fitting image of injustice and inequality between different races in America. However, it presents only one example of a further-reaching conflict. Inequality occurs in policing, but also in the educational system, in the workplace and in housing. Still, African Americans are more likely to be detained by the police or suspected of a crime; they have the largest number of high school dropouts; they are less likely to obtain a managerial position, and they often live in poorer, less developed parts of cities. In order to fulfil the original dream connected with the Statue of Liberty as well as the aims of the American Constitution, politicians should take these problems more seriously and offer effective solutions. Only then can the country truly claim its "golden door" is open to everyone in equal measure. **Comment**

*(535 words)*

**HÖRVERSTEHEN**

### Task 1: BBC News

You will hear several items from the BBC radio news. Choose from the list (A–H) which description applies to which news item (1–7). For each item there is only one correct answer. Put the letters (A–H) into the correct box. There is one more description than you need.

| | Description |
|---|---|
| A | Call for less pride and vanity |
| B | Conflict leading to migration |
| C | Favourable outcome |
| D | Highly skilled assault |
| E | Long-awaited decision |
| F | People affected by administrative failure |
| G | People suffering in conflict |
| H | Politician demanding solidarity |

| News item | 1 | 2 | 3 | 4 | 5 | 6 | 7 |
|---|---|---|---|---|---|---|---|
| Description A–H | | | | | | | |

## Task 2: Scottish History

Listen to a radio report. While listening, complete the table. Do not write complete sentences.

| | |
|---|---|
| **1** Information about who wrote the manuscript: | |
| **2** Original function of the manuscript: | |
| **3** Reason why the 1563 law only applied to Scotland: | |
| **4** Nature of interrogations: | |
| **5** Significance of publication: | |

## Task 3: Native Americans in Wyoming

Listen to a radio report. While listening, tick (✓) the correct answer (a, b, c or d). There is only one correct answer.

**1** Some inhabitants have to leave the Wind River Reservation because …

**a** ☐ life there does not appeal to them.

**b** ☐ the reservation is overcrowded.

**c** ☐ they cannot find an apartment.

**d** ☐ they try to find employment.

**2** Ken Hebah …

**a** ☐ has serious financial problems.

**b** ☐ is forced to stay with a relative.

**c** ☐ prefers to live with his extended family.

**d** ☐ wants enough room to host friends.

**3** The Department of Housing and Urban Development …

   **a** ☐ encourages landlords to rent to Native Americans.

   **b** ☐ found out that housing discrimination is rarely reported.

   **c** ☐ helps Native Americans to pay the rent.

   **d** ☐ reports housing discrimination to the courts.

**4** Landlord Dave Kellogg …

   **a** ☐ has tough regulations for future tenants.

   **b** ☐ refuses to rent to Native Americans.

   **c** ☐ regularly renovates his apartments.

   **d** ☐ specializes in housing for large families.

**5** Kellogg says that Native Americans …

   **a** ☐ cannot afford his apartments.

   **b** ☐ must include a CV in their applications.

   **c** ☐ often provide incorrect personal information.

   **d** ☐ usually cannot fulfil his conditions.

**6** The reporter, Melodie Edwards, says that Native Americans often …

   **a** ☐ cause financial damage to their landlords.

   **b** ☐ like to avoid renovation costs.

   **c** ☐ prefer to rent from other Native Americans.

   **d** ☐ wish to share their home with relatives.

**7** Lyle Konkol …

   **a** ☐ criticizes the checking of credit histories.

   **b** ☐ insists on equal rights for all.

   **c** ☐ suggests landlords should limit the number of tenants.

   **d** ☐ wishes to avoid legal complications.

**8** Jane Juve …

   **a** ☐ claims courts have acted inappropriately.

   **b** ☐ facilitates communication between Native Americans and others.

   **c** ☐ organizes workshops for Native American tenants.

   **d** ☐ works to improve the housing situation on the reservation.

Listen to a radio commentary. While listening, tick (✓) the correct answer (a, b, c or d). There is only one correct answer.

1  Stella Lau thinks her father …

a ☐ considers art an important part of education.

b ☐ expects her to put family before career.

c ☐ values financial success above all else.

d ☐ will force her to study a science.

2  Stella Lau …

a ☐ concludes their argument with a compromise.

b ☐ makes a well-considered, independent decision.

c ☐ meets her parents' hopes and wishes.

d ☐ seriously considers her father's advice.

*Bei den für Set 2 abgedruckten Aufgaben zum Hörverstehen handelt es sich um die Original-Aufgaben des Hörverstehensteils der zentral gestellten Kursarbeit 2018 in Rheinland-Pfalz.*

| Text | Jean Kwok: *Girl in Translation* |

1   After a bit of searching, I found the classroom and knocked weakly on the door.
A deep, muffled voice came from behind the door. "You're late! Come in."
I pushed it open. The teacher was a man. I learned later his name was Mr. Bogart.
He was extremely tall, so that his forehead was level with the top of the blackboard,
5   with a raspberry nose and a head bald as an egg. His green eyes seemed unnaturally
light to me in his wide face and his stomach stuck out from under his shirt. He was
writing English words on the blackboard, from left to right.
"Our new student *eye-prezoom*?" He gave a strange smile that made his lips disap-
pear, then he looked at his watch and his lips reappeared. "You're very late. What's
10   your *exsu*?"
I knew I had to answer so I guessed. "Kim Chang."
He stared at me for a second. "I know what your name is," he said, enunciating each
word. "What's your *exshus*?"
A few of the kids snickered. I took a quick look around: almost all black with two
15   or three white kids. No other Chinese at all, no help in sight.
"Can't you speak English? They said that you did." This came out as a kind of
grumbled whine. Who was he talking about? He took a breath. "Why are you late?"
This, I understood. "I sorry, sir," I said. "We not find school."
He frowned, then nodded and waved at an empty desk. "Go sit down. There."
20   I sat down in the seat he had indicated, next to a chubby white girl with frizzy hair
that stuck out in all directions. My fingers were shaking so much that I fumbled with
my pencil case. It opened and everything in it clattered on the floor. Now most of the
class laughed and I scrambled to pick up my things. I was so flushed I could feel the
heat not only in my face but in my neck and chest. The white girl also bent down and
25   picked up a pen and a pencil sharpener for me.
Mr. Bogart continued writing on the blackboard. I sat up straight and folded my
hands behind my back to listen even though I couldn't follow it at all.
He glanced at me. "Why are you *see something that*?"
"I sorry, sir," I said, but I had no idea what I'd done wrong this time. I looked around
30   at the other students. Most of them were sprawled in their chairs. Some had sunk so
low that they were practically lying down, some were leaning on their elbows, a few
were chewing gum. In Hong Kong, students must fold their hands behind their backs
when the teacher is talking, to show respect. Slowly, I loosened my arms and placed
my hands on the desk in front of me.
35   Shaking his head, Mr. Bogart turned back to the blackboard.
Our class went to the school cafeteria for lunch. I had never seen children behave
the way these Americans did. They seemed to be hanging from the beams on the ceil-
ings, shrieking. The lunchroom ladies roamed from table to table, yelling instructions
no one heard. I had followed the other children and slid a tray across a long counter.
40   Different ladies asked me questions and when I only nodded, they plopped foil-covered

28

packages on my plate. I wound up with this: minced meat in the form of a saucer, potatoes that were not round but had been crushed into a pastelike substance, a sauce similar to soy sauce but less dark and salty, a roll and milk. I had hardly ever drunk cow's milk before and it gave me a stomachache. The rest of the food was interesting,
45 although there was no rice, so I felt as if I hadn't really eaten.

After lunch, Mr. Bogart gave out sheets of paper with a drawing of a map.

"This is a pop *quick*," he said. "Fill in *allde captal see T's*."

The other kids groaned but many of them started writing. I looked at my piece of paper and then, in desperation, glanced at the white girl's sheet to try to see what we
50 were supposed to do. Suddenly, the sheet of paper slid out from under my fingers. Mr. Bogart was standing next to me with my test in his hands.

"No *cheap pen!*" he said. His nose and cheeks were flushed as if he were getting a rash. "You a *hero!*"

"I sorry, sir –" I began. I knew he wasn't calling me a hero, like Superman. What
55 had he said? Although I'd had basic English classes in school in Hong Kong, my old teacher's accent did not in any way resemble what I now heard in Brooklyn.

"'I'mmm'," he said, pressing his lips together. "'I'm sorry.'"

"I'm sorry," I said. My English mistakes clearly annoyed him, although I wasn't sure why.
60 Mr. Bogart wrote a large "0" on my paper and gave it back to me. I felt as if the zero were fluorescent, blinking in neon to the rest of the class. What would Ma say? I'd never gotten a zero before, and now everyone thought I was a cheat too. My only hope was to impress Mr. Bogart with my industry when we cleaned the classrooms after school. If I'd lost any claim to intelligence here, I could at least show him I was
65 a hard worker.

But when the last bell finally rang, all of the other kids ran out of the room. No one stayed behind to mop and sweep the floors, put up the chairs or clean the blackboards.

Mr. Bogart saw me hesitating and asked, "Can I help you?"

I didn't answer and hurried from the classroom.                    *966 words*

**Annotation**
line 12:   to enunciate: to say or pronounce words clearly

**1**  Sketch the problems Kim encounters on her first day at school in New York.

(30 %)

**2**  Analyse how the author manages to convey Kim's feelings of alienation.

(30 %)

**3**  Choose *one* of the following tasks:

(40 %)

**3.1**  Larry in *Crooked Letter, Crooked Letter* is a victim of bullying. Compare his and Kim's experiences at school.

**or**

**3.2**  In *Gran Torino*, the older Hmong speak their native language, the younger generation speaks both English and Hmong.

Comment on the importance of language for the integration of migrants.

**HÖRVERSTEHEN**

| **Transcript 1** **BBC News**

1 BBC News with Eileen McKue.

**1** A senior EU official has warned that the scale of migration across the Mediterranean from North Africa to Italy is untenable. About 10,000 people are reported to have attempted the journey in the past few days. The EU's Commissioner for Migration said
5 all EU member states had a humanitarian obligation to save lives.

**2** United Nations says at least 173 civilians have been killed this month in the Syrian city of Raqqa where western-backed forces are trying to drive out Islamic State militants. It's believed that up to 100,000 local people are trapped by the fighting.

**3** Relatives of the 96 Liverpool football fans who were killed at Hillsborough Stadium
10 nearly three decades ago have welcomed the announcement of criminal charges against six people. Those facing charges include the police commander on the day of the game in Sheffield.

**4** The Brazilian authorities have suspended the issuing of passports, as the country approaches its peak travel season, because of a budget crisis. The country is suffering
15 its worst recession in decades. The government said it would try to allocate more money for passports.

**5** Gunmen in Libya have attacked a UN convoy. Seven United Nations staff were seized near the western town of Surman. They have now been handed over unharmed to local security forces. The UN convoy was in the town to visit a migrant detention
20 centre.

**6** The European police agency has warned that the cyberattacks spreading around the world appear to be even more sophisticated than last month's devastating wave of attacks. It's said the latest version called "Petya" completely overrides the files making them irretrievable.

25 **7** And Pope Francis has been holding a ceremony to create five new cardinals. He told them not to be misled by the traditional description of cardinals as "Princes of the Church" but instead to be humble and help the poor.

BBC News.

*BBC WorldService, BBC News Summary, 2017/03/01, www.bbc.co.uk/programmes/p04tnn56*

**TIPP**

To match the descriptions with the respective news item, you should first of all identify the key words in the descriptions and then listen for similar key words in the news items. However, the listening text may also use synonyms of the key words. Therefore, focusing on the content is more helpful than waiting for an exact repetition of the words used in the descriptions. If you cannot match all the items after the first listening, it might be helpful to cross out the options you have already allocated. Then you can focus on the remaining ones and the items you had trouble with.

These text passages will help you find the correct answers:

1 News item **1** is a typical example where an exclusive focus on key words (without taking the larger context into account) can be misleading: While the item is about "migration" (ll. 2, 4), **B** is not the right answer. There is no mention of the conflict which makes people emigrate, but rather "[t]he EU's Commissioner for Migration" (l. 4), in other words, a politician, demands solidarity when he calls helping the migrants "a humanitarian obligation to save lives" (l. 5).

2 Description **G** might seem difficult to allocate because it seems rather general and therefore fitting to more than one item. However, the key words "[p]eople suffering" and "conflict" can best be connected to people being "killed" (l. 6) or "trapped by [...] fighting" (l. 8).

3 To match news item **3** to the fitting description, it is especially important that the incident at the football stadium took place "nearly three decades ago" (l. 10) and that "the announcement of criminal charges" (l. 10) has therefore long been overdue.

4 News item **4** is an especially tricky case. What you should recognise is that the "authorities" (l. 13) and "[t]he government" (l. 15) are mentioned twice and they have to deal with an unfavourable situation. When you deduce that the non-issuing of passports (cf. l. 13) will affect many people, especially in the "peak travel season" (l. 14), you have the right answer: People are affected by mistakes the government has made, in other words "by administrative failure" (**F**).

5 For news item **5**, only one sentence is really important, namely "They have now been handed over unharmed to local security forces" (ll. 18/19).

6 The word "sophisticated" (l. 22) can be seen as a synonym for "[h]ighly skilled" (**D**).

7 Pope Francis's call "to be humble and help the poor" (l. 27) and "not to be misled by the traditional description of cardinals as 'Princes of the Church'" (ll. 26/27) is a "[c]all for less pride and vanity" (**A**).

| News item | 1 | 2 | 3 | 4 | 5 | 6 | 7 |
|---|---|---|---|---|---|---|---|
| Description A–H | H | G | E | F | C | D | A |

32

1 **Lourdes Garcia-Navarro** *(host)*: And now for some 350-year-old gossip. London's Wellcome Library has digitized a manuscript called "Names of Witches in Scotland
1658". It records everyone accused of witchcraft in the country between 1658 and
1662. The list has also been posted on a genealogy website for those who may want
5 to find out if their own family members got caught up in Scotland's witch-hunting
fever. Christopher Hilton is the senior archivist at the Wellcome Library. He joins
us now from London.
Thanks so much for being with us.

**Christopher Hilton:** Thank you for having me.

10 **Garcia-Navarro:** So tell us about this manuscript, number 3,658, I believe. Who wrote
it? Where does it come from?

**Hilton:** Right. OK. Well, it's essentially a list of names produced in Scotland in 1658,
summarizing people accused of witchcraft. It didn't actually start out as a book. It
began as a set of loose papers in five separate handwritings, presumably sent in
15 from people dotted around Scotland in various locations. It's been collated, brought
together, in Edinburgh and then folded up very small at some stage, presumably so
that it could be carried around by a court messenger who was then convening trials
in various locations.

**Garcia-Navarro:** Well, let's step back a minute. Can you give us a bit of a history lesson?
20 You know, I'm sure a lot of our listeners have heard of the Salem witch trials in the
late 1600s or, you know, read *The Crucible* in high school. But what was it like in
Scotland during this time period?

**Hilton:** The prosecutions that were being talked about in this particular document were
launched under the Witchcraft Act of Scotland, which was passed in 1563. Now, at
25 the time that it was passed, Scotland was a completely independent kingdom. And
nothing like this Witchcraft Act existed in England and Wales, south of the border.
So there is a distinctly Scottish flavor to witchcraft trials. And it seems to have gone
on for 150 years or so. It was a fairly steady element in Scottish life.

**Garcia-Navarro:** So what was the criteria back then to accuse someone of being a witch?
30 **Hilton:** The Witchcraft Act is notoriously baggy actually, notoriously vague. You were
a witch if somebody thought you were a witch. I think we can hazard a guess as to
some of the things that went on. I'm sure that in some cases people were genuinely
casting spells and attempting to influence the world around them through what we
would understand as magic now. In other cases, they doubtless were attempting folk
35 medicine, carrying out things that we would see as more scientific.

**Garcia-Navarro:** And just to remind people, what happened to these people after they
were accused and possibly found guilty?

**Hilton:** You would be almost certainly interrogated in ways that breach any legal protocol now. As far as we're aware, about 4,000 people that we know of were accused
40 of witchcraft during the currency of the act. And about 2,000 people were executed.
So you had about a 50/50 chance of coming out of the process alive. But equally
well, it would – you know, it was clearly not good news to be accused.

**Garcia-Navarro:** Why do you think it's important to make these records public?

**Hilton:** I think there are a whole range of uses to which one could put them. One of the
45 things that this document does is make people aware that what we now think of as
scientific medicine is something that has evolved over time. It basically gets people
thinking about – what do we think of as being proper science? What do we think of
as being magic? What do we think of as alternative medicine? And have the boundaries changed? We may come to think of quantum chromodynamics or something
50 like that as – in the same way that we now think of witchcraft.

**Garcia-Navarro:** Christopher Hilton, senior archivist at the Wellcome Library, thank you
so much for being with us.

**Hilton:** Thank you for having me.

---

**TIPP**

It is really important to make good use of the time you have to read the assign-
ments before you listen to the recording for the first time: That way you will know
to which questions and answers (in the interview) you have to pay close attention.

The following text passages will help you to find the correct answers:
1  Here the question, "Who wrote it?" (ll. 10/11), should trigger your attention.
   The answer can be found in lines 13 to 15, "It began as a set of loose papers
   in five separate handwritings, presumably sent in from people dotted around
   Scotland in various locations."
2  "it's essentially a list of names produced in Scotland in 1658, summarizing
   people accused of witchcraft" (ll. 12/13); "it could be carried around by a court
   messenger who was then convening trials in various locations." (ll. 17/18)
3  "Scotland was a completely independent kingdom. And nothing like this Witchcraft Act existed in England and Wales, south of the border." (ll. 25/26)
4  "You would be almost certainly interrogated in ways that breach any legal
   protocol now." (ll. 38/39) You can either use the exact wording of the recording
   or simply describe the nature of the interrogations in your own words.
5  For number 5, there is once more a question in the interview that should trigger your attention, "Why do you think it's important to make these records public?" (l. 43). The answer can be found in Christopher Hilton's explanation: "One
   of the things that this document does is make people aware that what we now
   think of as scientific medicine is something that has evolved over time. It basically gets people thinking about – what do we think of as being proper science?
   What do we think of as being magic? What do we think of as alternative medicine? And have the boundaries changed?" (ll. 44–49)

| 1 | Information about who wrote the manuscript: | five different people from various locations in Scotland |
|---|---|---|
| 2 | Original function of the manuscript: | list of accused people carried around by court messenger to convene trials in various locations |
| 3 | Reason why the 1563 law only applied to Scotland: | Scotland an independent kingdom |
| 4 | Nature of interrogations: | would breach today's legal protocols / cruel |
| 5 | Significance of publication: | can clarify how the boundary between science and magic / our understanding of medicine / science has evolved |

## Transcript 3  Native Americans in Wyoming

1  **Ari Shapiro** *(host)*: A severe lack of housing on American Indian reservations means that many Native Americans who would prefer to live there are instead forced to rent a home in a community nearby. That's the case for the Wind River Reservation in central Wyoming. Some tribal members there are still struggling to find places to

5  live because of what they say is racial discrimination. Wyoming Public Radio's Melodie Edwards reports.

**Melodie Edwards** *(byline)*: Ever since last summer, Ken Hebah has been unable to find a place to live. The Eastern Shoshone member says he doesn't need much.

**Ken Hebah:** More like a – maybe, like, a one-bedroom just for me.

10  **Edwards:** Until Hebah finds his own place, he's living at his sister's house on the reservation. He's a nurse with good credit history, but he says somehow, landlords just won't rent to him.

**Hebah:** That's the first question: Do you party? Do you drink? Do you have a lot of people? They already assume I'm going to do something like that, and that's where

15  I feel I'm being discriminated because of my race.

**Edwards:** The most recent study from the Department of Housing and Urban Development shows that one in four Native Americans has experienced housing discrimination, but few get around to filing formal complaints. In the last ten years, only four people did so in this county, and Hebah wasn't one of them.

20  **Dave Kellogg:** This is an apartment house, and interestingly, this little trailer court is mine also.

**Edwards:** I'm taking a ride with landlord Dave Kellogg in his old VW Bug to see some of the apartment buildings he owns in the area.

There aren't …

25  **Kellogg:** I just basically rent the space.

**Edwards:** Yeah. Mostly, Kellogg rents affordable two-bedroom, one-bath apartments. But he's learned to set strict rules after shelling out $15,000 repairing one apartment complex he says was trashed by former tenants. Since then, he requires detailed credit histories and plenty of references.

30 **Kellogg:** The Native Americans are less able, in many instances, to meet the amount of information I want to have on the credit application.

**Edwards:** Like, can you give me some examples?

**Kellogg:** A lot of them don't have a bank account.

**Edwards:** Kellogg tries to be flexible, but he says he can't treat his rental business like 35 a charity. Still, there are some things he won't budge on, like only allowing one family per apartment. This rule might be the hardest for Native Americans because many want to live in extended families in the same home. Kellogg had a problem with one Native family a few years back.

**Kellogg:** All of a sudden, there was five kids in the apartment. And nobody wanted to 40 admit to where they came from or do anything about getting them out. So I – we ended the rental agreement with some damage, I might add.

**Lyle Konkol:** No, you cannot put a number on how many people can live in a unit.

**Edwards:** That's Lyle Konkol, field director for the Department of Housing and Urban Development in Wyoming. He says you especially can't put a number on family 45 members. Konkol says most landlords discriminate unknowingly. For instance, Kellogg was in his rights to use a strict credit application.

**Konkol:** Here's the key. If you treat them like you treat everybody else in your application process, that's acceptable. But everyone has to be treated the same.

**Edwards:** Konkol says in order to better know how pervasive such discrimination is, he 50 wishes more Native Americans would file complaints. Jane Juve is trying to help tribal members do just that. She's the liaison in the nearby city of Riverton between tribal and non-tribal communities. Since she's been on the job, she's found that many Native Americans are reluctant to file complaints because of longstanding mistrust of government agencies.

55 **Jane Juve:** Just because you report something doesn't mean you lose control of that process, OK? You don't.

**Edwards:** To that end, Juve recently offered a landlord training on Fair Housing law, and she made it easier to find the complaint form by posting it on the city's website. For NPR News, I'm Melodie Edwards on the Wind River Reservation.

60 (SOUNDBITE OF CLAP YOUR HANDS SAY YEAH SONG, "BLUE TURNING GRAY")

Have a close look at the sentence beginnings to know on which text passages you have to focus your attention. When you have identified the passage a certain sentence refers to, check all the possible sentence endings in detail: Which of them can immediately be discarded? Which use key words that reappear in the listening text? Which use other words or synonyms to describe the circumstances mentioned in the text? Make good use of both listening rounds by using the first to solve the easier tasks, the second to exclude any sentence endings about which you are still in doubt.

The following text passages will help you find the correct answer:

1 "Some tribal members there <u>are still struggling to find places to live</u> because of what they say is racial discrimination." (ll. 4/5) You might be tempted to choose solution **b**, "the reservation is overcrowded". However, on closer inspection, the more general sentence ending **c**, "they cannot find an apartment" is more fitting. There are probably not too many people on the reservation, the regulations just make it difficult for Native Americans to be granted access to the existing space.

2 "Until Hebah finds his own place, he's <u>living at his sister's house</u> on the reservation." (ll. 10/11)

3 "The most recent study from the Department of Housing and Urban Development shows that one in four Native Americans has experienced housing discrimination, but <u>few get around to filing formal complaints</u>. In the last ten years, only four people did so in this county" (ll. 16–19)

4 "he's learned to set <u>strict rules</u> after shelling out $15,000 repairing one apartment complex he says was trashed by former tenants. Since then, he requires <u>detailed credit histories and plenty of references</u>." (ll. 27–29)

5 "The Native Americans are less able, in many instances, to meet the amount of information I want to have on the credit application." (ll. 30/31)

6 "only allowing one family per apartment. This rule might be the hardest for Native Americans because <u>many want to live in extended families in the same home</u>." (ll. 35–37)

7 "If you treat them like you treat everybody else in your application process, that's acceptable. But <u>everyone has to be treated the same</u>." (ll. 47/48)

8 "She's the <u>liaison</u> in the nearby city of Riverton <u>between tribal and non-tribal communities</u>." (ll. 51/52) Once more, you might be tempted to think that **c** is correct because of the "training" (l. 57) Juve offered. However, when you listen closely, you will see that the mentioned training is for landlords, not for Native American tenants. Once more, the more general solution is the correct one.

1 Some inhabitants have to leave the Wind River Reservation because …

c ☑ they cannot find an apartment.

**2** Ken Hebah …

   **b** ☑ is forced to stay with a relative.

**3** The Department of Housing and Urban Development …

   **b** ☑ found out that housing discrimination is rarely reported.

**4** Landlord Dave Kellogg …

   **a** ☑ has tough regulations for future tenants.

**5** Kellogg says that Native Americans …

   **d** ☑ usually cannot fulfil his conditions.

**6** The reporter, Melodie Edwards, says that Native Americans often …

   **d** ☑ wish to share their home with relatives.

**7** Lyle Konkol …

   **b** ☑ insists on equal rights for all.

**8** Jane Juve …

   **b** ☑ facilitates communication between Native Americans and others.


## Transcript 4    Choosing a College Major

1   I'm a high school senior preparing for college. When my dad asks me about my plans, I dread telling him I want to study art. I already know the reaction I am going to get. I'm Stella Lau with a commentary from Youth Radio.

   My dad was recently driving me to school when we started arguing about my future.
5  "No, no, no!" he said. "People who major in arts aren't well educated and won't make enough money. Why don't you major in computer science like your cousins?"

   Now I understand where his worries are coming from. I'm going against my family's expectations. They're worried that I won't be able to be financially secure. And, art isn't as valued in my family than [*sic*] say STEM majors.

10  But, while this may all be true, I'm passionate and driven when it comes to art. I spend hours painting and drawing on my own. I even have my own online gallery.

   I know I might come off as delusional or stubborn, but I am confident I can make it as an artist. My family might not support it, but they're going to have to deal with it. And at least I am being true to myself.
15  For Youth Radio, I'm Stella Lau.

*Stella Lau / Youth Radio: "Choosing an Art Major over My Parents' Wish", http://youthradio.org/ journalism/education/choosing-an-art-major-over-my-parents-wishes/, © Youth Radio*

This task deals with a girl contrasting her father's plans for her future life with her own.

**1** In the first part of the radio commentary, you have to identify the underlying motif, which makes the father reject his daughter's plans. There are two instances where it becomes clear that Stella's father values financial success a lot: "People who major in arts aren't well educated and won't make enough money." (ll. 5/6); "They're worried that I won't be able to be financially secure." (l. 8)

**2** In lines 10 to 14, it becomes evident that Stella Lau is convinced of her career choice. This can be seen as an independent decision while all her arguments show that she has given a lot of thought to the issue.

**1** Stella Lau thinks her father …

  **c** ☑ values financial success above all else.

**2** Stella Lau …

  **b** ☑ makes a well-considered, independent decision.

 **SCHREIBEN**

**1** 

In this task you have to write a short summary of the excerpt focusing on the difficulties the narrator is confronted with. Read the text carefully before you start working on the assignment. Firstly, it is essential to establish the context of the scene: The events are narrated from the perspective of Kim, a young girl from Hong Kong who is new at an American school. You should then find a convincing structure for the main part of your answer: you can either follow the chronology of the text or focus on Kim's main problem areas, such as the language barrier, the cultural clash, the teacher's and the classmates' unfriendliness, etc., one by one. This sample solution takes a chronological approach.

Possible sections of this excerpt are:
- section 1: Kim has difficulty finding the school and arrives late
- section 2: Kim's first encounter with her new teacher and classmates
- section 3: dinner time at school
- section 4: afternoon lessons and end of school day

Start with a short introduction, in which you mention the basic facts about the excerpt. Use your own words as far as possible and do not quote from the text.

You could mention the following points:

**Introduction:** Kim's first day at her new school

**Main part:** Kim's difficulties at school
- Kim's late arrival (cf. ll. 1/2, 9, 17/18)
- unfriendly welcome by teacher and classmates:
  - language barrier (cf. for instance ll. 11, 16)
  - teacher Mr. Bogart: brusque, inconsiderate and demanding (cf. ll. 8–10, 12/13, 16–19, 28, 35)
  - outsider in comparison to her classmates: nearly all Black, no Chinese kids (cf. ll. 14/15), ridicule Kim (cf. ll. 14, 22/23), unruly and disinterested behaviour in Kim's eyes (cf. ll. 29–32)
- lunchtime: Kim is unaccustomed to …
  - the American kids' eating habits (cf. ll. 36–39)
  - the American food (cf. ll. 40–45)
- afternoon lessons:
  - Kim's failure in the pop quiz (cf. ll. 47–62)
  - Kim's intention to be industrious and helpful is misunderstood (cf. ll. 62–68)

---

The excerpt from Jean Kwok's novel *Girl in Translation*, which was published in 2010, tells how Kim Chang, a Chinese immigrant from Hong Kong, goes through her first day at her new school in Brooklyn. It is an unpleasant and trying experience because Kim is entering a completely strange environment and an unfamiliar culture. Introduction

Kim's school day gets off to a very bad start because the young Chinese girl has difficulty finding her way in the city. So, she arrives late to her first lesson. Main part: Kim's late arrival

Her new teacher notices her trouble in understanding him. Yet, he shows no sympathy and with his very brusque, inconsiderate and demanding manner, adds to Kim's uneasiness. unfriendly welcome by teacher

Her classmates, who are all of a different ethnicity to Kim's, are not much help either. Instead of supporting her and making her feel welcome in their group, they add to Kim's distress by laughing at her nervousness and language difficulties. In addition, Kim is singled out from the rest of the class through her disciplined behaviour. outsider in comparison to her classmates

This becomes especially evident at lunchtime when Kim is shocked and overwhelmed both by her classmates' unruly conduct and the unfamiliar food. As she cannot express herself properly, she just has to accept what is put on her plate. lunchtime

In the afternoon, she does not understand what she is supposed to do with the test the teacher has handed out. When she tries to look at what her neighbour is writing, she is accused of cheating. At the end of the lessons, she wants to help clean the room, like students in afternoon lessons

Hong Kong usually do, but her teacher misunderstands her intentions. So, Kim leaves in a very agitated and distressed state.

*(281 words)*

2

**TIPP**

When it comes to content and Kim's feelings of alienation, you will probably allude to many of the points you have already mentioned in task 1. For this task, however, your focus should be on the mode of presentation. That means you have to show <u>how</u> a certain message is conveyed. The first question you can ask yourself is: Who is telling the story? It is important to distinguish between author and narrator. The author is Jean Kwok. However, she does not tell the story directly, she has "invented" a narrator, the Chinese immigrant Kim Chang, who remembers her first day at her new school in Brooklyn from a first-person perspective. Other narrative techniques you should mention in your analysis are the general tone of the excerpt and some linguistic devices the author uses. However, be careful not to simply list quotes from the text or stylistic devices, but to put everything into a larger context and always interpret why and to what effect a certain technique is used. As to the structure of your solution, it is advisable to summarise the main content in the introduction before analysing the narrative process in the main part.

The main points are:

**Introduction:** Kim's first day at her new school in Brooklyn

**Main part:** analysis of narrative process
- first-person narration: Kim's perspective mainly exemplified by her language problems (cf. ll. 8, 10, 13, 52, 53)
- unfavourable description of Mr. Bogart:
  - unpleasant outward appearance and voice: "eyes [that are] unnaturally bright" (ll. 5/6), "his stomach stuck out from under his shirt" (l. 6), "strange smile" (l. 8), "a kind of grumbled whine" (ll. 16/17)
  - use of imagery: "raspberry nose and a head bald as an egg" (l. 5)
  - unpleasant behaviour: anger and impatience (cf. ll. 16/17, 19, 35, 52/53, 57–59)
- unfavourable description of Kim's classmates:
  - first "snicker" (l. 14), then "laugh" (l. 23) at Kim
  - exaggerated description of their disorderly sitting position in contrast to students in Hong Kong (cf. ll. 30–33)
  - another exaggerated description of unruly behaviour at lunchtime (cf. ll. 36–39)
  - second contrast to students in Hong Kong: behaviour after lessons (cf. ll. 66/67)

- linguistic devices that illustrate Kim's growing desperation:
  - detailed descriptions of things that are obvious for American / European readers but not for Kim ("writing [...] from left to right", l. 7)
  - kind of interior monologue style with elliptical anaphora ("No other Chinese at all, no help in sight.", l. 15) and questions (cf. ll. 17, 54/55)
  - comparison: "I felt as if the zero were fluorescent, blinking in neon to the rest of the class." (ll. 60/61)

  **Conclusion:** overall effect: vivid impression of Kim's loneliness and alienation

Kim's first day in her new class is not an easy experience. The author uses several narrative techniques to convey the atmosphere at the school and Kim's feelings of abandonment and alienation.

**Introduction**

To begin with, the events are presented from Kim's perspective in a first-person narration. This makes the account very direct and offers insight into Kim's thoughts and feelings. Kim's language problem is an especially impressive example: She knows some basic English which she learned at school in Hong Kong. However, she has great difficulty in understanding the native speakers in Brooklyn (cf. ll. 55/56). The author illustrates this by presenting the words Kim does not understand in false spelling, the way Kim hears them, e. g. "eye-prezoom" (l. 8), "exsu" (l. 10), "exshus" (l. 13), "cheap pen" (l. 52) or "hero" (l. 53). So, the reader, like Kim, has to guess or decode the meaning of the sounds.

**Main part:** first-person narration (exemplified by Kim's language problem)

Kim recalls her dislike of her teacher and classmates with words and expressions which have a negative connotation. Mr. Bogart is a man with "eyes [that are] unnaturally light" (ll. 5/6) and "his stomach stuck out from under his shirt" (l. 6). That he looks strange and unfamiliar to Kim is further illustrated by the use of imagery when his nose is called a "raspberry" (l. 5) and his bald head compared to an egg (cf. l. 5). He has "a strange smile" (l. 8), speaks in "a kind of grumbled whine" (ll. 16/17), becomes very angry at her alleged attempt to cheat (cf. ll. 52/53) and seems annoyed by her language mistakes (cf. l. 58).

unfavourable description of Mr. Bogart

Her new classmates are a loud, unruly and disinterested group. They laugh at Kim (cf. ll. 14, 22/23), sit in class in a disorderly fashion (cf. ll. 30–32), are noisy and disobedient at lunch (cf. ll. 36–39) and do not stay behind after class to help tidy the room (cf. ll. 66/67). This is a sharp contrast to what Kim was used to in Hong Kong.

unfavourable description of Kim's classmates

Kwok illustrates the shock Kim feels by employing several linguistic devices: Things that are obvious to an American or European person are described in a way that makes it clear that they are unusual for Kim. One example is that Mr. Bogart's writing "from left to right" (l. 7) is explicitly mentioned.

linguistic devices to illustrate Kim's growing sense of despair

Another means the author employs to show Kim's alienation is to present her thoughts in a kind of interior monologue. This becomes especially apparent in situations where she is completely overwhelmed and unsure of what to say or think. When she does not understand Mr. Bogart's questions and looks around for a classmate to help her, the elliptical anaphora of "No other Chinese at all, no help in sight" (l. 15) makes her growing desperation almost tangible. In a similar way, the questions she asks herself (cf. ll. 17, 54/55) exemplify the thoughts racing through her head when she is desperately trying to understand her teacher.

*kind of interior monologue*

The test where Kim is falsely accused of cheating is apparently the final straw for her. Her horror and embarrassment at being given a zero become apparent in the comparison that for her, the zero is "fluorescent, blinking in neon to the rest of the class" (l. 61). She feels like her shame is displayed openly.

*comparison*

Through all these means, the reader can directly share Kim's mounting confusion and desperation. In this way, the author arouses pity and sympathy for the lonely foreigner.

**Conclusion**

*(582 words)*

## 3.1 TIPP

This assignment requires you to compare Kim's experiences at school with Larry Ott's in *Crooked Letter, Crooked Letter*. Have a look again at your answer in task 1 where you summarised Kim's first day at school in New York. When it comes to Larry's school life, there are different scenes of the novel you could refer to: Try to come to a rather general assessment of his situation and find examples that show how he deals with it. A particularly striking scene is described in chapter 3 of the novel when Larry insults a Black classmate in order to impress his White peers. For a satisfactory comparison, you should think about aspects that both characters have in common, but also explain in which ways their situations and reactions differ from each other. Of course, you could also mention that you know a lot more about Larry than about Kim. So, you can only speculate about her future experiences.

The sample solution mentions the following points:

**Introduction:** Kim's and Larry's general situations at school

**Main part 1:** what Kim and Larry have in common
- both are outsiders
- both have a different ethnical background from the majority of their classmates

**Main part 2:** differences between Kim's and Larry's experiences and reactions
- Kim starts at a new school as a foreigner in a new country (main difficulties: language barrier, unfamiliar customs, racism)

- at Larry's recently desegregated school there are racial tensions between Black and White pupils, but Larry is also an outsider with the White kids (due to his character and interests)
- Larry's failed attempt to ingratiate himself with his White classmates by insulting a Black girl
- Kim's strategy to be as inconspicuous and industrious as possible

**Conclusion:** Kim and Larry both have difficulties in their schools, but perhaps Kim has a better chance of coping with the challenges in the long term

Kim Chang, a Chinese immigrant, starts school in New York. Larry Ott attends a recently desegregated high school in the Deep South of the USA. Generally speaking, for both Kim and Larry, school is an unpleasant experience.

*Introduction*

Kim and Larry are outsiders at their school and for both, there are instances in which they are singled out, embarrassed or even openly ridiculed or attacked. So, both feel uncomfortable in their peer group and are victimised in certain situations.

*Main part 1: what Larry and Kim have in common: both are outsiders*

One further thing that they have in common is that they are from an ethnical background that is different to that of the majority of their classmates. Kim is an immigrant, a newcomer and the only Chinese girl in her class. Larry is one of the few White pupils at a desegregated school where there are more Black than White kids.

*different ethnical background from the majority of their classmates*

However, there are also clear differences between the two students: First of all, Kim's experience of being an outsider mainly comes from her being a Chinese immigrant from Hong Kong and her unfamiliarity with the language and culture she encounters. She wants to integrate and to act in accordance with the rules. That is why she tries very hard to do what is expected of her and to avoid mistakes. However, this is made difficult by her lack of knowledge of English and her inability to understand all of her teacher's commands. Her teacher's and her classmates' unfriendly reactions to her difficulties add to her insecurity and tenseness, which she feels as a new student anyway.

*Main part 2: differences between Kim and Larry: Kim's difficult start at a new school*

Larry, on the other hand, is in a different situation. Even after several years of them going to a desegregated school, the atmosphere between Black and White children is rather tense. Contrary to the authorities' expectations, desegregation does not seem to work and the races do not mix. Instead, Black and White students mainly stay in separate groups and eye each other with suspicion. However, Larry does not only have problems with the Black kids. Due to being shy, an avid reader and not good at sports or other things considered cool and "manly", he is also an outsider among his White classmates – and even looked down upon by his own father.

*Larry's general outsider role (among both Black and White classmates)*

It is probably his utter loneliness and the lack of acceptance in all parts of his life that make Larry take rather drastic measures to try to belong and to impress his peers: To be accepted by his White classmates Ken and David and gain their respect, he insults Jackie Simmons, a Black schoolmate, calling her "Monkey Lips". This racist test of courage fails completely because it provokes angry retaliation from his outraged Black classmates and does not ingratiate Larry with the White boys either. Instead, they only laugh at him being beaten up and humiliated.

*Larry's failed attempt to ingratiate himself with his White classmates*

Kim, on the other hand, reacts rather differently to her experiences: She tries to be as inconspicuous as possible and to keep a low profile. Her main interest lies in showing herself as industrious and as willing to learn although sadly, her attempts also fail, particularly because of the cultural divide between the USA and Hong Kong.

*Kim's strategy to be as inconspicuous as possible*

All in all, neither Kim nor Larry has it easy at school. Yet, it seems that Kim has a better chance of coping with the challenges in the long term. Her problems seem to be of a more temporary nature than Larry's. After getting used to her new surroundings and provided that she will meet people with a less racist outlook than Mr. Bogart, she might be able to mix more with her classmates. Larry, on the other hand, has already internalised the bad opinion about himself that he is confronted with repeatedly. So, for him it is particularly hard to have the confidence to initiate new friendships. *(629 words)*

**Conclusion:**
*Kim probably has a better chance of coping in the long term*

**3.2** TIPP

This is a task where you should refer to the film *Gran Torino*, at least where it fits your overall argument. However, you can also go beyond the film and focus on recent events or the situation in your own country. You could for instance refer to the demographic developments in Europe (rising migration numbers), which initiated a debate about how best to integrate all these newcomers. The main part of your solution should mention the areas of everyday life in which good language skills are essential: work, communication (social contacts) and education. However, you can also include the view that learning the language of the host country is not a guarantee for integration. To prove this, you could mention terrorist attacks that were carried out by so-called "homegrown terrorists". You could also allude to Sue and especially Thao, who are competent English speakers, but are still confronted with integration and assimilation problems. To conclude, you could point out that language has a considerable significance for the integration of immigrants into host societies, but that language skills alone are not sufficient for a successful multicultural society.

The main points are:

**Introduction:** recent developments
- influx of refugees and asylum seekers
- integration difficult: language skills required

**Main part:** importance of language
- field of work: basic command necessary for training and employment (example of Thao's beginnings on the job market)
- private life: basic command necessary for social participation
- school/education: difficult, formal written language requirements complex, see PISA tests

**Objection:** learning the language of the host country no guarantee for integration
- examples: "homegrown terrorists"
- Thao: lack of acceptance and respect from Americans

**Conclusion:** knowing the language is a prerequisite for immigrants to successfully integrate, but not sufficient

In recent years, large numbers of refugees have made their way into Europe in their flight from wars, persecution and poverty. Integrating these newcomers into society has remained a formidable task, especially because many of the migrants cannot speak the language of the country they arrive in. However, there is general agreement that language plays a prominent role in avoiding the development of so-called "parallel societies" within a country, in which people of the same ethnic background live in ghettos without much contact with the "outside world".

For example, in the world of work, knowing the language is crucial to getting a job or starting a business. It is difficult or sometimes impossible for newcomers to be trained or employed when they do not have a basic command of the national language. Think of the situation in *Gran Torino*, when Walt Kowalski tries to find a job for Thao on the building site. The first question the boy is asked is, "Do you speak English?" Without a job, real integration proves difficult, and not just because of financial hardships connected to unemployment. High numbers of unemployed migrants can also be at the root of a dangerous vicious circle of misconceptions: xenophobic groups feel vindicated in their prejudices of "lazy foreigners" who do not want to work and exploit social services. The foreigners, who suffer from that lack of recognition, might consequently withdraw even more into their own communities.

*Introduction*

*Main part: importance of language in the field of work*

This leads me directly to my next point that language also plays an important role in people's private lives. Only when migrants can understand what others are saying and make themselves understood, can they begin to make friends, establish social contacts and take part in public and cultural life outside their native community. This is what true integration looks like in my opinion: only when they feel confident and accepted will migrants truly feel a part of their new home country and willingly identify with it.

private life

In everyday life, a limited vocabulary and some basic grammar are usually sufficient to make oneself understood. However, at school immigrant children are confronted with enormous language problems in reading, understanding and writing texts, because formal written language differs greatly from the spoken version. In Germany, for example, PISA tests showed that school children with an immigrant background are generally less successful and have lower marks than non-immigrant students. This is especially problematic because a poor performance at school leads to fewer employment opportunities and compounds the aforementioned vicious circle. Therefore, I would strongly advise the government to invest more money in public schools for language teaching and for the provision of extra tuition for immigrant students.

school / education

On the other hand, we should not forget that language alone does not solve all integration problems and is not a guarantee for mutual understanding. Take some of the terrorist attacks directed against the way of life in Western societies that have been spread all over the news. Many of these atrocities were carried out by young people who had been raised in the countries they attacked and spoke their languages perfectly.

**Objection:** knowing the language no guarantee for successful integration

Similarly, Thao is a competent English speaker, but plagued by self-doubt and still searching for his identity and his place in American society. His problems have more to do with a lack of acceptance from Americans and the dangerous counterculture the Hmong gang represents, which might be true for young people who are drawn into extremist circles, too.

example from *Gran Torino*

All in all, I would argue that language skills are a prerequisite for immigrants to successfully integrate into their new homeland. Expressing oneself, communicating with others, knowing how others think and what they believe in requires at least a basic command of the language of the host country. In my view, it is especially important to consider supporting migrant children a matter of urgency because their success at school and future employment chances depend to a large extent on their language competence. However, this is only the first step. Additionally, diversity must generally be accepted and welcomed more so that feeling inferior or rejected because of one's ethnic origins truly becomes a thing of the past.          *(687 words)*

**Conclusion**

**HÖRVERSTEHEN**

### Task 1: BBC News

You will hear several items from the BBC radio news. Choose from the list (A–G) which description applies to which news item (1–6). For each item there is only one correct answer. Put the letters (A–G) into the correct box. There is one more description than you need.

| | Description |
|---|---|
| A | Conflict escalates |
| B | Consequences of a disaster |
| C | Family tradition regulated |
| D | Forbidden custom defended |
| E | Soon on trial |
| F | Suspected of foul play |
| G | Threat of catastrophe |

| News item | 1 | 2 | 3 | 4 | 5 | 6 |
|---|---|---|---|---|---|---|
| Description A–G | | | | | | |

You will hear an excerpt from Barack Obama's autobiography *Dreams from My Father*, which was published before his presidency. While listening, tick (✓) the correct answer (a, b, c or d). There is only one correct answer.

1  When an airport guard approaches him, Obama …

   **a** ☐ wants to ask him a question.

   **b** ☐ is troubled by the guard's weapon.

   **c** ☐ worries he might have broken a rule.

   **d** ☐ expects to be asked for his documents.

2  The guard …

   **a** ☐ assumes Obama is a relative.

   **b** ☐ recognizes Obama right away.

   **c** ☐ wants to visit a relative in Texas.

   **d** ☐ has no idea of the size of the U.S.

3  Obama's expectations before his arrival in Kenya were …

   **a** ☐ realistic.

   **b** ☐ skeptical.

   **c** ☐ euphoric.

   **d** ☐ ambivalent.

4  Obama's luggage is …

   **a** ☐ sent back home.

   **b** ☐ still on the plane.

   **c** ☐ given to him by an attractive woman.

   **d** ☐ assumed to be on its way to another city.

5  During his conversation with Miss Omoro, Obama …

   **a** ☐ thinks about asking her out.

   **b** ☐ tells her about his past travels.

   **c** ☐ finds out she is in a relationship.

   **d** ☐ learns she is planning a trip to Britain.

6  The fact that his name is recognized makes him feel …

   **a** ☐ ecstatic.

   **b** ☐ flattered.

   **c** ☐ relieved.

   **d** ☐ accepted.

**7** Obama's half-sister Auma ...

a ☐ sees him for the first time.

b ☐ introduces him to his aunt.

c ☐ meets him with reservation.

d ☐ is in tears when they finally meet.

**8** On the whole, with this text Obama wants to ...

a ☐ help his listeners discover Kenya.

b ☐ illustrate difficulties of cross-cultural encounters.

c ☐ inform his listeners about his personal experiences.

d ☐ make others aware of risks and benefits of travelling.

## Task 3: Wallpaper

You will hear a radio report about the cultural history of wallpaper, which includes an interview with Lucinda Hawksley, the author of the book *Bitten by Witch Fever*. While listening, answer the questions. Do not write complete sentences.

1 What time period is the book *Bitten by Witch Fever* about?

2 What was the problem with wallpapers at the time?

3 What did wallpaper look like at the time?

4 What group of people made this new kind of wallpaper more popular?

5 Who was William Morris?

6 How do people interpret the story "The Yellow Wallpaper"?

7 What does the protagonist of "The Yellow Wallpaper" do with the wallpaper?

8 How is the protagonist's behaviour explained?

9 Apart from wallpaper, what other items were often green? *(Name one.)*

10 How is Oscar Wilde's lifestyle described?

*Bei den für Set 3 abgedruckten Aufgaben zum Hörverstehen handelt es sich um die Original-Aufgaben des Hörverstehensteils der Abiturprüfung 2019 in Rheinland-Pfalz.*

| Text | Kushanava Choudhury: The New World |

*This is an excerpt from the introductory chapter of* The Epic City, *Choudhury's literary portrait of Calcutta, the city of his birth, from where his family moved to the United States of America.*

1 Of all the people who came to Ellis Island in the first decades of the twentieth century, more than half went back. They never told us that on our seventh-grade class trip.

The American immigrant myth says that migration is a reset button. The New World offers deliverance from the past, liberation from the Old World's limited horizons. The
5 myth states: "The past is gone. The future awaits. Start over."

It never really works like that. That was the story no one ever told about America. The past is never left behind. It haunts every world you live in. Sometimes it drags you back.

By the time I visited Ellis Island on that class trip, I had already migrated halfway
10 around the world four times, flipping back and forth between continents like a dual-voltage appliance. My parents were Indian scientists, torn between nation and vocation. Twice they moved to America, twice they moved back. They were unwilling to leave their country and they were unable to stay. When he was around forty, my father quit his cushy job at a government research institute in Calcutta. He wanted one more
15 chance, he said [...].

So, when I was almost twelve, my parents and I moved to Highland Park, New Jersey.

Our move carried no Emma Lazarus cadences. We certainly had not arrived tempest-tossed, beating at the golden door. Our coming was equivocal, always tied to re-
20 turn. Living in New Jersey, we hardly saw ourselves as immigrants. My parents expected to go back to India, like many of their Bengali friends, someday, eventually. On Saturday nights, they gathered at each other's homes, ate fourteen-course meals brimming with various types of fish and meat, and derailed each other's sentences in locomotive Bengali, their conversations full of memories of Calcutta. Return, the duty of
25 return and the dream of return, were spoken of endlessly while eating platefuls of goat curry and hilsa fish. Few, of course, actually went back. There were too many good reasons not to. Nationalism and nostalgia did not pay the bills, raise children or advance careers. And yet that dream of a return to the great metropolis cocooned them like a protective blanket from the alien world all around.

30 As for me – my friends, my neighbourhood, my Calcutta life was gone. In New Jersey, I was in seventh grade in a public school that had almost no Indian students. Cocooning was not an option. I had to fit in fast. I wasn't assimilating as much as passing. So much of what went on inside my head was from another place. I had happy childhood memories of mid-morning cricket matches during summer vacations, of
35 games played in gullies, rooftops, courtyards and streets. When I moved, it was the streets of the city as much as my childhood that I left behind.

52

We had not had an easy few years in America. The man who had offered the job to my father had made promises he did not keep, and so my father was forced to find other work, work he grew to despise. From time to time, there would be talk of another
40 move, to Georgia, to Colorado, and I would pull down the posters in my room and prepare. We stayed put, the three of us adrift in the treacherous shoals of the lower middle classes, a world of chronic car trouble and clothes from K-Mart. In the fall of my senior year, a piece of good news finally came to our two-bedroom apartment. I had been accepted early to Princeton University.
45 Every immigrant who has lugged worthless foreign degrees through customs knows that where you go to college […] determines your lot in life. When the acceptance letter from Princeton arrived, my parents acted as if someone had come to our door with balloons and a giant cardboard cheque. It was their happiest day in America. But it wasn't mine.
50 It is probably universally true that education drives a wedge between us and our hometowns, our families, our earlier selves. But for the immigrant the gap is greater, that divergence in mentality more extreme. My trajectory was taking me farther afield, to Princeton, while a part of me was elsewhere, in another country, in another city. Through all my sojourns I had carried memories on my back like Huien Tsang's chair,
55 until at seventeen, I felt hunched over nostalgia like a middle-aged man. When the Princeton letter arrived, I had what my friend Ben called a "premature midlife crisis".
At night, I couldn't sleep. By day I sleepwalked through classes. Each evening, while my friends assembled at Dunkin' Donuts, complained about how there was nothing to do in our little town and roared together into the night on long aimless drives,
60 while they enjoyed the languor of spring and that sweet American affliction called senioritis, I stayed home and stewed. In my mind, I hatched a plan. I would go back.
India lives in its villages, Mahatma Gandhi had said. So, even though I was a city boy who had never spent a night in an Indian village, I wrote letters back home to arrange to teach in a village school. Instead of Princeton, I would take a year off and
65 head to rural Bengal, I told my parents. But in our two-bedroom apartment full of shared immigrant striving, such a detour was out of the question.
Instead I just drove. The black night, the shimmering yellow lines on inviting ribbons of asphalt, the radio jammed loud. Enveloped by night and noise, the mind gave way to a deeper calling. Just drive. It was the mantra of our Jersey youth, an exhorta-
70 tion, a command, an ideology, something hardwired in us as teenage boys. Night after night I took my parents' Toyota and just drove, without destination, without purpose, to escape. […]
After graduating from college, while friends set up their apartments in New York, Boston, and Los Angeles, I headed to Calcutta, to join the *Statesman*.      *994 words*

*Choudhury, Kushanava (2017). The Epic City. The World on the Streets of Calcutta. London: Bloomsbury. pp. xi-xvi*

**Annotations**
line 18:     Emma Lazarus: 1849–1887, author of "The New Colossus", a poem engraved on the base of the Statue of Liberty, which ends with the following verses: *Send these, the homeless, tempest-tossed to me: / I lift my lamp beside the golden door.*

line 42: K-Mart: inexpensive department store chain in the USA
line 44: Princeton University: prestigious university in New Jersey, USA
line 52: trajectory: (here) career path
line 54: Huien Tsang: Chinese Buddhist monk and scholar, travelled throughout India in ancient times
line 61: senioritis: (colloquial) decreased motivation to study displayed by senior students
line 74: *The Statesman*: an influential Indian English-language daily newspaper founded in 1875

---

### Aufgabenstellung

**1** Outline the biographical information given on the author and his parents. (30 %)

**2** Analyze how Choudhury's attitude towards the traditional view of American immigration is conveyed. (30 %)

**3** Choose *one* of the following tasks: (40 %)

**3.1** Assess to what extent the cartoon reflects what Choudhury and his family have experienced in the US.

© Dan Rosandich / cartoonstock

or

**3.2** You are participating in an international school project on identity. Write an article for the project website in which you discuss the importance of place in shaping one's identity.

*Bei den für Set 3 abgedruckten Aufgaben zum Schreiben handelt es sich um offizielle Musteraufgaben des Landes Baden-Württemberg.*

**HÖRVERSTEHEN**

| **Transcript 1**  BBC News

1  BBC News with Debbie Russ.

**1** The authorities in California are evacuating tens of thousands of people living down-stream of the tallest dam in the United States following fears that an overflow channel was about to collapse. Roads below the Oroville dam clogged with traffic as residents
5  heeded warnings to leave their homes. Engineers urgently want to plug a giant hole that's developed in the spillway.

**2** The French authorities have launched an investigation into whether the carmaker Renault has tried to cheat emissions tests with its diesel vehicles. Renault shares initially fell sharply before recovering much of their value. A company spokesman said
10  Renault did not use cheating software in its vehicles.

**3** Protest rallies have been held across the Southern Indian state of Tamil Nadu in support of a traditional form of bull taming banned by the Supreme Court. Supporters of Jallikattu say it's an important cultural event but animal rights activists have condemned the practice.

15  **4** The record setting heatwave that spawned 200 bushfires in the Australian state of New South Wales has abated, but firefighters are still tackling about 80 outbreaks. The largest was so vast it created its own weather system triggering a lightning storm.

**5** Six journalists working for opposition newspapers are expected to appear in court in Ivory Coast. They are charged with spreading false information following a mutiny
20  last week by soldiers demanding bonus payments.

**6** A town in Somalia has banned lavish weddings to encourage more young people to marry. The district commissioner of Beled Hawo near the Kenyan border told the BBC that a maximum of three goats could be slaughtered to feed guests and that hotel receptions would not be allowed.

25  That's the latest BBC News.

*BBC World Service, BBC News Summary, 2017/01/13, www.bbc.co.uk/programmes/p04nhff4*

**TIPP**

When looking through the short descriptions, you will notice that quite a lot of them seem to deal with similar issues at a superficial glance (e. g. "[c]onflict" in **A**, "disaster" in **B**, "catastrophe" in **G**, respectively "[f]amily tradition" in **C** and "custom" in **D**). So when listening for the first time and ideally making quick notes on the most important aspects of the news items, do not focus solely on the events or facts described, but also their consequences, the attitudes expressed with regards to them, etc.

1 "The authorities in California are evacuating tens of thousands of people living downstream of the tallest dam in the United States <u>following fears that an overflow channel was about to collapse</u>." (ll. 2–4) In other words, the "catastrophe" has not happened yet, but there are threats of it (description **G**).

2 "The French authorities have launched an <u>investigation into whether the carmaker Renault has tried to cheat emissions tests</u> with its diesel vehicles." (ll. 7/8) Here you might easily identify **E** and **F** as possible answers because some kind of criminal offence is dealt with. To decide which of the two is ultimately correct, you should once more focus on details such as the fact that it is not certain whether Renault really has been cheating (cf. the spokesman's denial in ll. 9/10). In other words, there are mere suspicions.

3 "Protest rallies have been held across the Southern Indian state of Tamil Nadu <u>in support of a traditional form of bull taming</u> banned by the Supreme Court." (ll. 11/12)

4 News item **4** also deals with a catastrophic event, in this case a natural disaster: "The record setting heatwave that spawned 200 bushfires in the Australian state of New South Wales <u>has abated, but firefighters are still tackling about 80 outbreaks</u>. The largest was so vast it created its own weather system triggering a lightning storm." (ll. 15–17) To find the fitting description, you should pay attention to the fact that the heatwave itself has already blown over, but the "[c]onsequences of [this] disaster" (description **B**) are the main concern.

5 "Six journalists working for opposition newspapers <u>are expected to appear in court</u> in Ivory Coast." (ll. 18/19)

6 "<u>A town in Somalia has banned lavish weddings</u> to encourage more young people to marry." (ll. 21/22) A wedding is a "[f]amily tradition" (description **C**). The second sentence of the news item tells you that there are quite detailed regulations in place, such as the number of goats allowed to be slaughtered (cf. ll. 22–24). Therefore description **C** fits.

| News item | 1 | 2 | 3 | 4 | 5 | 6 |
|---|---|---|---|---|---|---|
| Description A–G | G | F | D | B | E | C |

## Transcript 2  Barack Obama

Kenyatta International Airport was almost empty. Officials sipped at their morning tea as they checked over passports; in the baggage area, a creaky conveyor belt slowly disgorged luggage. Auma was nowhere in sight, so I took a seat on my carry-on bag and lit a cigarette. After a few minutes, a security guard with a wooden club started to walk toward me. I looked around for an ashtray, thinking I must be in a no-smoking area, but instead of scolding me, the guard smiled and asked if I had another cigarette to spare.

"This is your first trip to Kenya, yes?" he asked as I gave him a light.

"That's right."

"I see." He squatted down beside me. "You are from America. You know my brother's son, perhaps. Samson Otieno. He is studying engineering in Texas."

I told him that I'd never been to Texas and so hadn't had the opportunity to meet his nephew. This seemed to disappoint him, and he took several puffs from his cigarette in quick succession. By this time, the last of the other passengers on my flight had left the terminal. I asked the guard if any more bags were coming. He shook his head doubtfully.

"I don't think so," he said, "but if you will just wait here, I will find someone who can help you."

He disappeared around a narrow corridor, and I stood up to stretch my back. The rush of anticipation had drained away, and I smiled with the memory of the homecoming I had once imagined for myself, clouds lifting, old demons fleeing, the earth trembling as ancestors rose up in celebration. Instead I felt tired and abandoned. I was about to search for a telephone when the security guard reappeared with a strikingly beautiful woman, dark, slender, close to six feet tall, dressed in a British Airways uniform. She introduced herself as Miss Omoro and explained that my bag had probably been sent on to Johannesburg by mistake.

"I'm awfully sorry about the inconvenience," she said. "If you will just fill out this form, we can call Johannesburg and have it delivered to you as soon as the next flight comes in."

I completed the form and Miss Omoro gave it the once-over before looking back at me. "You wouldn't be related to Dr Obama, by any chance?" she asked.

"Well, yes – he was my father."

Miss Omoro smiled sympathetically. "I'm very sorry about his passing. Your father was a close friend of my family's. He would often come to our house when I was a child."

We began to talk about my visit, and she told me of her studies in London, as well as her interest in traveling to the States. I found myself trying to prolong the conversation, encouraged less by Miss Omoro's beauty – she had mentioned a fiancé – than by the fact that she recognized my name. That had never happened before, I realized; not in Hawaii, not in Indonesia, not in L.A. or New York or Chicago. For the first time in my life, I felt the comfort, the firmness of identity that a name might provide, how it could carry an entire history in other people's memories, so that they might nod and say knowingly, "Oh, you are so and so's son." No one here in Kenya would ask how to spell my name, or mangle it with an unfamiliar tongue. My name belonged and so I belonged, drawn into a web of relationships, alliances, and grudges that I did not yet understand.

"Barack!" I turned to see Auma jumping up and down behind another guard, who wasn't letting her pass into the baggage area. I excused myself and rushed over to her, and we laughed and hugged, as silly as the first time we'd met. A tall, brown-skinned woman was smiling beside us, and Auma turned and said, "Barack, this is our Auntie Zeituni. Our father's sister."

"Welcome home," Zeituni said, kissing me on both cheeks.

I told them about my bag and said there was someone here who had known the Old Man. But when I looked back to where I'd been standing, Miss Omoro was nowhere in sight. I asked the security guard where she had gone. He shrugged and said that she must have left for the day.

*Barack Obama:* Dreams from My Father: A Story of Race and Inheritance. *New York: Crown Publishers (1995) 2005*

**TIPP**

To choose the right sentence ending out of several options, it is important to identify the text passages the tasks refer to. Key words from the tasks will help you. Sometimes you have to interpret Obama's words for their general meaning because you will only rarely find a one-to-one correspondence between the audio text and the answer options.

The following text passages will help you:

1 "I [...] lit a cigarette. After a few minutes, a security guard with a wooden club started to walk toward me. I looked around for an ashtray, thinking I must be in a no-smoking area, but instead of scolding me, the guard smiled" (ll. 3–6)

2 The fact that the guard expects Obama to know his nephew who is studying in Texas, just because he too is from America, (cf. ll. 10/11) shows that he has no idea of the size of the U.S.

3 The passage, "The rush of anticipation had drained away, and I smiled with the memory of the homecoming I had once imagined for myself, clouds lifting, old demons fleeing, the earth trembling as ancestors rose up in celebration" (ll. 19–22), shows that Obama's expectations before his actual arrival in Kenya had been euphoric.

4 Although Obama meets an attractive woman at the airport, she cannot give him his luggage because his "bag had probably been sent on to Johannesburg by mistake" (ll. 25/26).

5 "I found myself trying to prolong the conversation, encouraged less by Miss Omoro's beauty – she had mentioned a fiancé – than by the fact that she recognized my name." (ll. 37–39) You can exclude **a** because Obama has already accepted that Miss Omoro is not single. They talk about her future travel plans, but she is interested "in traveling to the States" (l. 37). A journey to Britain (**d**) is not mentioned. Places where Obama has been before (**b**) come up in the audio text (cf. ll. 39/40), but they do not form part of his and Miss Omoro's conversation. He just remembers them.

6 "For the first time in my life, I felt the comfort, the firmness of identity that a name might provide, [...]. My name belonged and so I belonged" (ll. 40–45)

58

**7** Auma, whom he must have met before because they "laughed and hugged, as silly as the first time [they]'d met" (l. 49), introduces him to his aunt by saying: "'Barack, this is our Auntie Zeituni. Our father's sister.'" (ll. 50/51)

**8** The whole text is told from a first-person narrator, Barack Obama. We do not learn a lot about Kenya (**a**) or the risks and benefits of travelling (**d**) (besides losing one's luggage, which is only an incident of minor importance, however), nor are any difficulties of cross-cultural (**b**) encounters mentioned. Thus, Obama simply wants to inform the listeners about his personal experience.

**1** When an airport guard approaches him, Obama …

**c** ✓ worries he might have broken a rule.

**2** The guard …

**d** ✓ has no idea of the size of the U.S.

**3** Obama's expectations before his arrival in Kenya were …

**c** ✓ euphoric.

**4** Obama's luggage is …

**d** ✓ assumed to be on its way to another city.

**5** During his conversation with Miss Omoro, Obama …

**c** ✓ finds out she is in a relationship.

**6** The fact that his name is recognized makes him feel …

**d** ✓ accepted.

**7** Obama's half-sister Auma …

**b** ✓ introduces him to his aunt.

**8** On the whole, with this text Obama wants to …

**c** ✓ inform his listeners about his personal experiences.

---

| **Transcript 3** Wallpaper

1 **Richard Lea:** Lucinda Hawksley is an art historian and biographer whose latest tome *Bitten by Witch Fever* gathers together 275 facsimiles of the most sumptuous wallpapers ever created. But this astonishing collection of Victorian design contains a deadly secret: each one has been found to contain arsenic. When Hawksley joined
5 Claire Armitstead in the studio, she started by describing how Oscar Wilde, Charlotte Perkins Gilman and some eye-watering Victorian colour schemes began their murderous invasion into the houses of Britain.

**Lucinda Hawksley:** Well, in the 19th century, very vibrant wallpapers became incredibly fashionable, particularly borne by the aesthetic art movement, which Oscar Wilde

<sup></sup>10   was such a huge part of the aestheticism movement. And the reason that the colours were so incredibly vibrant is because they were created with arsenical paints, so paints that contained arsenic. And this became a huge social ill in the 19th century. So, these wonderful wallpapers were produced, everybody was slathering their homes with them and then, the doctors started to talk about this connection between

15   wallpaper and illness. And many people poo-pooed this idea, including the great wallpaper designer William Morris whose comment was the famous, "The doctors have been bitten as they were bitten by witch fever", where the title of the book comes from.

**Claire Armitstead:** "The Yellow Wallpaper", the story has been taken as a story about a

20   woman being suppressed in the home by her husband. But I was just really struck by this fact that actually, at the end of it, she is eating the paper, and we know that these particular colours were arsenical. So, would you think that was in her mind?

**Lucinda Hawksley:** I think that was definitely in her mind because there had been so much in the media before this that I think the author must have known. She would

25   have been very aware of the dangers of arsenic. Now, having said which, arsenic was normally, erroneously believed just to be in green colours, but actually it was in many different colours, particularly golds, yellows, blues, reds. But I do think that there must have been a knowledge on the part of Charlotte Perkins Gilman. She knew that arsenical wallpaper could cause people to become ill. But of course, the

30   arsenic poisoning that was caused by wallpaper or arsenic in general was much more of a physical sickness. And in "The Yellow Wallpaper", her heroine becomes very, very mentally ill. So, there is definitely the feminist writing of this novel that her heroine is being driven mad by domesticity. She is being stifled physically by the walls and what she sees in the wallpaper is a woman who's trying to get at her

35   and that's when she starts ripping the wallpaper off with her teeth. She is trying to get to the woman who she believes is trying to kill her.

**Claire Armitstead:** And then, you have Oscar Wilde and his green carnation, which is also, is the green of absinthe, isn't it? But he does associate the green with a toxic lifestyle, doesn't he, overtly?

40   **Lucinda Hawksley:** Absolutely. The green was the colour of absinthe but also very much the colour of arsenic. And he talks about it as being an arsenic green. And this is because it had become so incredibly controversial. The aesthetic artists, writers, bohemians embraced the idea of the kind of peacock greeny-blue colour and this was the colour that was so fashionable and that to create in a really wonderful vi-

45   brant way, not just in wallpapers, but in hair accessories, clothing, anything that people could wear was often done with arsenic paint or arsenic dye. And there'd been a huge controversy over it. And Wilde was playing up to this, in the way that he did, always, he loved to cause controversy. So, by deliberately colouring a carna- tion green, by putting it in green-coloured water before wearing it in his buttonhole,

50   he was just showing off to the world that he was being as unnatural as he could possibly be. And unnatural was a word that, as you know, was often applied to Oscar Wilde's lifestyle, not just in terms of his sexuality, but also in terms of the

way that he dressed and the way he behaved. So, he really loved to create this aura about himself.

*The Guardian Books Podcast. "Deadly Beauty with Ruth Padel and Lucinda Hawksley".*
*https://www.theguardian.com/books/audio/2016/dec/23/ruth-padel-and-lucinda-hawksley-books-*
*podcast*

---

**TIPP**

---

Normally, the questions for listening comprehension tasks follow the text chrono-logically. Here you will notice that the first two statements by Richard Lea and Lu-cinda Hawksley contain the answers to questions **1** to **4**. However, all the impor-tant aspects are mentioned several times, so you should have no trouble finding the right solutions. In a similar fashion, questions **6** to **8** all deal with the short sto-ry "The Yellow Wallpaper". Make sure that you focus on common interpretations for question **6**, on the content of the story for **7** and on the explanation for the pro-tagonist's behaviour for question **8**.

1  Throughout the lines 3 to 18, it becomes apparent that the period the book is about must be the 19th century, the so-called Victorian Age. Not only is Oscar Wilde, a famous writer of the Victorian Age, mentioned (cf. ll. 5, 9) but also the 19th century (cf. ll. 8, 12). The adjective Victorian (cf. ll. 3, 6) is explicitly re-ferred to several times as well.

2  "*Bitten by Witch Fever* gathers together 275 facsimiles of the most sumptuous wallpapers ever created. But this astonishing collection of Victorian design contains <u>a deadly secret: each one has been found to contain arsenic</u>." (ll. 2–4); "some eye-watering Victorian colour schemes began their <u>murderous</u> inva-sion into the houses of Britain" (ll. 6/7); "paints that contained arsenic. And this became a huge social ill in the 19th century. […] the doctors started to talk about this <u>connection between wallpaper and illness</u>." (ll. 12–15)

3  "*Bitten by Witch Fever* gathers together 275 facsimiles of the most <u>sumptuous</u> wallpapers ever created. But this <u>astonishing</u> collection of Victorian design" (ll. 2/3); "some <u>eye-watering Victorian colour schemes</u>" (l. 6); "Well, in the 19th century, <u>very vibrant wallpapers</u> became incredibly fashionable" (ll. 8/9); "And the reason that the colours were so <u>incredibly vibrant</u>" (ll. 10/11); "So, these <u>wonderful</u> wallpapers were produced" (l. 13)

4  "Well, in the 19th century, very vibrant wallpapers became incredibly fashion-able, <u>particularly borne by the aesthetic art movement</u>, which Oscar Wilde was such a huge part of the aestheticism movement." (ll. 8–10)

5  "And many people poo-pooed this idea, including the <u>great wallpaper designer William Morris</u> whose comment was the famous, 'The doctors have been bitten as they were bitten by witch fever'" (ll. 15–17)

**6** "'The Yellow Wallpaper', the story has been taken as a story about a <u>woman being suppressed</u> in the home by her husband." (ll. 19/20); "So, there is definitely the feminist writing of this novel that her heroine is being <u>driven mad by domesticity</u>." (ll. 32/33)

**7** "But I was just really struck by this fact that actually, at the end of it, <u>she is eating the paper</u>" (ll. 20/21); "she starts <u>ripping the wallpaper off with her teeth</u>." (l. 35)

**8** "So, there is definitely the feminist writing of this novel that her <u>heroine is being driven mad by domesticity</u>. She is being <u>stifled physically by the walls</u> and what <u>she sees in the wallpaper</u> is <u>a woman who's trying to get at her</u> and that's when she starts ripping the wallpaper off with her teeth. She is trying to get to the woman who she believes is trying to kill her." (ll. 32–36)
Since "at the end of it, she [the heroine] is eating the paper, and we know that <u>these particular colours were arsenical</u>" (ll. 21/22), she might be poisoned by arsenic wallpaper.

**9** "And then, you have Oscar Wilde and his <u>green carnation</u>, which is also, is <u>the green of absinthe</u>, isn't it? [...] The green was the colour of absinthe" (ll. 37–40); "The aesthetic artists, writers, bohemians embraced the idea of the kind of peacock greeny-blue colour and this was the colour that was so fashionable and that to create in a really wonderful vibrant way, not just in wallpapers, but in <u>hair accessories, clothing, anything that people could wear</u> was often done with arsenic paint or arsenic dye." (ll. 42–46)

**10** "But he does associate the green with a <u>toxic lifestyle</u>, doesn't he, overtly?" (ll. 38/39); "And there'd been a huge controversy over it. And Wilde was playing up to this, in the way that he did, always, <u>he loved to cause controversy</u>. [...] he was just showing off to the world that he was being as <u>unnatural</u> as he could possibly be. And <u>unnatural was a word that</u>, as you know, <u>was often applied to Oscar Wilde's lifestyle</u>, not just in terms of his sexuality, but also in terms of the way that he dressed and the way that he behaved. So, <u>he really loved to create this aura about himself</u>." (ll. 46–54)

**1** What time period is the book *Bitten by Witch Fever* about?
**Victorian Age/19th century**

**2** What was the problem with wallpapers at the time?
**contained arsenic/poison/caused illness/made people ill**

**3** What did wallpaper look like at the time?
**sumptuous/vibrant/bright/colourful/vivid/eye-watering colour schemes/ astonishing/wonderful**

**4** What group of people made this new kind of wallpaper more popular?
**aesthetic art movement**

**5**  Who was William Morris?

**a wallpaper designer/sb who did not believe that wallpapers caused illnesses**

**6**  How do people interpret the story "The Yellow Wallpaper"?

**woman suppressed by husband/woman being driven mad**

**7**  What does the protagonist of "The Yellow Wallpaper" do with the wallpaper?

**eats wallpaper/rips it off the wall**

**8**  How is the protagonist's behaviour explained?

**feels stifled by the walls/thinks she sees a woman who is trying to get at her/ is poisoned by arsenic wallpaper/is driven mad by domesticity**

**9**  Apart from wallpaper, what other items were often green?

**Oscar Wilde's green carnation/hair accessories/clothes/anything people could wear/absinthe**

**10**  How is Oscar Wilde's lifestyle described?

**unnatural/toxic lifestyle/loved to create a special aura/to provoke/to cause controversy**

**1**

**TIPP**

This first task is aimed at testing your skills in text comprehension and summary. You are not asked to interpret or analyse the text. Therefore, read the text closely and sum up the biographical information given on the author and his parents. "Biographical information" refers to everything that you get to know about their circumstances and background. In a short introduction, you can give some basic information about the text, the author and his family. Your main part can be divided into one part that provides details on the author's parents and a second part which describes the author himself.

You could structure your answer like this:

**Introduction:** basic information on the text and summary of its gist
- Choudhury family's back-and-forth migration between India and the USA (cf. ll. 9–11)
- family torn between nostalgia and hope for better opportunities in the USA (cf. ll. 24–28)

**Main part 1:** biographical information on the author's parents
- scientists from India (cf. l. 11)
- move to New Jersey, looking for a better job (cf. ll. 13–17)
- nostalgia for their life in India cultivated in a circle of Bengali friends (cf. ll. 19–29)
- job promises not kept; father has to take on jobs he despises, financial insecurity (cf. ll. 37–42)

**Main part 2:** biographical information on the author
- attends an American public school with no Bengali/Indian friends (cf. ll. 30/31)
- remembers his happy childhood in India (cf. ll. 33–36)
- only child (cf. l. 41)
- admitted to Princeton and unhappy about it (cf. ll. 42–44; 48–56)
- plans to move back to Bengal, which his parents prevent (cf. ll. 61–66)
- return to Calcutta after graduation to work for a newspaper (cf. ll. 73/74)

In the excerpt from his novel *The Epic City*, which was published in London in 2017, Kushanava Choudhury provides information on how he and his family experience their lives as immigrants in the USA. When the author was twelve years old, his family had already moved several times from Kushanava's birthplace Calcutta to the United States of America and back. Choudhury describes his parents as torn between the hope for a career abroad and nostalgia for their original home in India.

**Introduction**

Both Kushanava's father and mother are scientists. At around age 40, his father leaves a comfortable job at a governmental research institute in Calcutta to find new opportunities in Highland Park, New Jersey. However, the job promises that attracted the family to move turn out to be false, so Choudhury's father takes on work in several other fields, all of which he hates. Choudhury describes his family as being part of the lower middle class and as one that suffers from financial insecurity. As a result, they always have to be ready to leave their home again and move somewhere with better job prospects. In the end, they never go, although Kushanava's parents regularly assemble their Bengali friends, with whom they cultivate their nostalgia for their life in Calcutta, and dream of returning there. **Main part 1:** biographical information on the author's parents

For the author himself, who is apparently an only child, his early memories of life in Calcutta are precious, too. However, as he has to get used to being a student at an American public school with almost no other Indian kids, he cannot give in to nostalgia in the same way his parents do. After high school when he is admitted to Princeton, he is unhappy because he fears that university will further alienate him from his roots. He secretly plans to go to rural Bengal and teach children in a village there. However, his parents, for whom his admittance to a prestigious university is very joyful news, do not allow him to waste this opportunity. So, it is only after his college graduation that Kushanava returns to Calcutta and takes on a job as a newspaper reporter there. **Main part 2:** biographical information on the author

*(355 words)*

2 **TIPP**

In this task, you are asked to analyse the text and work out in which way the author's attitude is brought about. So, in a first step you should try to define what the traditional view of American immigration is and work out a hypothesis concerning the author's view of it. Then verify this attitude with proof from the text. You need to pay attention to explicit as well as implicit comments he makes and to the rhetorical devices he uses to illustrate his opinion. Give examples from the excerpt and make sure you write a coherent and well-structured text.

You could structure your solution like this:

**Introduction: traditional view of immigration:** you can start a completely new life leaving everything behind
– metaphor: "migration is a reset button" (l. 3)
– positive words: "deliverance", "liberation" (l. 4)
– parallel sentences with simple structure and use of imperative: "The past is gone. The future awaits. Start over." (l. 5)

**Main part: author's scepticism of this view**
- official immigration story is only a **"myth"** (ll. 3, 5)
  - statistical proof: majority of the 20th-century immigrants went back to their countries of origin (cf. ll. 1/2)
  - negations: "It never really works like that.", "the story no one ever told", "The past is never left behind." (ll. 6/7)
- Choudhury family history as a counterexample: **lack of continuity** and **home-sickness for India**
  - (very negative) personifications: "[The past] haunts every world you live in. Sometimes it drags you back." (ll. 7/8)
  - comparison: "like a dual-voltage appliance" (ll. 10/11)
  - rhyme: "torn between nation and vocation" (ll. 11/12)
  - antithesis: "unwilling to leave [...] unable to stay" (ll. 12/13)
  - repetition: "Return, the duty of return and the dream of return" (ll. 24/25)
  - personifications: "Nationalism and nostalgia did not pay the bills, raise children or advance careers." (ll. 27/28)
- immigration as a **negative experience:** examples from Choudhury family's and Kushanava's personal history
  - allusions: "Our move carried no Emma Lazarus cadences. We certainly had not arrived tempest-tossed, beating at the golden door." (ll. 18/19)
  - imagery: "that dream of a return to the great metropolis cocooned them like a protective blanket from the alien world around them." (ll. 28/29)
  - figurative language and concrete examples for financial difficulties: "the three of us adrift in the treacherous shoals of the lower middle classes, a world of chronic car trouble and clothes from K-Mart." (ll. 41/42)
  - Kushanava's negative reaction to the news of having been accepted to Princeton: comparison ("my parents acted as if someone had come to our door with balloons and a giant cardboard cheque.", ll. 47/48) and enumeration ("education drives a wedge between us and our hometowns, our families, our earlier selves.", ll. 50/51)
  - drastic images: "I had carried memories on my back like Huien Tsang's chair" (l. 54), "I felt hunched over nostalgia like a middle-aged man" (l. 55), "a 'premature midlife crisis'" (l. 56)
  - contrast: "After graduating from college, while friends set up their apartments in New York, Boston, and Los Angeles, I headed to Calcutta" (ll. 73/74)

**Conclusion**: deflation of the American immigration myth

Throughout the excerpt, Choudhury expresses a critical attitude towards the common view of American immigration. According to the text, immigration is traditionally seen as "a reset button" (l. 3). This image expresses the idea that newcomers entering the USA start from scratch, cutting all bonds to their countries of origin. This idea

Introduction: traditional view of immigration

is further stressed by the short, parallel sentences, "The past is gone. The future awaits.", which culminate in the easy-sounding directive to just "[s]tart over" (l. 5). That this new start should be a positive thing also becomes clear in Choudhury's use of words like "deliverance" and "liberation" (l. 4). So, immigrants' old lives and background should be something they want to and can easily leave behind.

However, Choudhury is very sceptical of this assumption and questions it. The first clear indication for his critical stance is that he calls the traditional view a "myth" (ll. 3, 5), which already hints at its fictionality. He refers to the statistical fact that the majority of the people who migrated to the USA in the early 1900s went back to their countries of origin (ll. 1/2) to substantiate his criticism. So, immigration is a step that can be reversed, and he criticises the official story for concealing this aspect (cf. l. 2). The sequence of negations in lines 6 and 7, "[i]t never really works like that", "the story no one ever told" and "[t]he past is never left behind", hammers this point home: The official story that is often told does not correspond with reality. **Main part: author's scepticism:** immigration story is only a **"myth"**

His criticism of the immigration myth becomes even more pronounced when he uses his own family history as an obvious counter-example: they moved between Bengal and the US several times during the author's youth (cf. ll. 9–12). In that context, he compares himself to "a dual-voltage appliance" (ll. 10/11), a clear contrast to the "reset button" (l. 3) image of the official version. The lack of continuity and an unambiguous home expressed in this image is further explored throughout the text: Both the idea that his parents were "torn between nation and vocation" (ll. 11/12), which is particularly memorable through the use of rhyming words, and the antithesis that "[t]hey were unwilling to leave their country and [...] unable to stay" (ll. 12/13) show a similar dilemma: their Bengali past is not something they gladly leave behind. Choudhury's family history: **lack of continuity**

Instead, the family always dreams of returning to their Indian home: The force of this unrelenting dream is clearly expressed in the repetition of "[r]eturn, the duty of return and the dream of return" (ll. 24/25). In several striking personifications, their strong feelings for the home they left behind become obvious: they seem to be in America for pragmatic reasons only because "[n]ationalism and nostalgia did not pay the bills, raise children or advance careers" (ll. 27/28). So, it seems to be true for the Choudhury family that the past "haunts" them and "drags [them] back" (ll. 7/8). **homesickness**

These last two personifications create an almost violent image, which underlines another message that is apparent throughout Choudhury's text: immigration to the USA is not an undisputedly positive experience. By stating that his family was not "tempest- immigration as a **negative experience:** allusion to Emma Lazarus's poem

tossed" (ll. 18/19) when they arrived in the US, he alludes to the famous poem which is engraved at the base of the Statue of Liberty and which can be described as the epitome of the American immigration myth. According to Choudhury, his family's "move carried no Emma Lazarus cadences" (l. 18), so he clearly contrasts their experience with the stereotypical image of the American immigrant who arrives in desperation and finds a much better life behind "the golden door" (l. 19).

Instead, the US is an "alien world" (l. 29) from which they need the protection of "cocoon[ing]" memories (cf. ll. 28/29). The image he uses to describe their financial situation underlines the family's difficulties: They are "adrift in the treacherous shoals of the lower middle classes" (ll. 41/42), in other words they never make it out of "chronic car trouble and clothes from K-Mart" (l. 42). *(financial) difficulties*

Choudhury's own psychological situation is an especially obvious example of how unfulfilling life in the USA can be: Although on the outside he attains success by being accepted by an American elite university, a fact that is celebrated by his parents "as if someone had come to [their] door with balloons and a giant cardboard cheque" (ll. 47/48), Kushanava himself only seems to see everything that he might be distancing himself from through education, namely "[his] hometown[...], [his] famil[y], [his] earlier sel[f]" (ll. 50/51) and suffers "a 'premature midlife crisis'" (l. 56). Choudhury uses the two drastic images of being "hunched over nostalgia like a middle-aged man" (l. 55) and "carr[ying] memories on [his] back like Huien Tsang's chair" (l. 54) to illustrate his obsession with his childhood recollections of Calcutta. He finally enacts another reverse migration when after graduation he does not move to an American city like his friends, but to Calcutta instead (cf. ll. 73/74). *Kushavana's personal example*

All in all, Choudhury's examples of his and his family's experiences enable him to deflate the American immigration myth. The USA is not the land of their dreams in which all of their longings are fulfilled. They always dream of returning to India instead. *(887 words)* **Conclusion**

**3.1** **TIPP**

To complete this task, you must first analyse the cartoon and work out its message. In a second step, you should compare the cartoon's message with the experiences described in the text, pointing out both similarities and differences.

You could mention the following points:

**Analysis of the cartoon**
- description of the cartoon
- explanation of the melting-pot concept: different ethnic and religious groups are fused into one distinct people
- criticism of the melting-pot concept: individual groups are pressured to assimilate ("somebody always gets burned" as the cartoon puts it)

**Experiences described in the text**
- Kushanava Choudhury's parents remain in their "Bengali bubble"; experience America as very different and protect themselves; dream of returning to India
- author himself has to assimilate, but like his parents dreams of returning to Calcutta

**Assessment**
- **parallels** between cartoon and text:
  - author and his family feel the pressure to assimilate in order to attain financial security
  - they suffer because they do not feel they belong and are instead outsiders in the American society
- **differences** between cartoon and text:
  - author and his family are probably not forced to suppress their traditions; they isolate themselves by choice, which American society allows them to do
  - Choudhury's career as the epitome of the American Dream

**Conclusion**
- the author's experience partially reflected in the cartoon (parallel between criticism of melting-pot concept and criticism of "American immigration myth")
- salad bowl as the more fitting concept for American society?

---

The cartoon by Dan Rosandich shows two men in front of a skyline of high-rise buildings. One of them is reading a newspaper with the headline "America: Melting Pot". He is obviously commenting on that headline when he says to the other man: "The problem with a melting pot is that somebody always gets burned."

*Analysis of the cartoon: description*

The melting pot is a metaphor for the way US society is supposed to deal with the various ethnic and religious groups who have immigrated to the country. According to this concept, all these groups are fused into one distinct people united by the ideals and beliefs that constitute the United States. Differences are overcome and former identities or customs discarded in favour of a homogeneous society.

*explanation of the melting-pot concept*

In more recent years, however, criticism of the melting-pot concept has come up, because it discourages diversity. The need to give up one's individual customs and to assimilate in order to become a valu-

*criticism of the melting-pot concept*

able member of society might feel like a form of oppression to people who see their cultural background as an important part of their identity. Such criticism is also the message of the cartoon: Individual ethnicities – especially those who are remarkably different in their customs and traditions –often "get burned", which means that their individuality is not recognised or even seen as a threat to an allegedly desirable homogeneous whole.

With this message, the cartoon reflects what Kushanava Choudhury and his family have experienced in the USA – at least to a certain extent. Choudhury describes how after their arrival, his parents remain in their "Bengali bubble" by surrounding themselves with friends from their country of origin and celebrating the dream of returning there. They want to protect themselves from an American environment that is very different to what they are accustomed to. Experiences described in the text: parents' "Bengali bubble"

Being a teenager going to an American public school, Choudhury himself has to "fit in fast". However, in his own words, he "wasn't assimilating as much as passing" (ll. 32/33). That means that he only pretends to be like everyone else. In his innermost feelings, he still longs for his childhood home in Calcutta and does not feel completely integrated. Choudhury's "passing"

So, arguably, both Choudhury himself and his parents feel the need to assimilate, which the cartoon alludes to, a need which causes them to suffer. His father has to accept jobs he despises, and Kushanava has to go to a college that promises economic success but also means sleepless nights because he actually has different plans for his life, far away from the USA. No place in the country they migrated to really feels like home to the Choudhury family, and their dreams of returning to Calcutta grow ever larger. In a way, they could be described as "getting burned" in the melting pot. Assessment: parallels between cartoon and text

On the other hand, it is not quite clear from the excerpt whether the Choudhury family are really expected to suppress their culture and traditions in their New Jersey environment. The way Kushanava's parents and their friends cultivate their nostalgia shows that they are quite unwilling to accept the USA as their home. It seems to be their own choice to remain outsiders, and the very fact that they can live in a parallel society without integrating into a cultural mainstream indicates that there is no melting pot that "burns" those who are different. differences between cartoon and text: existence of parallel societies seems to contradict melting-pot concept

In fact, Choudhury's career can even be described as the epitome of the American Dream. He realises his full potential by making use of the opportunities that the American educational system offered him. After graduation he is free to go his own way and does not have to conform to a certain prescribed identity. Choudhury's successful American Dream

In conclusion, it might be adequate to say that the cartoon at least partially reflects what Choudhury and his family have experienced Conclusion in the USA. The cartoonist's criticism seems to mirror Choudhury's problems with the "American immigration myth": it is not as easy to leave your old country behind as the myth and the melting-pot concept insinuate. Yet, Choudhury and his family do not really "get burned" by the American melting pot. Instead, the metaphor might even be seen as rather obsolete for an American society that – on the whole and despite the controversy about immigration that haunts it – manages to give space to a population from many different ethnic backgrounds. So, the more modern concept of the salad bowl in which all the different "ingredients" keep their separate identities and are not forced to give them up might be more accurate. That immigrants still face tremendous challenges when trying to feel at home in a new country is certainly true. Yet, perhaps it is rather the right balance between keeping one's identity and culture on the one hand and connecting to a common whole, the salad's dressing so to speak, which is sometimes hard to find, and not the concept itself which is at fault. *(816 words)*

**3.2** **TIPP**

An article for a website needs to be well-structured with a headline, an introduction, a main part and a conclusion. Make sure you keep to a formal register while writing it. As you are asked to "discuss" the importance of place in shaping one's identity, find arguments that support the thesis as well as those contradicting it. In your conclusion, you should sum up what you have said and decide which stance (for or against the importance of place) you would like to take.

The sample solution mentions the following aspects:

Headline

**Introductory paragraph:** short enumeration of factors shaping identity and definition of "place" in that context

**Arguments against the importance of place**
– in a globalised world, fixed locations do not seem to matter too much
– online activities make places seem irrelevant

**Arguments for the importance of place**
– a place is more than a mere geographical location, it also creates:
  • a specific mindset (example: rural area vs. big city)
  • a cultural identity
  • the availability of opportunities
– changes in place also create changes in identity:
  • example of immigrants
  • travel enriches perspectives

**Conclusion:** summary of the arguments

**Where we are makes us who we are** Headline

Identity is a complex and multifaceted concept that is shaped by a Introductory paragraph variety of factors, including customs and traditions, family and friends, experiences and education, etc. In this article, I will focus on the role that place plays in shaping our identities. Place takes on plural meanings. Firstly, it refers to our physical environment, that is, the geographical location where we are based. Seen from a wider perspective, it can also include the community and culture that surround us.

At a superficial glance, it sounds quite old-fashioned to attach too Arguments against the importance of place: globalisation much meaning to a certain place. After all, we live in a globalised world and at a time when international travel makes it easy to see and inhabit the whole globe. So, if the world seems to have turned small and any location can at least theoretically be our home for a certain amount of time, why should places still be fixed anchor points in our developments?

This seems even more relevant with regard to the amount of time we online activities spend online nowadays: many people work remotely, connect with colleagues from every corner of the earth and spend a large proportion of their leisure time on the Internet, too. So, how can place still be a shaping factor when it is entirely irrelevant for most of our activities from where we perform them?

Despite these questions apparently diminishing the role of place, it Arguments for the importance of place: place creates a certain mindset, cultural identity and the availability of opportunities remains highly significant in defining who we are. First of all, it is too simplified a view to regard place as simply a geographical spot. This becomes obvious when we consider the various ways our birthplace or the place where we grow up influences us even if we do not stay there for the rest of our lives: For example, calling a rural area home may instil us with a strong sense of community and connection to nature, while growing up in a city may foster a more independent and fast-paced mindset. Our surroundings also shape our cultural identity and beliefs, as the customs, traditions and values of a community are usually passed down through generations. Furthermore, place determines both whom we meet and the experiences and opportunities available to us, be it in education, the job market or recreational activities.

Secondly, the many changes our fast-paced world confronts us with changes in place also create changes in identity might be an argument for the importance of place rather than against it. Just think of immigrants and people of diaspora, for example. For them, maintaining a connection to their home country or culture often plays a significant role, which shows that even places that are no longer physically close can influence our lives. In that context, it is also important to note that identity is not fixed and can change over time. A person's identity can be shaped by their experiences and interactions with different places and cultures. Even if we only travel to a different country, this can broaden our perspective and expose us to new ideas, values and ways of life.

In conclusion, place plays a significant role in shaping our identity. **Conclusion** It influences the way we see ourselves, the values and beliefs we hold and the opportunities and experiences available to us. Considering the significance of place and accepting it in its many facets can help us appreciate the diversity and richness of our world and teach us to be more empathetic and understanding of others. This is particularly true when we recognise that both identity and place are not fixed and unchangeable concepts but that the interactions and experiences we have with different places make us who we are.

*(606 words)*

**HÖRVERSTEHEN**

### Task 1: Purple Door Coffee Shop: Changing Lives One Cup at a Time

Listen to a recording about how a project is helping young homeless people in Denver. While listening, tick (✓) the correct answer (a, b or c). There is only one correct answer.

**1** The aim of the scheme is …

   **a** ☐ to give homeless young people a job.

   **b** ☐ to raise money to provide shelter for homeless young people.

   **c** ☐ to give homeless young people a chance to change their lives.

**2** The young people are found through …

   **a** ☐ advertisements.

   **b** ☐ suggestions by partner organisations.

   **c** ☐ voluntary internships.

**3** A big problem of young homeless people is that they …

   **a** ☐ lack many basic life skills.

   **b** ☐ often fight each other.

   **c** ☐ do not eat healthily.

**4** The coffee shop owners …

   **a** ☐ provide an education for the young people.

   **b** ☐ meet once a week to talk about their employees.

   **c** ☐ help their employees to manage their lives.

**5** What Kevin likes about working at the "Coffee Shop" is …

   **a** ☐ gaining new ideas through the programme.

   **b** ☐ the approach the owners adopt towards their employees.

   **c** ☐ that employees can talk openly to the owners.

**6** The owners feel that the best thing is seeing the people in the scheme …

**a** ☐ grow up.

**b** ☐ gain self-confidence.

**c** ☐ enjoy themselves.

---

| **Task 2: Teen Business Owner Creates Recipe for Success** |
| :--- |

Listen to a recording about a teenager who has started her own business.
While listening, fill in the missing information. If not specified, one aspect is enough.

| | | |
| :--- | :--- | :--- |
| **1** | How Bree feels when baking: | |
| **2** | How her great-grandmother influenced Bree: | |
| **3** | What Bree's mother advised her daughter to do: | |
| **4** | What role Bree's mother has in the business today: | •<br><br>• |
| **5** | What Leo Harrington thinks of Bree's work: | •<br><br>• |
| **6** | What Bree has learnt through working in her bakery: | •<br><br>• |
| **7** | What ingredient(s) make(s) Bree's sweets special: | |

Listen to a recording about journalism and its audiences. While listening, complete the sentences with information from the text.

1   The book *Journalism in Context* by Angela Phillips mainly deals with

_____

_____.

2   The democratisation process that Internet enthusiasts once expected was about

_____

_____.

3   More than interviews and second-hand information, journalists' sources today also include

_____

_____.

4   In contrast to "pro-sumers", journalists are still the ones who

_____

_____.

5   Journalists today have more power than they used to because

_____

_____.

| Text | What So Many People Don't Get about the US Working Class |

1 My father-in-law grew up eating blood soup. He hated it, whether because of the taste or the humiliation, I never knew. His alcoholic father regularly drank up the family wage, and the family was often short on food money. They were evicted from apartment after apartment.

5 He dropped out of school in eighth grade to help support the family. Eventually he got a good, steady job he truly hated, as an inspector in a factory that made those machines that measure humidity levels in museums. He tried to open several businesses on the side but none worked, so he kept that job for 38 years. He rose from poverty to a middle-class life: the car, the house, two kids in Catholic school, the wife who

10 worked only part-time. He worked incessantly. He had two jobs in addition to his full-time position, one doing yard work for a local magnate and another hauling trash to the dump.

Throughout the 1950s and 1960s, he read *The Wall Street Journal* and voted Republican. He was a man before his time: a blue-collar white man who thought the union

15 was a bunch of jokers who took your money and never gave you anything in return. Starting in 1970, many blue-collar whites followed his example. This week, their candidate won the presidency.

For months, the only thing that's surprised me about Donald Trump is my friends' astonishment at his success. What's driving it is the class culture gap. One little-known

20 element of that gap is that the white working class (WWC) resents professionals but admires the rich. Class migrants (white-collar professionals born to blue-collar families) report that "professional people were generally suspect" and that managers are college kids "who don't know shit about how to do anything but are full of ideas about how I have to do my job," said Alfred Lubrano in *Limbo*. Barbara Ehrenreich recalled

25 in 1990 that her blue-collar dad "could not say the word *doctor* without the virtual prefix *quack*. Lawyers were *shysters* … and professors were without exception *phonies.*" Annette Lareau found tremendous resentment against teachers, who were perceived as condescending and unhelpful.

Michèle Lamont, in *The Dignity of Working Men*, also found resentment of profes-

30 sionals – but not of the rich. "[I] can't knock anyone for succeeding," a laborer told her. "There's a lot of people out there who are wealthy and I'm sure they worked darned hard for every cent they have," chimed in a receiving clerk. Why the difference? For one thing, most blue-collar workers have little direct contact with the rich outside of *Lifestyles of the Rich and Famous*. But professionals order them around every day.

35 The dream is not to become upper-middle-class, with its different food, family, and friendship patterns; the dream is to live in your own class milieu, where you feel comfortable – just with more money. "The main thing is to be independent and give your own orders and not have to take them from anybody else," a machine operator told Lamont. Owning one's own business – that's the goal. That's another part of Trump's

40 appeal.

Hillary Clinton, by contrast, epitomizes the dorky arrogance and smugness of the professional elite. [...] Worse, her mere presence rubs it in that *even women* from her class can treat working-class men with disrespect. Look at how she condescends to Trump as unfit to hold the office of the presidency and dismisses his supporters as
45 racist, sexist, homophobic, or xenophobic.

Trump's blunt talk taps into another blue-collar value: straight talk. "Directness is a working-class norm," notes Lubrano. As one blue-collar guy told him, "If you have a problem with me, come talk to me. If you have a way you want something done, come talk to me. I don't like people who play these two-faced games." Straight talk is
50 seen as requiring manly courage, not being "a total wuss and a wimp," an electronics technician told Lamont. Of course Trump appeals. Clinton's clunky admission that she talks one way in public and another in private? Further proof she's a two-faced phony.

Manly dignity is a big deal for working-class men, and they're not feeling that they have it. Trump promises a world free of political correctness and a return to an earlier
55 era, when men were men and women knew their place. It's comfort food for high-school-educated guys who could have been my father-in-law if they'd been born 30 years earlier. Today they feel like losers – or did until they met Trump.

Manly dignity is a big deal for most men. So is breadwinner status: Many still measure masculinity by the size of a paycheck. White working-class men's wages hit the
60 skids in the 1970s and took another body blow during the Great Recession. Look, I wish manliness worked differently. But most men, like most women, seek to fulfill the ideals they've grown up with. For many blue-collar men, all they're asking for is basic human dignity (male varietal). Trump promises to deliver it.                    *825 words*

*Williams, Joan C. (2016) "What So Many People Don't Get about the US Working Class."* Harvard Business Review. *16 November 2016*

## Annotations

line 24:    Alfred Lubrano. *Limbo: Blue-Collar Roots, White-Collar Dreams.* Hoboken, 2004.
line 24:    Barbara Ehrenreich (*1941): author, essayist, political activist
line 27:    Annette Lareau. *Unequal Childhoods, Class, Race, and Family Life.* Berkeley, 2003.
line 29:    Michèle Lamont. *The Dignity of Working Men.* Cambridge, 2009.
line 34:    *Lifestyles of the Rich and Famous:* American TV series (1984–1995)
line 41:    Hillary Clinton: Democratic presidential candidate who ran against Donald Trump in the 2016 campaign
line 50:    wuss, wimp: weakling
line 51:    clunky: (here) inept, not skillful
lines 59/60:    hit the skids: (here) suddenly fell
line 63:    varietal: version

**1**  Sum up what the article says about the US working class.                (30 %)

**2**  Analyze the way in which the author conveys her message.                (30 %)

**3**  Choose *one* of the following tasks:                                    (40 %)

**3.1**  "… most men, like most women, seek to fulfill the ideals they've grown up with." (ll. 61/62)

Assess to what extent this is true for Larry in *Crooked Letter, Crooked Letter*.

**or**

**3.2**  You are taking part in an international school project called *The American Dream in Film*.

Write an article for the project website, commenting on whether social mobility as presented in *Gran Torino* is something worth striving for.

*Bei den für Set 4 abgedruckten Aufgaben zum Schreiben handelt es sich um offizielle Musteraufgaben des Landes Baden-Württemberg.*

HÖRVERSTEHEN

| Transcript 1 | **Purple Door Coffee Shop: Changing Lives One Cup at a Time** |

1   **Paula Vargas:** Kevin Person had been homeless for a quarter of his life. Today, he works at this espresso bar and is transitioning into a home.

  **Kevin Person:** The struggle to get a job even when you have a house nowadays, but when you don't have a house, trying to get a job is so much harder.

5   **Paula Vargas:** The mission of the Purple Door Coffee Shop goes beyond serving coffee. The owners want to turn lives around and for two years the non-profit has hired three to four young adults per year. They work with shelters like Urban Peak, where Kevin was staying, for recommendations on who to hire. Kim Easton, who runs Urban Peak, says the partnership is vital to this community.

10   **Kim Easton:** When someone has lived in chronic stress and trauma for as long as these young people have, every day fighting for survival, they haven't had the opportunity nor the example of how to learn conflict management, how to manage money, how to cook a meal, how to pay their rent on time – nor do they understand even why that's important.

15   **Paula Vargas:** Purple Door co-founder, Madison Chandler, and her partner meet with each worker once a week. They discuss 52 topics ranging from mental health, finance, hygiene and customer service, and provide a life coaching tour; they will help their employees put their past behind them. But there are success stories.

  **Madison Chandler:** Our very first guy that ever graduated from the programme; he's
20   been working at an Auto Parts Warehouse since he left, which has been over a year now.

  **Paula Vargas:** Kevin appreciates the chance to learn new skills. He says the programme is giving him things he never had.

  **Kevin Person:** They seem to have the philosophy that they don't want to change us, they
25   want to help us change ourselves and to have, like, a purpose and a goal that's, like, tangible.

  **Madison Chandler:** The more rewarding things are watching somebody start to believe in themselves and to believe that they can achieve a life for themselves that they have dreamed of, or to believe that they are worth it.

30   **Paula Vargas:** As for Kevin, who turns 25 this month, living off the streets in a home and having a job will be the best gift he gives himself. For VOA news, Paula Vargas in Denver.

*Paula Vargas: "Purple Door Coffee Shop: Changing Lives One Cup at a Time."*
*In:* Voice of America News, *29 May 2015*

**TIPP**

These text passages will help you find the correct answer:
1 "The mission of the Purple Door Coffee Shop goes beyond serving coffee. The <u>owners want to turn lives around</u>" (ll. 5/6)
2 "They work with shelters like Urban Peak, where Kevin was staying, <u>for recommendations on who to hire</u>." (ll. 7/8)
3 "they haven't had the opportunity nor the example of how to learn conflict management, how to manage money, how to cook a meal, how to pay their rent on time – nor do they understand even why that's important." (ll. 11–14)
4 "Purple Door co-founder, Madison Chandler, and her partner meet with each worker once a week. They discuss 52 topics ranging from mental health, finance, hygiene and customer service, and <u>provide a life coaching tour</u>; they will help their employees put their past behind them." (ll. 15–18)
5 "Kevin <u>appreciates</u> the chance to learn new skills. He says the programme is giving him things he never had." – "They [...] have the philosophy that they don't want to change us, <u>they want to help us change ourselves and to have</u>, like, <u>a purpose and a goal that's</u>, like, <u>tangible</u>." (ll. 22–26)
6 "The more rewarding things are watching somebody <u>start to believe in themselves</u> and to believe that they can achieve a life for themselves that they have dreamed of, or to believe that they are worth it." (ll. 27–29)

1 The aim of the scheme is …
  c ☑ to give homeless young people a chance to change their lives.

2 The young people are found through …
  b ☑ suggestions by partner organisations.

3 A big problem of young homeless people is that they …
  a ☑ lack many basic life skills.

4 The coffee shop owners …
  c ☑ help their employees to manage their lives.

5 What Kevin likes about working at the "Coffee Shop" is …
  b ☑ the approach the owners adopt towards their employees.

6 The owners feel that the best thing is seeing the people in the scheme …
  b ☑ gain self-confidence.

**Faith Lapidus:** For Bree Britt nothing is more enjoyable, soothing and fulfilling than working in the kitchen.

**Bree Britt:** I can be in the worst of moods and … once I get started baking it's just … something turns on where I'm just … in my whole … another world.

**Faith Lapidus:** Here she says she can be innovative and creative.

**Bree Britt:** I'd like to compare myself to an artist, sort of a painter for his canvas which … I'm the baker so, of course my cupcakes and cookies, and all my sweet desserts are my canvas. I think I'm going to do something with, maybe, a banana.

**Faith Lapidus:** Bree started cooking with her great-grandmother when she was five years old.

**Lillie Walter** *(great-grandmother)*: Well, I've always tried to help them learn to cook.

**Faith Lapidus:** Bree perfected her great-grandmother's recipes and came up with her own. When she was 12, she told her mother she wanted to open a bakery.

**Bree Britt:** She told me to really think about, you know, the sacrifices and the things that I'll have to go through. You know … I wasn't going to be just a normal teenager … or a normal kid anymore. So, she told me to really think about it.

**Charmaine Britt** *(Bree's mother)*: I thought it was going to be fly-by-night. Something that she just would get tired of eventually and once she saw how much work it would be. So my deal was we'll start online – the only way we can start making money is we'll do it online.

**Faith Lapidus:** It made enough money that Charmaine Britt became her daughter's business partner. They rented a shop and opened Bree's Sweet Treats. Charmaine runs the store during the day until Bree gets out of school.

**Leo Harrington** *(customer)*: I guess it's going to be key lime today.

**Faith Lapidus:** Leo Harrington, a neighbouring barber shop owner, comes almost every day.

**Leo Harrington:** The flavour … she has all kind … a great assortment.

**Faith Lapidus:** He admires what Bree's accomplished.

**Leo Harrington:** I watch her diligence; school and then here – baking all evening, getting ready for the next day.

**Faith Lapidus:** It's challenging but Bree says studying and running a business taught her how to better manage her time.

**Bree Britt:** It has also taught me hard work and responsibility … and it has also taught me to be more aware of people and when they come into the store, more … friendlier, that I can say. It's … it's taught me a lot.

**Faith Lapidus:** Whether it's vanilla or chocolate, key lime or strawberry, there is a secret behind Bree's recipes.

**Charmaine Britt:** Her cupcakes are made … are flavoured with fresh fruits or more of the extracts, more so than of sugar.

**Faith Lapidus:** But sugar or not, Bree's treats are sweet enough to keep them coming back for more.

**Customer:** They're so pretty!

**Faith Lapidus:** For writer Faiza Elmasry, I'm Faith Lapidus, VOA news.

*Faiza Elmasry: "Teen Business Owner Creates Recipe for Success."*
*In:* Voice of America News, *17 April 2015*

---

**TIPP**

These text passages will help you find the correct answer:
1 "I can be in the worst of moods and ... once I get started baking it's just ... something turns on where I'm just ... in my whole ... <u>another world</u>." (ll. 3/4); "Here she says she can be <u>innovative and creative</u>." (l. 5)
2 "I've always tried to <u>help them learn to cook</u>." (l. 11)
3 "She told me <u>to really think about</u>, you know, <u>the sacrifices</u> and the things that I'll have to go through. You know ... I wasn't going to be just a normal teenager ... or a normal kid anymore. So, she told me <u>to really think about it</u>." (ll. 14–16)
4 "It made enough money that Charmaine Britt <u>became her daughter's business partner</u>." (ll. 21/22); "Charmaine <u>runs the store during the day</u> until Bree gets out of school." (ll. 22/23)
5 "He <u>admires what Bree's accomplished</u>." (l. 28); "I watch her <u>diligence</u>; school and then here – baking all evening, getting ready for the next day." (ll. 29/30)
6 "Bree says studying and running a business taught her how <u>to better manage her time</u>." (ll. 31/32); "It has also taught me <u>hard work</u> and <u>responsibility</u> ... and it has also taught me <u>to be more aware of people</u> and when they come into the store, more ... <u>friendlier</u>, that I can say. It's ... it's taught me a lot." (ll. 33–35)
7 "Her cupcakes are made ... are <u>flavoured with fresh fruits</u> or more of the extracts, more so than of sugar." (ll. 38/39)

| 1 | How Bree feels when baking: | innovative / creative / in another world |
|---|---|---|
| 2 | How her great-grandmother influenced Bree: | taught her to cook / taught Bree to bake / taught her great-granddaughter her recipes |
| 3 | What Bree's mother advised her daughter to do: | to be prepared to make sacrifices / to really think about it |
| 4 | What role Bree's mother has in the business today: | • Bree's business partner<br>• runs store during the day |
| 5 | What Leo Harrington thinks of Bree's work: | • admires what she accomplished<br>• admires her discipline / diligence |

| 6 | What Bree has learnt through working in her bakery: | zwei aus:<br>• to better manage her time<br>• (to take) responsibility<br>• hard work<br>• friendliness towards other people |
|---|---|---|
| 7 | What ingredient(s) make(s) Bree's sweets special: | fresh fruits / flavoured with fresh fruits / the extract of fresh fruits |

## Transcript 3 Journalism and Its Audiences

1 **Tess Woodcraft** *(reporter):* Hello this is Pod Academy and I am Tess Woodcraft. Journalism and how we interact with it is changing but what exactly are those changes and do they matter? I caught up with Professor Angela Phillips, author of *Journalism in Context*, just before she was due to speak at the […] Future of Journalism
5 conference in Cardiff.

**Angela Phillips:** I'm interested in the way in which news journalism is changing, and, in particular, how news audiences are changing in relation to changes in the industry. So I've looked at audiences in my book, *Journalism in Context,* but I've also been looking at young audiences … young news audiences in an international con-
10 text to see how young people are accessing news.

**Tess Woodcraft:** So, what's been happening with journalism?

**Angela Phillips:** Since the rise of the Internet, there have been big changes, not only in how news journalism is produced, but also in how it is consumed. And, these two things are, kind of, in lockstep. At the end of the last century, the beginning of this
15 one, there were a lot of people who were very enthusiastic about the kind of changes. They saw the Internet as being a means of democratising news. They saw audiences being much more involved in news production and they talked about journalists becoming less elitist, more involved in their audiences, and that journalism would become much more of a collaborative process.

20 **Tess Woodcraft:** To a certain extent that's happened, hasn't it? We see, for example, the Shoreham Airshow – ordinary people's videos of the crash.

**Angela Phillips:** In very marginal ways this "pro-sumer" revolution – the idea of the consumer that also produces – has come to pass, but not in anything like the way in which those web enthusiasts imagined it would. What we have today is people –
25 bystanders with cameras. So, whereas before journalists would have gone and interviewed people about what they saw and it would have been sort of secondary – second-hand information – now if there is a big event like an air crash, like a bombing, there will always be people in the vicinity who have camera phones and will very often put that information into social media where journalists can access it. But
30 actually this doesn't make them journalists, they are still sources. And although that information moves around – might make it on Twitter or on Facebook or on You-Tube – most of what happens is that it is curated by journalists who bring it together and construct a narrative around the information and then repackage it in a different

84

place and a different way. So, although one can look ... so, really it is not collabo-
35 rative.
What we're seeing is journalists who in many ways have more power than they used
to have – they have the power to find their way into places where they would never,
never otherwise have managed to be. The likelihood of a journalist being in the right
place at the right time when a bomb goes off are *[sic]* miniscule. So the difference
40 we have is that we now have access – to pictures in particular – that we didn't have
access to before, but that doesn't really fundamentally change the job of journalists
or the relationship between journalist and audience in any way.

*Tess Woodcraft/Angela Phillips, Pod Academy, 8 September 2015.*
*http://podacademy.org/podcasts/journalism-and-its-audiences/*

---

**TIPP**

The following passages might help you find the correct information:
1  "I'm interested in the way in which news journalism is changing, and, in particular, how news audiences are changing in relation to changes in the industry." (ll. 6−8)
2  "Since the rise of the Internet [...] there were a lot of people who were very enthusiastic about the [...] changes. They saw the Internet as being a means of
   democratising news. They saw audiences being much more involved in news
   production and they talked about journalists becoming less elitist, more involved in their audiences, and that journalism would become much more of a
   collaborative process." (ll. 12−19)
3  "What we have today is people – bystanders with cameras [...] if there is a big
   event like an air crash, like a bombing, there will always be people in the vicinity who have camera phones and will very often put that information into social
   media where journalists can access it." (ll. 24−29)
4  "information moves around [...] what happens is that it is curated by journalists
   who bring it together and construct a narrative around the information and then
   repackage it in a different place and a different way." (ll. 31−34)
5  "What we're seeing is journalists who in many ways have more power than
   they used to have – they have the power to find their way into places where
   they would never, never otherwise have managed to be. [...] So the difference
   we have is that we now have access – to pictures in particular – that we didn't
   have access to before" (ll. 36−41)

1  The book *Journalism in Context* by Angela Phillips mainly deals with **the changes
   in news audiences/how people react to a changing news industry**.

2  The democratisation process that Internet enthusiasts once expected was about
   **audiences being more involved in news production/journalists becoming less
   elitist/journalism becoming more collaborative**.

**3** More than interviews and second-hand information, journalists' sources today also include **bystanders'/eye-witnesses' videos/photos/information (on social media).**

**4** In contrast to "pro-sumers", journalists are still the ones who **curate/bring together/construct narratives around/repackage information.**

**5** Journalists today have more power than they used to because **they have access to more material (than ever before)/find their way into new places (where they would not have ever been before)/have access to pictures they didn't have access to before.**

## SCHREIBEN: OFFIZIELLE MUSTERPRÜFUNG

**1**  `TIPP`
___

You are expected to sum up the information in the text about the American working class. As the whole article deals with the US working class, there is not really a part which is irrelevant for your answer. However, you should still try to be as concise as possible and leave out unnecessary aspects. For instance, when it comes to the information given in lines 1 to 17, make sure that you use the example of the author's father-in-law as a basis for more general observations on the US working class and do not get lost in details.

You could mention the following points:

**Introduction:** example of author's father-in-law for typical experiences of US working class, such as poverty (cf. l. 3), difficulties in finding affordable housing (cf. ll. 3/4), lack of education (cf. l. 5)

**Main part:** other typical characteristics of the US working class
- mistrust of institutions and professionals:
  • unions seen as useless (cf. ll. 14/15)
  • admiration of successful and rich people (cf. ll. 20/21, 30−32)
  • rejection of professionals (cf. ll. 20, 22−28, 34)
- ideal of independence:
  • making more money but within their own class (cf. ll. 35−37)
  • having a business of their own (cf. ll. 37−39)
- ideal of manliness:
  • resentment for female politicians (cf. ll. 41−43)
  • appreciation of straight talk (cf. ll. 46/47)
  • rejection of political correctness (cf. l. 54)
  • emphasis on manly dignity and breadwinner status (cf. ll. 53−58)

In her article "What So Many People Don't Get about the US Work-     **Introduction**
ing Class", which was published in the *Harvard Business Review* in

November 2016, the author Joan C. Williams uses the example of her father-in-law to illustrate some of the features of the US working class. Some typical difficulties members of this social group face include poverty, trouble in finding an affordable apartment which they are not kicked out of, and a lack of education because working class children often have to drop out of school and work in order to contribute to the family income.

Another typical feature of the US working class is mistrust of institutions and highly educated professional and academic people. Instead, members of the working class tend to admire successful self-made people and consider their wealth as justified if they see it as the result of hard work. While few working-class people have any first-hand experience with the wealthy, they meet managers, doctors, professors, teachers and lawyers in their everyday life. From the workers' point of view, these are bossy and condescending without being really equipped to give them advice. *mistrust of institutions and professionals*

As mentioned before, it is not wealth that members of the working class reject, but a certain way of being patronised which clashes with their ideal of independence. Many of them do want to earn more money and they are willing to work hard in order to become self-reliant and ideally have their own business. However, they do not want to cross the class barriers and become "middle-class" as the professionals they look down on. *ideal of independence*

White working-class men in particular often have a very traditional understanding of their role: they appreciate expressing their thoughts openly and disdain political correctness. Saying what is on your mind without giving attention to sensitivities is seen as a sign of strength and courage. Many men do not want to be humiliated and put a high value on manly dignity and being the breadwinners of their families. Thus, they especially resent female politicians, who seemingly condescend on less educated men, and are attracted to politicians like Donald Trump, who does not care about political correctness. *ideal of manliness*

*(356 words)*

2  **TIPP**
_____

In a first step, you need to work out the author's message, i. e. her intention in publishing her article. In a second step, point out which rhetorical devices she uses to make her message convincing. Make sure to not only list the devices you have found, but also explain why they are used. Your text should be well-structured and coherent. That means that you do not have to go through the text chronologically and name the aspects you find remarkable in an order that fits to the text. Instead, group your findings into larger paragraphs, according to the aims they are supposed to achieve.

The sample solution is structured like this:

**Introduction: message and intention**
- author wants to help her educated readers to understand the mentality of the White working-class men:
  - title "What So Many People Don't Get about the US Working Class": only indirectly addressing the readers ("So Many People"), informal language ("Don't Get about the US Working Class")
  - source of the article: *Harvard Business Review* (aimed at educated readership)
- author wants to explain why so many members of the working class voted for Donald Trump:
  - "the only thing that's surprised me about Donald Trump is my friends' astonishment at his success" (ll. 18/19)
  - "the class culture gap" (l. 19)

**Main part: further means to get her message across**
- **personal example** of father-in-law:
  - drastic example of having to eat blood soup (cf. l. 1), aimed at grabbing the reader's attention
  - antithesis "good, steady job he truly hated" (l. 6) illustrating the dilemma of the working class
  - paratactical sentence structures with anaphora of "He" (cf. ll. 5–12) establishing father-in-law as a perfect example
- author's **empathy and sympathy** with the working class:
  - informal language: e. g. "bunch of jokers" (l. 15), *"quack"* (l. 26), *"shysters"* (l. 26), *"phonies"* (ll. 26/27), "dorky" (l. 41), "[to] rub[...] it in" (l. 42)
  - quotes of working-class people: e. g. "who don't know shit about how to do anything but are full of ideas about how I have to do my job" (ll. 23/24), "[I] can't knock anyone for succeeding, [...] There's a lot of people out there who are wealthy and I'm sure they worked darned hard for every cent they have" (ll. 30–32)
  - speaking from the workers' perspective: "Worse, her mere presence rubs it in that *even women* from her class can treat working-class men with disrespect. Look at how she condescends to Trump as unfit to hold the office of the presidency and dismisses his supporters as racist, sexist, homophobic, or xenophobic." (ll. 42–45), "Further proof she's a two-faced phony." (l. 52)
  - distances herself from the concept of manliness of the working class ("men were men and women knew their place", l. 55): "Look, I wish manliness worked differently." (ll. 60/61)
  - however, understands the workers' perspective ("all they're asking for is basic human dignity (male varietal)", ll. 62/63) and Trump's appeal: short, simple sentences ("This week, their candidate won the presidency.", ll. 16/17;

"That's another part of Trump's appeal.", ll. 39/40; "Of course Trump appeals.", l. 51; "Trump promises to deliver it.", l. 63) and metaphor ("It's comfort food for high-school-educated guys", ll. 55/56)
- author's **authority and scholarly expertise:**
  - quotations from and references to scholarly works (cf. ll. 21–24, 24–27, 27/28, 29–39, 46–51)
  - references to historical background knowledge (cf. ll. 59/60)

**Conclusion**

Joan Williams wrote her article shortly after Donald Trump had been elected president of the United States. As it was published in the *Harvard Business Review*, it is clearly aimed at highly educated people who, like the friends Williams mentions (cf. ll. 18/19), were surprised at Donald Trump's popularity with the White working class. It is clearly Williams' intention to bridge "the class culture gap" (l. 19) and help members of the upper middle class understand the mentality of the workers who resent them so much and admire people like Trump instead. The implicit reproach of the title "What So Many People Don't Get about the US Working Class" does not address the reader directly, but with its informal language it is aimed at getting their attention by surprising and challenging them in a friendly way.

*Introduction: message and intention*

The opening paragraph supports this message with its highly personalised content: the author tells her readers about her father-in-law who had to eat "blood soup" even though he hated it (cf. l. 1), provoking a kind of fascinated disgust. The antithesis of the "good, steady job he truly hated" (l. 6) grabs the reader's attention with its paradox. At the same time, it illustrates a typical dilemma of the working class: they need to work in order to make a living, but they do not like the work they have to do. The paratactical structure of many sentences in the second paragraph, anaphorically starting with "He" (cf. ll. 5–12), establishes Williams' father-in-law as a perfect example of a blue-collar worker with a surprising political leaning: he was one of the first workers who – against older traditions – voted Republican.

*Main part: personal example of father-in-law*

Throughout her text, the author uses informal, colloquial language, like "bunch of jokers" (l. 15), *"quack"* (l. 26), *"shysters"* (l. 26) and *"phonies"* (ll. 26/27), that either directly or indirectly quotes her father-in-law or other members of the working class. Her description of Clinton's "dorky" arrogance who "rubs [her superiority] in" (ll. 41/42) also includes these informal expressions. By employing working-class vocabulary Williams shows her empathy with members of this social group, and the direct quotes in lines 23 and 24 as well as in lines 30 to 32 give them a voice in a text that is read by people who do not normally get in contact with them. That way, Williams

*author's empathy and sympathy with the working class: informal language and quotes*

also establishes authenticity and demonstrates that she knows how the working class speaks and thinks. In the passages on Hillary Clinton (cf. ll. 42–45, 52) she even takes their perspective without clearly marking her comments as quotes and thereby invites her readers to see the world through the workers' eyes too.

When it comes to the working-class concept of manliness, she provocatively summarises it as "men [being] men and women [knowing] their place" (l. 55). Even though Williams distances herself from this concept and directly addresses her readers towards the end of the text with the powerful words, "Look, I wish manliness worked differently" (ll. 60/61), she still demonstrates that she knows how the workers feel. They want nothing more than "basic human dignity" (ll. 62/63) which, although it is qualified by the slightly ironic addition of "male varietal", should be an understandable wish from anyone. In a similar way, the short, simple sentences that are used to refer to Trump's election (cf. ll. 16/17, 39/40, 51, 63) underline that his success might not be a desirable outcome for neither Williams herself nor the majority of her readers, but it can still be understood from the working class's perspective. This is further stressed by the metaphor that Trump's rhetoric is "comfort food" (l. 55) for many people who otherwise feel left behind by modern US society.

*distance yet understanding*

Williams supports her argument by quoting works from intellectuals like Alfred Lubrano (cf. ll. 21–24, 46–49), Barbara Ehrenreich (cf. ll. 24–27), Annette Lareau (cf. ll. 27/28) and Michèle Lamont (cf. ll. 29–39, 49–51) who confirm the author's personal observations with their analyses of the mindset of the working class. With these references to scholarly works as well as with the demonstration of her insight into historically important developments (cf. ll. 59/60), Williams signals to her mostly highly educated readers that her article is based on research and establishes herself as a competent author.

*author's **authority and scholarly expertise***

Williams' combination of light, entertaining language, telling personal examples and fitting quotes from academic literature make hers a very readable and convincing essay that manages to raise empathy for workers like her father-in-law. So, it might help upper-middle-class readers see what they "Don't Get about the US Working Class".

*Conclusion*

*(770 words)*

**3.1** TIPP

For this assignment, you are expected to change your perspective and engage with Larry's values and ideals. In a first step, you should explain the quote from the text and in a second step, you need to assess to what extent it applies to Larry's motivations and behaviour as described in the novel *Crooked Letter, Crooked Letter*. It makes sense to differentiate between Larry's youth and his adulthood in order to find out whether his experiences in his youth still influence his behaviour as an adult. For each of your points, give examples from the novel. Make sure to write a well-structured and coherent text with an introduction, a main part and a conclusion.

The sample solution mentions the following points:

**Introduction: explanation of the quote:** a person's values and ideals are mostly formed by their family members

**Transition to main part:** the influence of one's family's ideals can also be a negative one (see Larry)

**Main part 1: Larry's youth**
- father as a main influence: blue-collar worker who fulfils an ideal mentioned in the article:
  - works in his own shop and is the sole breadwinner
  - likes straight talk
  - despises "effeminate" men and wants Larry to be strong and tough
- Larry notices his father's contempt for weakness and feels that he cannot live up to his father's ideals of masculinity:
  - feels unsuited for "male work"
  - loses fight with Silas
  - date with Cindy turns into a disaster
  - as a result, he sees himself as a complete failure

**Main part 2: Larry's adult years**
- his father's ideals still guide him and on a superficial level, he fulfils them:
  - he becomes a successful mechanic in the army
  - returns to his family home and runs his father's shop
- ostracism of his hometown drives him to loneliness and desperation:
  - books are his only companions
  - he is still aware of his father's ideals but has given up living up to them
- Silas's confession brings about a change in attitude: he wants to take his life into his own hands

**Conclusion:** Larry's case confirms the thesis: even though he cannot fulfil them, his father's ideals drive him throughout his life; only after his time in hospital might he have found a way to emancipate himself from this negative influence

A person's values, norms and ideals are formed by the people that have a big influence on them, especially during their childhood and youth. In most cases, it will be your family that determines your outlook on life. The values your parents endorse, the lifestyle they live, the ideals they explicitly or implicitly proclaim will influence the way you live your life even after you have grown up and left your family, maybe to have a family of your own. This can also apply to the social class you belong to: as Williams' examples from the White working class show, many people want to stay in the same class as their parents and do not even aspire to climb the social ladder.

Of course, there are counterexamples when people decidedly reject the values their parents have set as an example. Both economically and morally speaking, there are cases in which it is exactly the circumstances a person has grown up in that they try to escape in later life. Yet, even if someone might rationally grasp that their parents' ideals are not good for them, it may be very difficult to really shake off the expectations and attitudes they have known for years. This is also true for Larry, the protagonist of *Crooked Letter, Crooked Letter*.

**Transition to main part:** possibly negative influence

When we take a look at his childhood and youth, the most dominant influence is certainly his father, a blue-collar worker similar to the ones presented in Williams' article. Carl Ott works as a mechanic in his own shop. He is a self-reliant businessman and the sole breadwinner in the family. Moreover, he is a friend of straight talk and is quite outspoken in his condescension on "effeminate" men or anyone who shows weakness. He is popular with his male friends and customers, and he expects his wife to know her place and his son to follow his example. In other words, he wants Larry to be strong and tough, and openly shows his disappointment when he is not.

**Main part 1: Larry's youth:** Carl's influence and ideals of manliness

Larry cannot but notice his father's contempt, and his continued failure to live up to his ideals of masculinity drive him to deep desperation. After his first attempts at working at his father's repair shop that are negatively commented on by Carl, he feels completely unsuited for this kind of "male work". He loses the fight with Silas, which his father has provoked, is unpopular with his peers and even his date with Cindy – the only moment in his life in which he receives some recognition from his father and his peers – turns into a complete disaster.

Larry's failure to live up to his father's ideals

Nevertheless, in his early adult years, his father's ideals still guide Larry: when he joins the army, he becomes a mechanic and, to his own surprise, gets recognition for his skills. This leads him to take over the repair shop after his father's death. When his mother moves into a nursing home, he also inherits and takes charge of the family's property. He stays within the same social class, works in his father's profession, lives in his family's house – on a superficial level, he fulfils his father's ideals as an adult despite his failure in his youth.

**Main part 2: Larry's adult years:** Larry superficially fulfils his father's ideals

However, his lack of self-confidence and even more the prejudices and the ongoing ostracism of his small hometown drive him into isolation and loneliness. He cannot integrate into the community and lives a solitary life without a partner or even a friend on his farm. So,

loneliness and desperation

he is still not the kind of man his father wanted him to be: he is introverted and only interested in books, which his father despised, and the repair shop has no customers, which makes Larry dependent on his inheritance for a living. The fact that he goes through the motions of running a business even though he has no customers shows that his father's ideals obviously still drive him, but in a completely negative way. He only pretends to fulfil them. To a certain extent, Larry seems to be aware of that, and has resigned himself to the solitary life of a social outcast without showing any initiative to alter his situation.

Only when he finds out that Silas has betrayed him by not telling anyone that he was the last one to have seen Cindy does something seem to change inside Larry. In an act of defiance, he asks for a room of his own in the hospital, without Silas. The time of recovery he spends there also brings about a new attitude: he shows some determination and secretly departs from the hospital in the middle of the night with the plan to take his life into his own hands.

*change in Larry's attitude*

In conclusion, Larry could be described as a confirmation of the thesis voiced in the quote. Although he fails to live up to his father's ideals in many respects, he still seeks to fulfil them even after Carl's death. The fact that this failure drives him into a kind of silent resignation asserts the ongoing challenge of these ideals. The determination to change his life that he shows at the end of the novel could be seen as a sign that he finally finds a way to shake off his father's ideals in a positive and productive way. However, whether he can succeed, and whether Chabot will give him a chance to become a respected man of the community, remains open.    *(898 words)*

**Conclusion**

---

**3.2**  ⬛ TIPP▷

---

This assignment asks you to focus on social mobility as one aspect of the American Dream. It makes sense to start your text by explaining social mobility within the context of the American Dream and then apply this concept to the film. The assignment uses the verb "comment", which means you need to argue whether social mobility as shown in the film is something worth striving for. The film provides you with arguments for or against the thesis by showing how successful and happy the characters are when they are trying to climb the social ladder or how they fare when they have succeeded. *Gran Torino* tells an ambiguous story in this respect. In your article, however, you need not deal with all possible pros and cons, but you can decide beforehand whether you want to support the thesis that social mobility is presented as something worth striving for or whether to oppose it. The solution suggested here focuses on the negative aspects of social mobility and shows that the American Dream does not consist of economic advancement alone, but also has social aspects that need to be taken into account. Of course, you are also free to argue in favour of the statement, for instance by emphasising Thao's positive development in the course of the film more strongly. As you are writing an article, make sure your text includes the typical features of this format: Give it a clear structure with an interesting headline, an introduction that describes what you are going to write about, a main part with arguments and examples, and a conclusion that sums up your line of thought.

The sample solution is structured like this:

**Headline**

**Introduction**
- introductory sentence with a plot summary of *Gran Torino*
- introduction of the topic of the American Dream and social mobility
- leading question: is social mobility depicted as something worth striving for?

**Main part**
- Walt as an embodiment of the American Dream: hard-working, successful, self-reliant; but also bitter and lonely
- Walt's sons and their families as examples of social advancement and economic success, but they only have materialistic interests
- social advancement requires a sense of community and connection to others: Thao and Walt as examples

**Conclusion:** *Gran Torino* suggests that social mobility is only worth striving for if accompanied by a sense of community

## Who wouldn't want a Gran Torino?

*Gran Torino*, directed by Clint Eastwood and released in 2008, tells the story of a Korean War veteran named Walt Kowalski who forms an unlikely friendship with a young Hmong boy named Thao. One of the themes the film explores through this relationship is social advancement and the conditions necessary for an individual to achieve it. Upward social mobility is one of the key aspects of the American Dream. It embodies the promise that you can move up the socio-economic ladder through hard work and determination, and it is this promise that makes the US so attractive. Or does it? Is social mobility something worth striving for? *Gran Torino* presents a rather nuanced view of this concept.

Walt, the film's protagonist, embodies the ideals of the American Dream in many ways. He is a hard-working, self-made man who has achieved success through his own efforts. He owns a house and a beautiful Gran Torino for which he is envied by everyone who sees it. He maintains the house and his garden all by himself, knows how to fix appliances that are broken, and seems to be completely self-sufficient, at least economically. However, as the film progresses, it

*Margin notes:*
Headline
Introduction
Main part:
Walt, whom social mobility has made bitter and lonely

94

becomes clear that his success has come at a cost. He is a bitter racist and a deeply unhappy man, haunted by his past and his experiences in the Korean War. After the death of his beloved wife, he spends most of his days sitting on his porch, living off beer and beef jerky. It seems as though his self-sufficiency is also caused by his inability to form any deep relationships beyond his marriage. He cannot connect with his sons, and the friendship with his mates at the bar seems rather superficial. As his neighbourhood becomes more and more inhabited by Asian immigrants, he withdraws into his racism and denies any friendly contact with the newcomers, bitterly disappointed that the traditional lifestyle he has become accustomed to and the upward social mobility of his area seem to be slipping away.

His sons, however, have obviously climbed the social ladder. They have left the working class behind, seem to make more money than their father (Walt says his son's job gives him the "license to steal"), and at least one of their children is planning to go to college. They seem to be quite happy, but are they? Walt's granddaughter is only interested in Walt's possessions (his sofa and especially his Gran Torino), and also Walt's son probably speaks highly of the retirement home to Walt simply because he wants Walt to move out of his house so he can have it for himself. Upward social mobility, the film suggests, can spoil your character. *Walt's sons and their families with their solely materialistic interests*

The second main character of the film, Thao, seems to show the positive side of social mobility: At the beginning of the film, Thao is a shy boy without direction and as a result gets drawn into a gang and finds himself in a vicious cycle of violence. He finds a new direction in life when he gets a job and later inherits Walt's Gran Torino. And yet, even in his case, it becomes clear that it is not the economic advancement alone that is fulfilling. More importantly, Thao forms a friendship with Walt and becomes involved in the community. He begins to change, becomes more responsible and more confident. This is what enables him to overcome his initial resignation and aimlessness and to start working. Walt, too, finds a way to get over his bitterness by opening up to his new neighbours and accepting the friendship that Sue, Thao's warm-hearted and quick-witted sister, offers him. Thus, the film highlights an aspect of the American Dream beyond pure materialism and consumerism: the chance to find freedom, prosperity and happiness in an equal and open society. *importance of sense of community and connection to others*

In conclusion, while *Gran Torino* presents a complex and nuanced view of social mobility, it ultimately suggests that it is something worth striving for, but only if it is accompanied by a sense of community and connection, and by a sense of purpose and meaning. So, the film's message is not just about upward mobility but also about being part of a larger whole and understanding the importance of friendship. **Conclusion**

*(711 words)*

**HÖRVERSTEHEN**

### Task 1: The Problem of Species Extinction

Listen to a recording about the problems of species extinction and climate change. VOA reporter Rosanne Skirble is talking to Kate Burns from the Al Bustan Zoological Centre and ecology professor Mark Urban. While listening, tick (✓) the correct answer (a, b or c). There is only one correct answer.

**1** According to Kate Burns, breeding rare animals ...

   **a** ☐ cannot stop them from becoming extinct in the wild.

   **b** ☐ must be done on a large scale to preserve the genetic diversity of a species.

   **c** ☐ only makes sense if there are too few wild animals left.

**2** Rosanne Skirble sees the reason for many species becoming extinct in ...

   **a** ☐ the overall negative impact of human life.

   **b** ☐ natural processes like the earth's temperature rising.

   **c** ☐ a lack of laws which regulate hunting and poaching.

**3** Experts believe that ...

   **a** ☐ global warming will reach a peak during this century and then fall again.

   **b** ☐ extinctions will become worse if climate change continues as predicted.

   **c** ☐ the earth is already 4.3 degrees warmer than before the industrial revolution.

**4** Mark Urban thinks that ...

   **a** ☐ it is too late to save many endemic species.

   **b** ☐ one in six species will not survive if current pollution continues.

   **c** ☐ species in Australia or South America should learn to adapt to other parts of the world.

**5** Mark Urban mentions a connection between species extinction and ...

   **a** ☐ world hunger.

   **b** ☐ crime and security.

   **c** ☐ the ability to cure diseases.

**6** The tone of the recording is …

   **a** ☐ humorous.

   **b** ☐ warning.

   **c** ☐ accusatory.

---

**Task 2: Happiness by Design: Finding Pleasure and Purpose in Everyday Life**

Listen to a report on what makes us happy. While listening, fill in the missing information. If not specified, one aspect is enough.

| | | |
|---|---|---|
| **1** | The two things Professor Dolan talks about in his book *Happiness by Design*: | • <br> • |
| **2** | Two things that are essential for the first client's happiness: | • <br> • |
| **3** | How Dolan knows what makes people happy: | • <br> • |
| **4** | What makes most people miserable: | |
| **5** | What kind of time is least valuable to most people: | |
| **6** | Why it is important how we use our time: | |
| **7** | Two instant measures of being happier: | • <br> • |
| **8** | How to achieve happiness according to Dolan: | |
| **9** | Two activities that do not make us happier: | • <br> • |

Listen to a report on a Black South African student who threw a bucket of excrement over a statue of Cecil Rhodes. This kicked off a protest movement that is shattering the way the country sees its past. While listening, fill in the gaps. It is not necessary to use the exact same words from the text.

1 Chumani Maxwele, the son of a poor miner from the Eastern Cape, South Africa, re-

alised one day that the apartheid past was still **(1)** _____.

The realisation made him feel **(2)** _____, because it had not

been what he had been taught growing up. His generation had been told they were the

5 "**(3)** _____": an exceptional generation in South African history, the first one

raised with almost no direct **(4)** _____ of apartheid's terrors. In

school and at home, parents and grandparents of Maxwele's generation often reminded

the young people how different life was for them and how much they had to be

**(5)** _____.

10 On the morning of 9 March, Maxwele travelled by **(6)** _____ out to

Khayelitsha, picked up one of the buckets of shit that he found in the street, and brought

it back to the campus of the University of Cape Town (UCT), where, in 2011, he had

gained a scholarship to study **(7)** _____. He took it to a bronze statue

of the 19th-century **(8)** _____ colonialist Cecil John Rhodes. Rhodes had

15 been one of the main architects of South Africa's **(9)** _____. "Where

are *our* heroes and ancestors?" Maxwele shouted to a gathering, curious crowd. Then

he opened the bucket and hurled its contents into Rhodes's **(10)** _____.

*Eve Fairbanks: "Why South African Students Have Turned on Their Parents' Generation."*
*In: theguardian.com, 18 November 2015. Copyright Guardian News & Media Ltd 2017*

| Text | Mitch Landrieu: Speech on the Removal of Confederate Monuments in New Orleans |

1 Thank you for coming.

The soul of our beloved City is deeply rooted in a history that has evolved over thousands of years; rooted in a diverse people who have been here together every step of the way – for both good and for ill. It is a history that holds in its heart the stories of
5 Native Americans […], the enslaved people from Senegambia, Free People of Color, the Haitians, the Germans, both the empires of France and Spain. The Italians, the Irish, the Cubans, the south and central Americans, the Vietnamese and so many more.

You see – New Orleans is truly a city of many nations, a melting pot, a bubbling caldron of many cultures. There is no other place quite like it in the world that so
10 eloquently exemplifies the uniquely American motto: e pluribus unum – out of many we are one. But there are also other truths about our city that we must confront. New Orleans was America's largest slave market: a port where hundreds of thousands of souls were bought, sold and shipped up the Mississippi River to lives of forced labor, of misery, of rape, of torture. America was the place where nearly 4,000 of our fellow
15 citizens were lynched, 540 alone in Louisiana; where the courts enshrined "separate but equal"; where Freedom riders coming to New Orleans were beaten to a bloody pulp. So when people say to me that the monuments in question are history, well what I just described is real history as well, and it is the searing truth.

And it immediately begs the questions, why there are no slave ship monuments, no
20 prominent markers on public land to remember the lynchings or the slave blocks; nothing to remember this long chapter of our lives; the pain, the sacrifice, the shame … all of it happening on the soil of New Orleans. So for those self-appointed defenders of history and the monuments, they are eerily silent on what amounts to this historical malfeasance, a lie by omission. There is a difference between remembrance of history
25 and reverence of it.

For America and New Orleans, it has been a long, winding road, marked by great tragedy and great triumph. But we cannot be afraid of our truth. As President George W. Bush said at the dedication ceremony for the National Museum of African American History & Culture, "A great nation does not hide its history. It faces its flaws and
30 corrects them." So today I want to speak about why we chose to remove these four monuments to the Lost Cause of the Confederacy, but also how and why this process can move us towards healing and understanding of each other. So, let's start with the facts.

The historic record is clear, the Robert E. Lee, Jefferson Davis, and P. G. T. Beau-
35 regard statues were not erected just to honor these men, but as part of the movement which became known as The Cult of the Lost Cause. This "cult" had one goal – through monuments and through other means – to rewrite history to hide the truth, which is that the Confederacy was on the wrong side of humanity. First erected over 166 years

after the founding of our city and 19 years after the end of the Civil War, the monu-
40 ments that we took down were meant to rebrand the history of our city and the ideals
of a defeated Confederacy. It is self-evident that these men did not fight for the United
States of America. They fought against it. They may have been warriors, but in this
cause they were not patriots. These statues are not just stone and metal. They are not
just innocent remembrances of a benign history. These monuments purposefully cel-
45 ebrate a fictional, sanitized Confederacy; ignoring the death, ignoring the enslavement,
and the terror that it actually stood for.

After the Civil War, these statues were a part of that terrorism as much as a burning
cross on someone's lawn; they were erected purposefully to send a strong message to
all who walked in their shadows about who was still in charge in this city. Should you
50 have further doubt about the true goals of the Confederacy, in the very weeks before
the war broke out, the Vice President of the Confederacy, Alexander Stephens, made
it clear that the Confederate cause was about maintaining slavery and white supremacy.
He said in his now famous "cornerstone speech" that the Confederacy's "cornerstone
rests upon the great truth, that the negro is not equal to the white man; that slavery –
55 subordination to the superior race – is his natural and normal condition. This, our new
government, is the first, in the history of the world, based upon this great physical,
philosophical, and moral truth."

Now, with these shocking words still ringing in your ears … I want to try to gently
peel from your hands the grip on a false narrative of our history that I think weakens
60 us. And make straight a wrong turn we made many years ago – we can more closely
connect with integrity to the founding principles of our nation and forge a clearer and
straighter path toward a better city and a more perfect union. […]          *867 words*

*Landrieu, Mitch: "Speech on the Removal of Confederate Monuments in New Orleans",*
*May 19, 2017, https://www.theadvocate.com/pdf_1683c300-3ce1-11e7-83b6-cb1d4ff55ec9.html*

**Annotations**

| | |
|---|---|
| headline: | Mitchell (Mitch) Landrieu: American politician and lawyer who was Mayor of New Orleans from 2010 to 2018 |
| line 5: | Senegambia: loose confederation between the West African countries of Senegal and Gambia |
| line 5: | Free People of Color: people of mixed African and European descent who were not enslaved |
| line 16: | Freedom riders: civil rights activists who rode interstate buses into the segregated southern United States in the 1960s |
| lines 27/28: | George W. Bush: US President from 2001–2009 |
| line 31: | Lost Cause of the Confederacy: ideological movement which views the American Civil War (1861–1865) as an honorable struggle for the Southern way of life while downplaying the role of slavery in triggering the war |
| line 34: | Robert E. Lee: commander of the Confederate States Army |
| line 34: | Jefferson Davis: President of the Confederate States |
| lines 34/35: | P. G. T. Beauregard: general of the Confederate States Army |

**1**   Outline what Mitch Landrieu says about monuments in New Orleans.    (30 %)

**2**   Analyze the way Mitch Landrieu conveys his message.    (30 %)

**3**   Choose *one* of the following tasks:    (40 %)

**3.1**  "A great nation does not hide its history. It faces its flaws and corrects them." (ll. 29/30)

Referring to at least one central chapter in American history, comment on this statement by George W. Bush.

**or**

**3.2**  For the blog called *Who deserves a monument in the 21st Century?* write a blog entry suggesting a public person from the English-speaking world whose political, cultural or scientific work has inspired and changed the lives of many people. In your blog entry, assess the achievements of this person and give reasons for your choice.

*Bei den für Set 5 abgedruckten Aufgaben zum Schreiben handelt es sich um offizielle Musteraufgaben des Landes Baden-Württemberg.*

HÖRVERSTEHEN

**Transcript 1**  The Problem of Species Extinction

1 **Rosanne Skirble:** In the United Arab Emirates, the rare bongo antelope is on the brink of extinction says Kate Burns, a veterinary nurse at Al Bustan Zoological Centre, which houses several of the animals. Burns hopes to breed more.

**Kate Burns:** Each individual counts. Mhmm, there is only 47 left in the wild. Mhmm,
5 so, yeah, breeding, we need to maintain the genetic diversity of the species and that means, you know, swapping, swapping animals, swapping experience.

**Rosanne Skirble:** Humans are pushing this species and others to extinction. While hunting and poaching certainly play a role, so do urban sprawl and oil extraction. Climate changing emissions from power plants, buildings and transport also threaten
10 biodiversity. Climate models predict the Earth's temperature will increase from two to six degrees Celsius this century. Experts say a 4.3-degree increase above pre-industrial times is a tipping point, which will lead to the worst impacts of climate change. Extinctions will accelerate, says University of Connecticut ecology professor Mark Urban.

15 **Mark Urban:** We reached the point where we had 16% extinction risk for species. So one in six species could be endangered if we don't do anything about controlling greenhouse gases.

**Rosanne Skirble:** Urban reviewed 131 articles on species extinction for an analysis, which appears in the journal *Science*. He says some regions of the world will be
20 harder hit than others.

**Mark Urban:** The small land masses play a role, places with lots of endemic species like Australia and South America. Mhmm, these are species that are already constrained to, to small ranges and so even a small shift in those ranges could endanger them.

**Rosanne Skirble:** Climate change will alter species and the habitats in which they live,
25 Urban warns. Their loss will spread disease and have other unintended consequences.

**Mark Urban:** If you think about our food security and we have crops. Well, it's very important to understand, say, the rainfall pattern in the future, and, and the ability of those crops to still be grown. But what we're neglecting are the biotic interac-
30 tions. So, what if we lose a, a really important predator of a pest in that field and suddenly that pest increases and decreases the crop yields.

**Rosanne Skirble:** Urban says his study gives policy makers and the public added incentive to adopt new strategies, to conserve and protect the most threatened species. Rosanne Skirble, VOA News, Washington.

*Rosanne Skirble, "One in Six Species Threatened with Extinction."*
*In:* Voice of America News, *30 April 2015*

This listening text contains quite a lot of background noises. Don't let them distract you and try to focus on what the speakers are saying. Also, don't worry if you do not know all the vocabulary in the text. You do not have to understand each and every word in order to be able to solve the task.

These text passages will help you find the correct answers:

1 "Burns hopes to <u>breed more</u>. [...] Mhmm, so, yeah, breeding, we need to <u>maintain the genetic diversity</u> of the species and that means, you know, swapping, swapping animals, swapping experience." (ll. 3–6)

2 "<u>Humans</u> are pushing this species and others to extinction. While <u>hunting</u> and <u>poaching</u> certainly play a role, so do <u>urban sprawl</u> and <u>oil extraction</u>. <u>Climate changing emissions from power plants, buildings and transport</u> also threaten biodiversity." (ll. 7–10) All the mentioned problems are manmade.

3 "Climate models predict the Earth's temperature will increase from two to six degrees Celsius this century. Experts say a 4.3-degree increase above pre-industrial times is a tipping point, which will lead to the worst impacts of climate change. <u>Extinctions will accelerate</u>, says University of Connecticut ecology professor Mark Urban." (ll. 10–14)

4 "one in six species could be endangered if we don't do anything about controlling greenhouse gases." (ll. 16/17)

5 "If you think about our <u>food security</u> and we have crops. Well, it's very important to understand [...] the <u>ability of those crops to still be grown</u>. [...] So, what if we lose a, a really important predator of a pest in that field and suddenly that pest increases and <u>decreases the crop yields</u>." (ll. 27–31)

6 The text is about a serious topic, namely species extinction. Especially in the end when it is explained that "Urban says his study gives policy makers and the public added incentive to adopt new strategies, to conserve and protect the most threatened species" (ll. 32/33), it becomes clear that it should be seen as a warning and an encouragement to do more against climate change in the future.

---

1 According to Kate Burns, breeding rare animals …

   b  ☑️ must be done on a large scale to preserve the genetic diversity of a species.

2 Rosanne Skirble sees the reason for many species becoming extinct in …

   a  ☑️ the overall negative impact of human life.

3 Experts believe that …

   b  ☑️ extinctions will become worse if climate change continues as predicted.

4 Mark Urban thinks that …

   b  ☑️ one in six species will not survive if current pollution continues.

**5** Mark Urban mentions a connection between species extinction and …

  **a** ☑ world hunger.

**6** The tone of the recording is …

  **b** ☑ warning.

---

| **Transcript 2** | **Happiness by Design: Finding Pleasure and Purpose in Everyday Life** |

1  **Professor Paul Dolan:** For me happiness is in our experiences of life. Things that we feel day to day, moment to moment. And I talk about pleasure and purpose.

OK, so my name's Paul Dolan, I'm at London School of Economics and my book is called *Happiness by Design – Finding Pleasure and Purpose in Everyday Life.*

5  So, happy lives are ones that contain some balance; it's not the same for everybody and it's not in equal measure. But some kind of balance between things that we find fun on the one hand and things that we find fulfilling on the other.

Well, it is a subjective experience. I think everything ultimately matters because it makes us feel better, so I can describe to you I think the things that I find pleasurable

10  and the things that I find purposeful. And I can also probably give you a good sense of how much I find them pleasurable and how much I find them purposeful. And equally, of course, things that I find painful and things that I find pointless, so I think we are now getting a better insight into the quantitative nature of those elements.

 **Client 1:** Happiness for me is a very ethereal thing, I think. By that I mean that it is very

15  difficult to say what it is, and it can be different, at different stages of my life. But in essence, happiness for me, as I've grown older, is quite a few intangible things, things which make me think that life is worth it, so it's spending time with the people I want to be with, it's not just living from moment to moment but actually just being in the moment and doing the things that are actually most important. So the

20  places that are really important for me, and often, actually, it's later on that you realise the happiest times. Well, I'm getting better at that.

 **Professor Paul Dolan:** We're getting many observations on many people over many years, and there seems to be something sensible coming through from the answers people give us. We get associations with some things that you would expect them

25  to be associated with, you know, poverty makes people miserable but being rich doesn't make people happier. So, you know, there are some nice insights coming through from this data. Time that we spend with other people that makes us feel nice, time spent on trains and on tubes and on buses, not so nice.

 **Client 2:** The things that make me happy are: spending time with my friends and family,

30  going out for dinner, going to watch my football team play football, playing with my cat.

 **Professor Paul Dolan:** Well, I think how we use our time is absolutely critical, it's the scarcest resource we've got, right? The few moments that we've been talking now, or that I've been talking now, are a few moments closer to death and it's time I

won't ever get back, so I think it's incumbent on us all to think about how we use
that time and just reorientate some of it away from things that we're finding painful
and pointless. And spend a bit more time, you know, with things that we find pleasurable and purposeful which would include spending more time with people that
we like being with; would include spending a bit more time outdoors, maybe listening to music, all of these things, I think most of us know if we stop and think for a
moment, would make us feel a bit happier. The interesting question is why we don't
do more of it? And helping others, too, makes us feel nice, too. So all these things
that we would get good feedback for if we paid attention to those experiences but
one of the reasons why we don't do those things more is we don't pay attention to
those experiences as much as we might, we tell ourselves big stories about the things
that we think should make us happy, buying more stuff, earning more money, the
kind of narratives and stories that we tell ourselves or we're told by other people
that sometimes deviate us off the path of using our time in those ways that make us
happier.
Yeah, I mean, I think we all know people, you know, who like to moan. It probably
makes them happy moaning, too, but there are some people that are just tempera-
mentally, naturally, you know, happier. But I think the important thing is that all of
us could be a little bit happier by doing some more of the things that make us feel
good. And the critical thing is to design environments that make it easier for us to
do those things. You know, if you've got a friend that you want to speak to, plan a
time in the diary that you speak to them, the same time every week, and then habits
will get formed and automatically you speak to that person without having to think
too hard about doing so. So all of us, wherever we start from, I think, can nudge
ourselves a little bit happier.

*Paul Dolan / Lee Millam, Pod Academy, 5 October 2014.*
*http://podacademy.org/podcasts/happiness-design/*

---

**TIPP**

These text passages will help you find the correct answer:
1 "And I talk about pleasure and purpose." (l. 2); "So, happy lives are ones that
contain some balance; [...] some kind of balance between things that we find
fun [...] and things that we find fulfilling" (ll. 5–7)
2 "But in essence, happiness for me, as I've grown older, is quite a few intangible things, things which make me think that life is worth it, so it's spending
time with the people I want to be with, it's not just living from moment to moment but actually just being in the moment and doing the things that are actually most important. So the places that are really important for me" (ll. 15–20)
3 "We're getting many observations on many people over many years, and there
seems to be something sensible coming through from the answers people give
us." (ll. 22–24)

4 "you know, <u>poverty</u> makes people miserable but being rich doesn't make people happier." (ll. 25/26)

5 "Time that we spend with other people that makes us feel nice, <u>time spent on trains and on tubes and on buses, not so nice</u>." (ll. 27/28)

6 "I think how we use our time is absolutely critical, it's <u>the scarcest resource we've got</u>, right? The few moments that we've been talking now, or that I've been talking now, are a few moments closer to death and <u>it's time I won't ever get back</u>" (ll. 32–35)

7 "And spend a bit more time, you know, with things that we find pleasurable and purposeful which would include <u>spending more time with people that we like being with</u>; would include <u>spending a bit more time outdoors</u>, maybe <u>listening to music</u>, all of these things, I think most of us know if we stop and think for a moment, would make us feel a bit happier. [...] And <u>helping others</u>, too, makes us feel nice, too." (ll. 37–42)

8 "So all these <u>things that we would get good feedback for if we paid attention</u> to those experiences" (ll. 42/43)

9 "we tell ourselves big stories about the things that we think should make us happy, <u>buying more stuff</u>, <u>earning more money</u>, the kind of narratives and stories that we tell ourselves or we're told by other people that sometimes deviate us off the path of using our time in those ways that make us happier." (ll. 45–49)

| 1 | The two things Professor Dolan talks about in his book *Happiness by Design*: | • pleasure<br>• purpose |
|---|---|---|
| 2 | Two things that are essential for the first client's happiness: | *zwei aus:*<br>• people he likes<br>• places that are important<br>• enjoying each moment |
| 3 | How Dolan knows what makes people happy: | • through observations<br>• through people's answers |
| 4 | What makes most people miserable: | poverty |
| 5 | What kind of time is least valuable to most people: | time spent on public transport |
| 6 | Why it is important how we use our time: | we won't get it back / scarcest resource we have |
| 7 | Two instant measures of being happier: | *zwei aus:*<br>• spending time with loved ones<br>• spending more time outside<br>• listening to music<br>• helping others |

| 8 How to achieve happiness according to Dolan: | paying attention to pleasurable experiences |
|---|---|
| 9 Two activities that do not make us happier: | • buying more stuff<br>• earning more money |

## Transcript 3   Why South African Students Have Turned on Their Parents' Generation

1 The apartheid past, Maxwele realised, was still shaping his life. The realisation made him feel more and more angry, because it had not been what he had been taught growing up. His generation had been told they were the "born frees": an exceptional generation in South African history, the first one raised with almost no direct memory of apart-
5 heid's terrors. "They're like nothing that's ever been!" bleated a promo segment for *Born Frees*, a reality TV show that began airing in South Africa in 2004. In school and at home, their elders often reminded them how different life was for them and how much they had to be grateful for.

On the morning of 9 March, Maxwele travelled by minibus taxi out to Khayelitsha,
10 picked up one of the buckets of shit that sat reeking on the kerbside, and brought it back to the campus of the University of Cape Town (UCT), where, in 2011, he had gained a scholarship to study political science. He took it to a bronze statue of the 19th-century British colonialist Cecil John Rhodes that held pride of place on campus, just downhill from the convocation hall. Rhodes had been one of the main architects of South Africa's
15 segregation. "Where are *our* heroes and ancestors?" Maxwele shouted to a gathering, curious crowd. Then he opened the bucket and hurled its contents into Rhodes's face.

*Eve Fairbanks: "Why South African Students Have Turned on Their Parents' Generation."*
*In: theguardian.com, 18 November 2015. Copyright Guardian News & Media Ltd 2017*

---

**TIPP**

In this task, you do not need to fill in the gaps with the exact words from the text. However, your solution has to make sense in the context given.

---

Chumani Maxwele, the son of a poor miner from the Eastern Cape, South Africa, realised one day that the apartheid past was still **(1) shaping/influencing his life**. The realisation made him feel **(2) more and more/increasingly angry**, because it had not been what he had been taught growing up. His generation had been told they were the "**(3) born frees**": an exceptional generation in South African history, the first one raised with almost no direct **(4) memory/recollection** of apartheid's terrors. In school and at home, parents and grandparents of Maxwele's generation often reminded the young people how different life was for them and how much they had to be **(5) grateful/thankful/glad for**.

107

On the morning of 9 March, Maxwele travelled by (**6**) **minibus taxi** out to Khayelit-sha, picked up one of the buckets of shit that he found in the street, and brought it back to the campus of the University of Cape Town (UCT), where, in 2011, he had gained a scholarship to study (**7**) **political science/politics**. He took it to a bronze statue of the 19th-century (**8**) **British** colonialist Cecil John Rhodes. Rhodes had been one of the main architects of South Africa's (**9**) **segregation**. "Where are *our* heroes and an-cestors?" Maxwele shouted to a gathering, curious crowd. Then he opened the bucket and hurled its contents into Rhodes's (**10**) **face**.

 **SCHREIBEN: OFFIZIELLE MUSTERPRÜFUNG**

1 **TIPP**

Read the text carefully and then briefly sum up Mitch Landrieu's arguments why the Confederate monuments in New Orleans should be removed. In lines 30 to 32, the mayor explicitly states, "So today I want to speak about why we chose to remove these [...] monuments to the Lost Cause of the Confederacy, but also how and why this process can move us towards healing and understanding of each other." So, you will probably find the main argument in the vicinity of this statement. Use your own words and do not quote from the text. Start with an introductory sentence that gives the reader some basic information on the text at hand.

You can structure your solution like this:

**Introduction:** general information on the text

**Main part:** Landrieu's main points against statues of Confederate leaders
– one-sided and misguided view of history:
  • Confederacy inhumane (cf. l. 38)
  • lack of recognition for African American history (cf. ll. 44–46)
– biased version of history un-American and ultimately weakening for the coun-try:
  • Confederacy contradictory to American ideals (cf. ll. 41–43)
  • focus on all aspects of history ultimately strengthening (cf. ll. 58–62)

In the given speech from May 2017, the mayor of New Orleans, Mitch Landrieu, argues why monuments remembering Confederate leaders should be removed. | **Introduction**

Mayor Landrieu's main point is that these monuments represent a one-sided and misguided view of history. According to Landrieu, leaders of the Confederacy receive honours inappropriate to the in-humane ideology for which they fought. Their glorification is espe-cially problematic as it coincides with the city's lack of recognition for the sufferings and trials that African Americans faced. | **Main part:** one-sided and misguided view of history

More broadly speaking, Landrieu is committed to the founding principles of the United States and says that these monuments contradict them. Their removal, on the other hand, will serve as a sign of solidarity among all Americans and thus enable a better future.

biased version of history un-American and weakening

*(123 words)*

**2** **TIPP**

Read the text closely and find patterns showing how Landrieu wants to convince the audience of his opinion that bringing down the monuments is the right thing to do. When you are asked to examine means and strategies, these can be stylistic devices, but also other means, such as addresses to the audience, a certain choice of words, facts and figures that add credibility to a text and many more. Make sure that you explain how the detected strategies work. In order not to simply list elements you have found, it is often useful to group your findings into certain categories for different aims. It is perfectly all right to digress from the text chronology to create a logical and coherent analysis. Start with a short introduction in which you explain what you are going to do, then describe your findings and end with a short conclusion summing up your results.

You could structure your answer like this:

**Introduction**

Main part: means and strategies
- creation of a **feeling of community and togetherness:**
  - addresses to the audience through use of pronouns and possessive determiners "you"/"your" (cf. ll. 8, 49, 58, 59) and "we"/"us"/"our" (cf. ll. 2, 11, 14, 21, 27, 32, 40, 59, 60, 61)
  - New Orleans as "our beloved City" (l. 2) → appeal to patriotism
  - "us" vs. "them" against historical and modern Confederates (cf. ll. 22/23, 42/43)
  - New Orleans as an inclusive place ("a city of many nations, a melting pot, a bubbling caldron of many cultures", ll. 8/9)
- **emotional and drastic description of African Americans' suffering:**
  - to not hide away from "the searing truth" (l. 18)
  - "Freedom riders [...] beaten to a bloody pulp" (ll. 16/17)
  - many enumerations: "souls were bought, sold and shipped [...] to lives of forced labor, of misery, of rape, of torture" (ll. 13/14), "the pain, the sacrifice, the shame" (l. 21), "ignoring the death, ignoring the enslavement, and the terror" (ll. 45/46)
  - numbers to substantiate his report with facts and figures (cf. ll. 14/15)
- representation of **Confederates as un-American anti-patriots:**
  - contrast: history of the USA and of New Orleans "marked by great tragedy and great triumph" (ll. 26/27)

- double contrast: "these men did not fight for the United States of America. They fought against it" (ll. 41/42), "They may have been warriors, but [...] they were not patriots" (ll. 42/43)
- allusion to Declaration of Independence ("[i]t is self-evident that", l. 41; "the founding principles of our nation", l. 61)
- **encouragement** that healing is possible:
  - quote by former President Bush (cf. ll. 27–30)
  - extended metaphor for journey (cf. ll. 60–62)

**Conclusion**

Mayor Landrieu is convinced that the monuments dedicated to Confederate leaders should be brought down. In order to make his audience agree with his conviction, he uses a number of means and strategies.

First, he connects to the audience by addressing them directly, for example in line 8 where he starts his explanations with "You see" or from line 49 onwards when he tries to shock them with the Vice President of the Confederacy's racist message. Throughout the text, there are also numerous occurrences of the pronouns "we" and "us" as well as the possessive determiner "our" (ll. 2, 11, 14, 21, 27, 32, 40, 59, 60, 61). Thereby, the mayor makes it clear that he shares a common interest with his audience, which becomes especially evident when he talks of New Orleans as "our beloved City" (l. 2) or when he warns that holding on to "a false narrative [...] weakens us" (ll. 59/60). Every patriotic New Orleanian will feel addressed and will want their city to prosper.

In this context, he also distances himself and his audience from historical Confederates as well as their modern followers by calling them "they" (e. g. ll. 42/43) or "those self-appointed defenders of history" (ll. 22/23). With these clearly assigned roles in mind, he makes an effort to include everyone else by using a metaphor to point out the multiethnicity of his city. He calls it "a city of many nations, a melting pot, a bubbling caldron of many cultures" (ll. 8/9).

This picture of a positive place is directly contrasted with the suffering of African American people, which Landrieu highlights throughout the text. He uses quite an emotional, partly even drastic language, for instance when he talks about the "Freedom riders [who] were beaten to a bloody pulp" (ll. 16/17). Numerous enumerations further provoke his audience's sympathy for the plight of African Americans and show that Landrieu, in contrast to The Cult of the Lost Cause, does not hide away from "the searing truth" (l. 18) of slavery: when he calls the victims of slavery "souls [who] were bought, sold and shipped" (l. 13)

*Sidenotes:*

Introduction

creation of a **feeling of community and togetherness:** use of pronouns, appeal to patriotism

"us" vs. "them", inclusivity of New Orleans

**emotional and drastic description of African Americans' suffering:** vivid language, numerous enumerations

to America to lead "lives of forced labor, of misery, of rape, of torture" (ll. 13/14), he makes it clear that behind each of the "hundreds of thousands" (l. 12) lies an individual story of hardship and suffering. He clarifies that "the pain, the sacrifice, the shame" (l. 21) took place in New Orleans and that the monuments in question are "ignoring the death, ignoring the enslavement, and the terror" (ll. 45/46).

By supporting his claims with numbers (cf. ll. 14/15), Landrieu shows that he has thoroughly researched the topic. Thus, he substantiates his moving plea for justice with hard, tangible facts.

*numbers*

That an inclusive American history is "marked by great tragedy and great triumph" (ll. 26/27) contradicts the one-sided story that the monuments represent. With the double contrast that the leaders of the Confederates "did not fight for the United States of America. They fought against it" (ll. 41/42) and that "[t]hey may have been warriors, but [...] they were not patriots" (ll. 42/43), Landrieu characterises them as wrong and un-American. Using a beginning phrase similar to that of the Declaration of Independence, "[i]t is self-evident that" (l. 41), the mayor further stresses that everyone truly interested in the American values, or as he puts it, in "the founding principles of our nation" (l. 61), must be against reverence for the anti-patriotic Confederates.

*representation of* **Confederates as un-American anti-patriots**

What the mayor wants to accomplish by destroying these wrong heroes' monuments is expressed in a known patriot's words, namely former President Bush's, who appealed to his fellow countrymen to "face [the country's] flaws and correct[...] them" (ll. 29/30). With an extended metaphor that centres around the motif of a journey, Landrieu wants to encourage his listeners that healing is possible. The "wrong turn" (l. 60) that has been taken can be corrected and "a clearer and straighter path" (ll. 61/62) lies ahead on the "long, winding road" (l. 26) of American history.

**encouragement** *that healing is possible*

Summing up, one can say that Mitch Landrieu promotes an idea of reconciliation and correction of the terrible flaws of history. In that way, he hopes to persuade everyone to follow him out of the "false narrative" (l. 59) of the Lost Cause of the Confederacy and into a better future for America. *(734 words)*

**Conclusion**

---

**3.1**  **TIPP**

---

When given a quote to comment on, it is important to interpret the quote and to describe what it says in your own words before you comment on it. In the following text, the interpretation of the quote is integrated into the introductory passage. The main part assesses whether what G. W. Bush said about great nations and the way they deal with their flaws can be applied to the US. You are to refer to at least one chapter of American history and evaluate whether the nation has actually admitted that mistakes have been made and whether these have been corrected. The solution suggested here focuses on the history of minorities in the USA. Make sure you write a coherent text with an introduction, a main part and a conclusion. Your solution should also clearly show your agreement (or disagreement) with ex-President Bush's words with regard to the USA.

The sample solution is structured like this:

**Introduction**
- interpretation of history is a political issue; nationalist/authoritarian regimes interpret history in a way that serves their interests; democracies ideally allow an open discussion
- Bush's statement points out that admitting mistakes and correcting them makes a nation strong

**Main part:** application of the quote to US history of dealing with minorities
- history provides examples of mistakes: the way settlers treated the Native Americans; slavery and racial segregation
- USA seems to have learned from its mistakes: slavery and segregation have been abolished, all citizens, independent of their ethnic origin, share equal rights
- closer look reveals that discrimination still exists: Black Lives Matter movement highlights examples: police violence, racial profiling, racial bias in the criminal justice system, discrimination in everyday life

**Conclusion:** USA is on the way to becoming a great nation: wrongs can be openly addressed, but are not always thoroughly righted

How a nation deals with its own history has always been a political issue. The interpretation of a country's past is an instrument with which rulers tend to justify their current decisions. Nationalist or authoritarian regimes, in particular, often try to prescribe a certain attitude that serves to maintain their power. Mistakes from times ago are ignored or reinterpreted in such a way that they show the leadership in a positive light. In contrast to that, a democratic state with a strong civil society will ideally give free rein to an open discussion about the evaluation of historical events. George W. Bush's statement emphasises that it is this way of dealing with its own history that makes a nation strong. The willingness to learn from mistakes opens up political room for manoeuvre and can provide a path to improvement and new moral strength.

*Introduction: admitting mistakes and correcting them makes a nation strong*

However, even in democracies, there is a danger that the socially strongest group will claim the sovereignty of interpretation on various issues. Thus, how a nation deals with its weakest members, for instance the minorities living there, might be the best test for its greatness.

*Main part: application of the quote to US history of dealing with minorities*

From its very beginning, American history has provided several examples of how a nation can make mistakes. In settling the North American continent, the White Europeans that were to become the "American nation" ignored the Native peoples' rights and committed atrocious crimes against them. Slavery and, after its abolishment, the segregation of the races represent further examples.

examples of mistakes

At first glance, the answer to the question of whether the USA can be termed a great nation in George W. Bush's sense seems to be yes: slavery as well as segregation have long been abolished, and every ethnic minority is granted the same civil rights these days. The US has faced the flaw of discrimination and corrected it.

USA seems to have learned from its mistakes

However, a closer look at the current state of affairs reveals that the flaw still exists. The Black Lives Matter movement in particular has put its finger in this wound by pointing out how African Americans are still being discriminated against. The murder of the Black teenager Trayvon Martin by a White neighbourhood-watch volunteer, who was acquitted in the ensuing trial, brought this movement about. It is still fuelled by recurring cases in which Black men are killed by White policemen even though there is no obvious threat. Racial profiling by the police and implicit and explicit racial bias within the criminal justice system is perceived as one of the main problems of modern US society. African Americans are unfairly stopped or treated by the police, and they very often have to face longer sentences in prison than White people who commit similar offenses. Across many realms of American life, Black people are not treated equally to their White compatriots. Applying for a mortgage, eating out in a restaurant or trying to buy an expensive item in a shop can often lead to mortifying experiences for Black people. Furthermore, they are systematically disadvantaged when voting and at the workplace.

discrimination still exists; example of Black Americans

So, is the USA a great nation? Bush's statement names two aspects: "A great nation does not hide its history. It faces its flaws and corrects them." I agree that recognising and admitting mistakes is the first step towards healing and improvement. Therefore, it seems as if the US is at least on its way to becoming a great nation. Unlike powerful authoritarian states like Russia or China who oppress any kind of criticism, the US enables its citizens to name the wrongs that have been done. While the Civil Rights Movement in the 1950s and 60s still faced partly violent, state-sanctioned opposition, the Black Lives Matter Movement is nowadays free to point out the many ways Black people are discriminated against. The US faces its flaws. But does it correct them? The policeman that ignominiously killed George Floyd by putting his knee on Floyd's neck for almost ten minutes in 2020 was charged with and later convicted of second-degree murder. One could say that this was a step towards more justice. However, the unfair treatment that Black people suffer from in

**Conclusion:** USA on the way to becoming a great nation

their everyday lives is still going on. In order to become a truly great nation, the USA must not only name, but finally also correct the flaw of racial inequality. *(715 words)*

3.2 **TIPP**

A blog entry can use colloquial language, but should still be coherent and well-structured with a headline, an introduction, a main part and a conclusion. The solution proposed here uses information from the text for its introduction in order to establish a context for the question of who deserves a monument in the 21st century. After mentioning this question in the second paragraph, the blog entry goes on to explain why Martin Luther King would be the right choice, especially as a counterstatement against the Confederate monuments that have been removed. While it might be easiest to write about someone like him, who fits the context of the article, you are of course free to choose every other public person whose achievements you think worth celebrating. As a blog entry, the text also makes a political statement in its conclusion, pointing out that erecting monuments is not the right way forward: you should not glorify single persons, you should rather become active and promote their messages.

The sample solution uses the following structure:

Headline

**Introduction:** Confederate monuments have been removed because they endorsed racist ideas

**Main part**
- MLK represents a counter-programme to the discriminatory ideology of the Confederacy
- MLK was a controversial hero: hated by segregationists as well as the FBI, even civil rights activists thought his protests were too weak, his private life was not faultless
- a society with deep divisions needs MLK's principles of non-violence and his protest forms of civil disobedience; he worked for his dream of a harmonious society; his aim is not accomplished yet

**Conclusion:** more important than a monument to MLK is that his mission must be continued

### Who could it be but Martin Luther King?

In a recent move, the mayor of New Orleans decided to take down statues like those of Robert E. Lee and Jefferson Davis from their pedestals. According to Landrieu, these men's monuments were not just put up because of their historic achievements, but they were designed to celebrate the cause of the Confederacy. In other words, they were meant to glorify a past of which the United States should

Headline

Introduction: reference to removal of Confederate statues

actually be ashamed. You see, these generals of the Confederate Army fought against the ideals of the USA that everyone is equal and that all US citizens should become one unit. Instead, they fought for the White race's supremacy over all other races, but especially over Black people who were enslaved to serve their White "masters". So, why should anyone want to keep those monuments?

Now that these figures have been quite rightly removed, the question arises as to who should be put on a pedestal in their place. In my eyes, Martin Luther King would be the most obvious candidate. His ideas represent a counter-programme to the divisive and discriminatory ideology of the Confederacy and point to a path that the United States must still follow in the 21st century, because let's face it, even 50 years after MLK's death, the cause he fought for is still not won. Throughout his public life, Martin Luther King was a controversial figure. It was not only the segregationists of the South who hated him. The FBI considered him to be highly dangerous, because he brought public disorder. Even many other civil rights activists distanced themselves from him because they thought that his forms of protest were too weak. On top of that, failures in his private life often gave cause for criticism and concern.

However, his ideas of non-violent resistance have not lost one bit of their relevance. In a society marked by deep divisions and in which violence increasingly appears as a legitimate means of asserting one's own claims, Martin Luther King's principles can point the way forward. It was clear to him that violence could not be overcome with violence. At the same time, he was also quite outspoken when it came to naming the mechanisms of White dominance. He knew that it was not enough to simply proclaim the equality of the races and ethnicities. His non-violent actions of resistance, the speeches, rallies and acts of civil disobedience, confronted the unjust structures of power head-on. He proclaimed the "dream" of a harmonious society, but he knew that dreaming was not enough. He knew that it was hard work to achieve changes in attitudes as well as changes in how power was exerted. He was assassinated before his mission was fulfilled, and like I said, it sadly still has not been, more than fifty years later.

So, if statues remind us of the values we should hold dear, the ideals Martin Luther King fought for are definitely worth remembering. However, I'm not sure whether erecting new monuments is the right way forward. Much more important than putting MLK on a pedestal would be to get to work and continue his mission. Without question, he and all the other civil rights activists would still protest against the state American society is in today.

*(550 words)*

**Main part:**
Martin Luther King as a good choice for a statue

controversies surrounding MLK

MLK's principles of non-violent resistance and his unfulfilled dream

**Conclusion:**
continuation of MLK's mission more important than his statue

## Material

© *Frédéric Deligne*

**Aufgabenstellung**

### I. Monologue

**1** Describe and interpret the cartoon. Explain the critical message the cartoonist wants to convey.

**2** Elaborate on where and how you use mobile devices. Discuss advantages as well as risks of your use of mobile devices.

### II. Dialogue

**1** Discuss what a positive use of mobile devices could look like in your opinion.

**2** "For adolescents, it is not always easy to find their own way." Discuss this statement. Take social networks as a starting point and include other aspects of life as well.

## I. Monologue

1

In a first step, describe the cartoon. You should not mention every single detail. Instead, focus on aspects that might be significant for the interpretation of the cartoon's message. For this interpretation, answer questions such as "What are bigger themes the cartoonist alludes to?", "What developments and behaviours is he criticising?", "What is the message the cartoonist wants to convey?", etc.

- cartoon by Frédéric Deligne
- caption: "Class photos aren't what they used to be"
- topic: how the use of mobile devices can impact our social lives in negative ways
- typical school situation: class photo, teacher in front of the students who are partly standing on chairs
- instead of a "normal" class photo, the teacher is turning her back to the class and taking a selfie with the students in the background; all the students are doing the same: taking selfies with the rest of the class in the background
- → result: no real class photo, but many selfies which centre on individuals and only show the other people's backs
- in body language, turning one's back to someone means that you do not value the other person
- no one is paying attention to each other, distance between the teacher and the students underlines this (distance could be seen as not only physical, but also emotional)
- tragically, the people in the photo do not even seem to notice their lack of real contact
- caption sounds nostalgic and encourages the viewer to think critically about the current state of affairs
- humorous depiction, yet, profound problems are addressed in the cartoon:
  - often no attention paid to others → no sense of community, everyone is isolated and behaves egoistically; while teacher and her students might not notice their isolation immediately, they will probably one day realise their loneliness and miss having serious relationships with others
  - many are unable to limit their use of digital devices and do not know how to react even if they notice that their habits are unhealthy
  - adults often bad role models → do not behave responsibly with regard to digital devices
- message: digital devices should be used critically and responsibly, because their uncontrolled use can have serious consequences

**2**

For this task, you should think about your own habits regarding the use of digital devices. You could start by giving examples of concrete situations in which you use your mobile phones, tablets, etc. Then continue with the chances and risks of such situations. Even if you see something as entirely positive or negative, try to also consider potentially opposing standpoints. Expressing a balanced view can be particularly challenging but will earn you top marks for this task.

Of course, your own solution can vary greatly from the sample answer suggested here. Yet, you can use it to memorise some helpful phrases. Furthermore, you could record yourself while answering tasks 1 and 2 with the help of the bullet points to get an impression of the time limit you will have in your exam.

The following questions could help you collect ideas for your answer:
- What digital devices do I use regularly? In what circumstances?
- Has my use of digital devices ever created problems?
- In which cases are digital technologies preferred over analogue ones?
- Would I miss out on anything important if I went without my mobile phone, tablet, etc. for a certain amount of time?
- Are there situations in which I would rather not use my mobile phone, tablet, etc.?

### Where and how do you use mobile devices?

- to inform myself → search engines, specialised websites, social networks, etc. can offer a huge amount of information (e. g. I can chat with people who share my interests and whom I would never have met in real life)
- to organise myself by help of my mobile phone: watch, calendar, online timetables, etc.
- to communicate with (large groups of) friends without having to be physically present/to communicate in foreign languages by the help of translation apps
- to listen to music, watch films and play online games
- to find recipes, ideas for gifts, travel advice, suggestions for different activities, clubs or volunteer work, advice how to repair something, etc.
- to take photos and videos (and share them online)

### What are possible advantages or risks in these situations?

Advantages:
- information is easily accessible → searching for information takes less time, which leaves me free to spend more of it on other activities
- no longer necessary for children to have a huge (and financially costly) support network → more social justice because access to a good education is no longer mainly determined by where somebody comes from and their family background
- keeping in touch is facilitated by social networks, even if friends move far away or are abroad for some time

118

Risks:

- overwhelming amount of information, also fake news → necessary skill: filtering and verifying information; otherwise: social networks can dumb people down or even endanger them
- new inequalities because only some people learn to use social media correctly and effectively
- relationships turn more superficial if they are only maintained online
- hate speech / negativity / polarised opinions / filter bubbles: many people only stay in surroundings where their own opinions are reinforced and people tell them what they want to hear; anonymity of the Internet makes it easy to disparage opposing opinions; bots often even intentionally polarise and emotionalise discussions

---

| II. Dialogue

1 **TIPP**

As you can see, the dialogue starts with a topic similar to the one you and your partner have talked about in your monologues. You can show your communicative skills by going back to things your partner has said, asking questions and elaborating on some of the aspects mentioned before. During your dialogue, it is no problem if you slightly branch off to topics other than the ones mentioned in the assignment. However, you should always come back to the task and round off your conversation with some kind of concluding statement. Try to give concrete examples, e. g. from school, your family, your friends, to illustrate your points and to encourage your partner to participate in the conversation.

In the following text, you will be shown one possible beginning for a dialogue as well as a list of subjects that could be addressed in the discussion. Useful phrases have been underlined – you can also use our "MindCards" (cf. „Hinweise zu den digitalen Zusätzen") to practise more of these connectives, useful sentence beginnings, etc.

**A:** Okay, so let's start discussing a positive use of mobile devices. I would like to comment on something you said before. Is it okay for you if I start?

**B:** Of course, please do.

**A:** When you were talking about your friends who were glued to their smartphones all the time, I remembered similar situations that bothered me too. In my opinion, digital devices should support people and not control their lives. Let me give you an example that shows how a healthy use of smartphones could work: I have a friend who has managed to control his usage very effectively. It is not that he doesn't use his smartphone or other electronic devices at all. Still, it is sometimes very difficult to get in touch with him on social networks. He always tells us that he does like us a lot, but he doesn't look at his smartphone screen more than 15 times a day. Of course, that can sometimes be a bit irritating, <u>but to be quite honest</u>, I think it's a brilliant way of keeping yourself in check. <u>What do you think about it</u>?

**B:** <u>On the one hand</u>, <u>I agree with you</u> that that's a brilliant idea. I also think that we shouldn't lose control when it comes to our smartphone use. <u>However</u>, I don't believe that counting the times I look at my smartphone screen would be the best method for me. <u>To my mind</u>, it would be better to determine a time limit for my smartphone usage. <u>For instance</u>, I ...

*Possible topics to continue with:*
- digital detox week
- keeping private lives and school/work completely separate; healthy work-life balance
- parental control of app use
- learning how to distinguish between truth and fake news (different strategies, such as comparing different sources of information, ...)
- trying to avoid filter bubbles: using various (reliable) sites for information, finding out where pieces of information come from, intentionally seeking contact with people who have different opinions, ...
- not giving away too much on the Internet, for instance not posting personal photographs, etc.
- not clicking on advertisements
- not clicking on links that make exaggerated promises, for example with regard to beauty, health, celebrities, etc. (often advertisements or even viruses)
- acting responsibly when making purchases on the Internet: often criminals only pretend to sell something in order to trick people out of their money or bank data
- caution with instant messenger apps (addiction/constant availability/impossibility to disconnect, cyberbullying, ...)

2   **TIPP**

Once more, it makes sense to connect your answer for task 2 with that for task 1. For instance, you could start by pointing out how difficult it is to find a healthy way of dealing with social media. Advice from others who might know more about the topic could be helpful here as well as in other areas of life. You can branch off to talk about some of these areas in which you have to make your own way. Some examples could be finding the right job, striking a good work-life balance, living abroad or at home, agreeing or disagreeing with a certain political attitude, getting politically engaged, etc. The sample solution shows you how you could progress from task 1 to task 2 and lists some subjects you could elaborate on.

**B:** This discussion <u>leads us perfectly</u> to the second task we were given, namely finding our own way in life. <u>Don't you think</u>?

**A:** <u>Oh yes</u>, <u>absolutely</u>.

**B:** <u>As we have just agreed</u>, there are so many dangers connected to the use of digital media, which really worries me a lot. <u>On the other hand</u>, it is simply not possible to go completely without digital devices, which is why we need to be competent in using them. But how can we become competent without experiencing things for ourselves, which will logically entail making a few mistakes too? <u>What I find really difficult is</u> that many adults seem to expect us to know perfectly well how to handle all the dangers on the Internet and at the same time limit the time we spend online. I mean how can it even be possible to do that? If you search for some information, for instance, you can't know in advance how long it will take to find what you're looking for. Add to that the time that you need to try out different research strategies in order to verify whether something you have found is true or false. So, of course, you will have to spend a lot of time on the Net to become a competent user …

**A:** <u>I couldn't agree more</u>. Very often, adults want us young people to behave like experts and at the same time we are supposed to obediently listen to their advice. How can we strike a perfect balance between independence and a willingness to accept help? <u>I mean</u>, there aren't many adults who are really good role models because their own digital media use is far from perfect. <u>For this reason</u>, it would be best for them to just let us find our own way even if it means that we make mistakes while learning. For me, that is a normal part of life and cannot be avoided. <u>This is not only true for</u> the correct usage of the Internet, but also applies to other areas of life …

### *Possible topics to continue with:*

- finding the right job (possible criteria: salary, passion/interests, job security, …)
- work-life balance
- deciding where and how to live (city vs. country, abroad vs. in one's own country, alone vs. sharing a home with friends or even people you have never met before)
- volunteerism
- how to protect the environment
- political opinions, political engagement

## Material

© *Theresa McCracken/*
*cartoonstock.com*

### Aufgabenstellung

#### I. Monologue

**1** Describe and interpret the cartoon. Explain the critical message the cartoonist wants to convey.

**2** Comment on the cartoon. Elaborate on whether you have ever experienced something similar to the situation shown in the cartoon. Illustrate the role social networks play in your life and that of people around you.

#### II. Dialogue

**1** Discuss what a positive use of mobile devices could look like in your opinion.

**2** "For adolescents, it is not always easy to find their own way." Discuss this statement. Take social networks as a starting point and include other aspects of life as well.

## I. Monologue

1

**TIPP**

As the second exam candidate, you can link what you are going to say to fitting aspects your partner has mentioned in their monologue. In the sample solution, suitable phrases to create these links have been underlined. The sample solution here is rather lengthy in order to give you as much input as possible. Do not worry if you are more concise in your own solution.

- cartoon by Theresa McCracken
- published on cartoonstock.com
- topic: similar to the material given to candidate A, the cartoon criticises some of the effects digital devices can have on our social lives
- two children are sitting in a car being driven by a woman; they are probably on holiday with their mother
- in front of the Grand Canyon, the children are asking their mother to stop the car so they can look at this natural wonder, but their mother is merely taking a photo with her mobile phone while driving past; according to her, the children can look at the Grand Canyon on the photos she is about to post on Facebook
- like in the other cartoon, there are two groups of people in the photo:
  - mother (sitting at the wheel)
  - children (sitting in the rear)
- separation between the two groups underlined by the structure of the Grand Canyon with its deep gorge
- only the mother has a mobile phone, the children do not
- criticism of the mother's behaviour:
  - not interested in her children: does not look at them at all, not even in the rear view mirror; of course, she has to focus on the road but that does not prevent her from taking photos while driving
  - constantly in a rush: does not even take the time to stop and take the photo from outside the car
  - not interested in real-life experiences: does not understand her children's wish to see the Grand Canyon; thinks that looking at Facebook photos is an equally fulfilling experience; apparently does not even regret not being able to see the Grand Canyon other than through the lens of her phone
  - Facebook image seems to be more important to her than her children's wishes and a unique experience
- message: for some, their image on social media is more important than real-life experiences; disinterest in unique experiences, inability to live in the moment and devaluation of people with whom the present moment is shared

**TIPP**

Of course, there are many individual solutions possible here. Depending on the time you took to answer task 1, you can choose a rather lengthy or a rather concise style for task 2. However, make sure that you keep to the assignment and illustrate your points with examples from your own experiences. Try to finish your monologue with a kind of conclusion. In a broader sense, social networks can also include messenger services or AI services.

The following questions could help you collect ideas for your answer:
- Have I ever experienced something similar to the situation shown in the cartoon? Has my behaviour mirrored the mother's or the children's behaviour in the cartoon?
- How have I felt in the above-mentioned situations? How might others around me have felt?
- Have there ever been conflicts between those around me and me about social media?
- What are advantages and disadvantages of social media in my own/my friends' lives?
- What is my opinion on social media making money out of my/its users' personal data?

If you are not active on social media yourself, you can always answer these questions with your friends or acquaintances in mind.

### Have you ever experienced something similar to the situation shown in the cartoon?

- Last weekend, I was at a bar with a few of my friends. One girl didn't really participate in our conversations because she was busy writing messages on her mobile phone. It was sad that she wasn't really "there" and to be honest, I was both irritated and disappointed by her behaviour.
- Last year, during a class trip, I didn't like my friends taking pictures all the time. I would have preferred just being myself and just experiencing the moment instead of feeling under observation all the time.
- Sometimes in restaurants you can see parents who aren't really interested in looking after their children and spending time with them. They prefer just giving them a mobile phone or tablet to look at so that it will keep them occupied.
- Once I participated in a language course abroad. Afterwards, I found a photo of our group online. One of the other participants had posted it on a big social network, with people's names showing up next to their faces. He didn't even bother to ask us for permission beforehand, so I felt really exploited and didn't like that at all.
- In my opinion, it is often young people who use social networks widely whereas their parents or other adults try to prevent them from being too active there. On the other hand, I have also seen parents posting (intimate) pictures of their small children, which doesn't really respect their right to privacy at all.

**What role do social networks play in your life and that of people around you?**

- I often use them to look for information for my lessons at school or for my leisure activities. Last year, I was also active on a social network where you could post short messages. However, I noticed how much time I was spending on this particular site, and I always felt obliged to read and answer other people's messages. So, I decided to delete this particular app.
- My parents often complain about us young people using our mobile phones all the time. However, we can all profit from great ideas we can find on the Internet, such as recipes, ways to repair things, etc. When we use ideas we find online for a project the whole family likes, I do not think the Internet comes at the cost of personal contact and relationships.

## II. Dialogue

*Lösungsvorschläge zum Dialog vgl. Part A*

PRÜFUNGSAUFGABEN

**TEIL I: LISTENING COMPREHENSION**

You will hear each recording twice. After each listening, you will have time to complete your answers.

| Task 1: Film reviews | (6) |
| --- | --- |

You will hear excerpts from six film reviews.
Match each review (1 to 6) with one of the descriptions (A to G). For each review there is only one correct description. There is one more description than you need.
You now have 45 seconds to read the assignment.

| | Description |
| --- | --- |
| **A** | Encounters between rich and poor |
| **B** | The abuse of power and its cover-up |
| **C** | A biography shaped by illegal activities |
| **D** | A comparison of stereotypical lifestyles |
| **E** | A movie star's long history of drug-addiction |
| **F** | The rise and fall of a politician in a corrupt world |
| **G** | A sports contest as a metaphor for the film industry |

| Film review | 1 | 2 | 3 | 4 | 5 | 6 |
| --- | --- | --- | --- | --- | --- | --- |
| Description | | | | | | |

You will hear a podcast about the history of Jim Crow and its connection to the current debate about blackface. While listening, answer the questions below.
You need not write complete sentences.
You now have one minute to read the assignment.

| 1 According to the speaker, what did the Jim Crow laws embody? | • **hate** <br> • |
|---|---|
| 2 What has recently led to a new public discussion about Jim Crow? | |
| 3 What was the purpose of the Jim Crow impersonations in the past? | |
| 4 What was typical of the Jim Crow stage performance? *(Name two aspects.)* | • <br> • |
| 5 Where did Thomas D. Rice get his inspiration for the Jim Crow character from? | |
| 6 What was the consequence of Rice's performance? | |
| 7 According to Daryl Davies, what does the perception of blackface depend on? | |
| 8 Which positive example of the use of blackface does Daryl Davies mention? | |
| 9 Which incident led to TV host Megyn Kelly losing her job? | |

**Annotations**
buffoon:    someone who does silly and amusing things
vernacular:  form of language spoken by a particular group of people

You will hear an interview about the rise of the online service *The Mindful Chef*.
While listening, tick (✓) the correct answer (a, b, c or d). There is only one correct
answer.
You now have two minutes to read the assignment.

**1** *The Mindful Chef* is an online recipe box delivery service that has …

   **a** ☐ moved to London recently.

   **b** ☐ been operating since 2001.

   **c** ☐ received a prestigious prize.

   **d** ☐ run counter to recent trends.

**2** When the partners started their business, they …

   **a** ☐ were desperate for money.

   **b** ☐ were disillusioned with their jobs.

   **c** ☐ had been toying with the idea for a while.

   **d** ☐ had been persuaded by business friends.

**3** According to Giles Humphries, this new start would allow them to …

   **a** ☐ grow closer to their friends.

   **b** ☐ make the most of their skills.

   **c** ☐ feel more satisfied in their job.

   **d** ☐ use their working time more flexibly.

**4** Looking back, Humphries says that coming home late from work they …

   **a** ☐ had no idea what to eat.

   **b** ☐ did not feel stressed at all.

   **c** ☐ were too exhausted to go shopping.

   **d** ☐ were unable to go to their gym classes.

**5** In the summer of 2014, Humphries observed Devon fishermen …

   **a** ☐ preparing traditional sea food.

   **b** ☐ offering their catch door to door.

   **c** ☐ changing the natural food chain.

   **d** ☐ using modern media to sell their fish.

**6** At the beginning of their business, Humphries and his co-founders …

**a** ☐ did the packing themselves.

**b** ☐ used cargo bikes to avoid traffic jams.

**c** ☐ built storage facilities for their ingredients.

**d** ☐ suffered from constantly working night shifts

**7** In their marketing strategy, they relied on …

**a** ☐ UK-wide advertising.

**b** ☐ pictures shown on social media.

**c** ☐ flyers distributed during deliveries.

**d** ☐ cooperation with local newspapers.

**8** Success came after Humphries and his co-founders …

**a** ☐ automated the packaging.

**b** ☐ employed a public relations team.

**c** ☐ hit the half-a-million pounds mark.

**d** ☐ tackled initial problems successfully.

*\* Der Prüfungsteil „Reading Comprehension" wird in Ihrem Abitur nicht abgeprüft und wurde deshalb hier weggelassen.*

| Text | Us vs Them: the Sinister Techniques of "Othering" – and How to Avoid Them |

1 We are in the midst of a rapidly changing world. More than 300 million people are currently living outside their homelands. Ethno-nationalism is on the rise – from the Rohingya people forced out of Myanmar in what many are calling the world's latest genocide, to neo-Nazis marching through the streets of Charlottesville, Virginia, in an
5 action President Trump pointedly refused to condemn.

Humans can only process a limited amount of change in a short period of time without experiencing anxiety. It's a natural human reaction – but how we respond to that anxiety is social. When societies experience big and rapid change, a frequent response is for people to narrowly define who qualifies as a full member of society – a process
10 I call "Othering". An alternative response is seeing the change in demographics as positive, and regarding the apparent other as enhancing our life and who we are. This is what I refer to as "belonging and bridging". Othering is not about liking or disliking someone. It is based on the conscious or unconscious assumption that a certain identified group poses a threat to the favoured group. It is largely driven by politicians and
15 the media, as opposed to personal contact. Overwhelmingly, people don't "know" those that they are Othering.

So while today's global anxiety has been precipitated by globalisation, technology and a changing economy, demographics play a crucial role in the process of Othering. The attributes of who gets defined as Other differ from place to place, and can be based
20 upon race, religion, nationality or language. It is not these attributes themselves that are the problem, of course, but how they are made salient, and how they are manipulated. I am therefore particularly concerned with how Othering shows up in today's power structures: how it is used to divide and dehumanise groups, and capture and reshape government and institutions. For society's leaders and culture play an over-
25 sized role in helping us make sense of change – and so greatly affect our responses to anxiety.

In the United States, politicians used to engage in what scholar Ian Haney-Lopez calls "dog whistles" – they could make references to Others but only in a coded way; never saying "those Mexicans" or "those Muslims", for example. President Trump,
30 however, has opened a space where people are emboldened to be more explicit. We now have not only our nation's leadership but many of our information networks amplifying these explicit calls to exclude and dehumanise. The rhetoric and language coming from Trump has begun to both define and normalise Othering. This is a threat to all the things we value. When Mexicans can be called "rapists and drug dealers" in
35 direct contradiction to the facts, it becomes a much easier step to call for their deportation, and for a literal wall to divide us. The language being used by many national

leaders not only activates people's anxiety and fear around a perceived Other, it creates new processes of exclusion and dehumanisation.

While it is common to focus only on economic changes to explain the rise of right-
40 wing nationalists and Othering, the loss of economic power is not the only thing stir-
ring anxiety around the globe. […] Conservative elites know how to strategically create and use fear of a perceived Other, by organising and manufacturing fear. When
Nixon began using the term "law and order", his popularity was cemented among a
certain base because he was appealing to a specific kind of conservative white fear:
45 not primarily about jobs, but rather the changing social order. This was not precipitated
by a specific economic downturn, yet the outcome of Nixon's strategy was the securing
of an economy rigged for the rich. People don't just figure out on their own that col-
lectively they need to be afraid of another group. Leadership plays a critical role. Often
people who have been living with one another for years are made to feel suddenly that
50 those differences have become threatening.

The recent rhetoric around people who are undocumented in the US, many of whom
have lived here for their whole lives, has created a culture of fear for millions, has
demonised children, and has created suspicion and anger in communities where none
had existed before. […] The stories we tell, and live, are not about facts but our values,
55 fears and hopes – all of which, to a certain degree, are malleable. Our narratives don't
just reflect them, they also shape them. While anxiety about change is natural, Othering
is not. Othering is socially and culturally constructed.

So how do we respond to our collective anxiety today? Either we "bridge", reaching
across to other groups and towards our inherent, shared humanity and connection,
60 while recognising that we have differences; or we "break", pulling away from other
groups and making it easier to tell and believe false stories of "us vs them", then supporting practices that dehumanise the "them". Part of the solution to Othering must
come from the stories we tell. As the world undergoes profound shifts, how do we
build true societies of belonging? […] If we are to combat the rising tide of extremism
65 across the globe, we must actively create bridges across difference, and resist strategic
exploitation of our collective anxiety. For when we bridge, we not only open up to
others, we also open up to change in ourselves – and actively participate in co-creating
a society to which we can all belong. The opposite of Othering is not "saming", it is
belonging. And belonging does not insist that we are all the same. It means we recog-
70 nise and celebrate our differences, in a society where "we the people" includes all the
people.                                                                 *938 words*

*Powell, John A., "Us vs Them: the Sinister Techniques of 'Othering' – and How to Avoid Them",*
*theguardian.com, November 8, 2017, accessed on July 17, 2020, slightly adapted,*
*Copyright Guardian News & Media Ltd 2021*

**Annotations**
line 43:   Nixon: Richard Nixon, Republican president (1969–1974)
line 59:   humanity: (here) the state of being human rather than an animal or a machine

1   "… we 'bridge', reaching across to other groups and towards our inherent, shared
    humanity and connection, while recognising that we have differences;" (ll. 58–60)

    Briefly explain the quote in the context of the article and analyse what enables Sue
    to "bridge" as well as how she "bridges" in *Gran Torino*.

Choose *one* of the following:

**2a**  In *Crooked Letter, Crooked Letter,* Silas experiences different kinds of loss.
    Assess his ways of dealing with them.

**or**

**2b**  "The greatest nations are defined by how they treat their weakest inhabitants."

*(2010) © Jorge Ramos, Mexican-American journalist*

Explain Ramos's statement and discuss whether, according to his definition, the
US is a great nation in the 21st century.

## Lösungsvorschlag

 **TEIL I: LISTENING COMPREHENSION**

| **Transcript 1** | Film reviews |

**1** It's about, you know, Frank Sheeran, the, the main character who is a real man and him looking back at his life of crime. And it says so much, I think, about the futility of crime, and just what happens when you are sort of the middleman doing everyone's dirty work, and there is no one left to look after you at the end, and your family has turned on you and, you know, you have just countless numbers of people's blood on your hands.

**2** I know it can also seem a little obvious in some ways. I felt it was beautiful to see it kind of worked through in this meta way in this film, which, why using the racing world as its, as its subject, this really is, it seems to me, about the kind of very, very, working of the movie business now, especially when you deal with big studios.

**3** This is a movie that is made in South Korea, and has had a level of impact that Korean films typically do not in the United States and in other countries. And this is a movie that puts the haves and have-nots front and center, but in ways that are really subversive and that are not banal or kind of expected. I mean this is a really surprising movie. I think it's the best of a number of movies that have taken on class this year.

**4** I felt this movie had the most fun with it and did a lot with it. Because that's one of the central questions as one character wants to move to L.A. and the other has wanted to stay in New York. And so there is theater and there's TV and it's, you know, people put on sunglasses as soon as they are in L.A. and then the Brooklyn people all have, like, lattes. And this is an interesting way that it plays with that.

**5** But it's the rigorous understatement of the assistant that makes it so powerful in its vision of how easily the Harvey Weinsteins of the world could exploit their absolute authority for years with little fear of consequence. Moment by moment, it pulls us into a world where predatory behavior is concealed behind closed doors and the silence of a hushed workplace becomes its own kind of complicity.

**6** *Judy* begins with one of several flashbacks to the teenage Garland on the set of *The Wizard of Oz* showing us how the industry created and destroyed her in the same breath. Her body and image are ruthlessly controlled by the powerful MGM studio head Louis B. Mayer, who puts her on a strict diet and gives her barbiturates and amphetamines, setting in motion the substance abuse problem that she will struggle with for the rest of her life.

In this task you will hear short fragments or snippets of film reviews. These fragments have to be matched with the respective descriptions. In order to match the fragments and definitions correctly, it is essential for you to find signal words and know their synonyms. That is why you should learn word families or lexical fields with umbrella terms. This will enable you to find the necessary information fast.

- **1 – C:** There are some signal words in the description (**C**) which show you that the film is a biography and that it is about illegal activities: in the film review the name of the protagonist is mentioned (which may suggest a biographical film), but expressions like "life of crime" (l. 2), "futility of crime" (ll. 2/3), "dirty work" (l. 4) and "people's blood on your hands" (ll. 5/6) also indicate that the film is about illegal activities. That is why **E** and **F** cannot match as the definition is about more than corruption or drug abuse.
- **2 – G:** In the audio, "racing world" (ll. 8/9) and "big studios" (l. 10) are mentioned, which belong to the same word families as the terms "sports contest" and "film industry" in description **G**.
- **3 – A:** The synonyms here are "rich and poor" (in description **A**) and "haves and have-nots" in the audio fragment (l. 13).
- **4 – D:** Here you need to notice that the audio snippet is built as a comparison (see description **D**): the speaker talks about "one character [...] and the other", "theater and [...] TV", "people [...] in L.A., and then the Brooklyn people" (ll. 17–19). There are also "stereotypical lifestyles" (**D**) mentioned: "people put on sunglasses [...] in L.A." and "Brooklyn people all have, like, lattes" (ll. 18–20).
- **5 – B:** General knowledge can be of help here: the audio names Harvey Weinstein, who exploited his position as a movie producer and was charged with sexual abuse, and the definition also mentions an "abuse of power" (**B**). There are also synonyms for "abuse of power" and "its cover-up" in the audio: "exploit their absolute authority" (ll. 22/23) and "predatory behavior [which] is concealed behind closed doors" (l. 24), as well as "silence" (l. 24) and "complicity" (l. 25). Note that "cover-up" is different from "corruption", which is why **F** is not an option here.
- **6 – E:** General knowledge can help you here too: the audio mentions the actress Judy Garland, who played Dorothy in the movie *The Wizard of Oz*. This points to definition **E**, which refers to a "movie star". The term "drug-addiction" in the definition corresponds to the mentioning of "barbiturates and amphetamines" (ll. 29/30) in the audio as well as to a "substance abuse problem" (l. 30).

| Film review | 1 | 2 | 3 | 4 | 5 | 6 |
|---|---|---|---|---|---|---|
| Description | C | G | A | D | B | E |

## Transcript 2    The History of Jim Crow and Blackface

1  Jim Crow, you've no doubt heard this name before. It's a name that has stood for hate
and for the laws, the Jim Crow laws, that made racial segregation in the South legal
until the Civil Rights Movement in the 1960s. Now that ugly name has re-emerged in
the American vernacular thanks to the recent political scandals unfolding in Virginia,
5  where both the governor and attorney general have admitted to wearing blackface in
their past. "I took responsibility for content that appeared on my page in the Eastern
Virginia Medical School yearbook. That was clearly racist and offensive."

So, what's the connection between Jim Crow and blackface? Well, back in the
1830s Jim Crow wasn't yet a symbol of inequality. He was a fictional character in
10  minstrel shows who, to entertain his audiences, danced like a buffoon and spoke with
an exaggerated imitation of Black slave vernacular. Intended to be comedic, minstrel
shows were first performed in New York with White actors who wore tattered clothing
and used shoe polish to blacken their faces, according to the Smithsonian's National
Museum of African American History and Culture. While society now considers don-
15  ning blackface as clearly racist, according to historians, the practice, especially on
stage, was celebrated by Whites in the South following the Civil War.

Who was behind Jim Crow? A man, a White man, named Thomas Dartmouth Rice.
Rice was born in 1808 in New York. As a teenager he began travelling the country as an
actor. According to a University of South Florida history of minstrel shows, Rice was a
20  dancer and a singer who drew from his observations of Blacks in the South to create an
extremely exaggerated and stereotypical Black buffoon. While he wasn't the first White
comic to perform in blackface, Rice was the most popular of his time and as a result
the character of Jim Crow spread, becoming a common stage persona. The big lips, the
lack of education, the poor clothing, that's how Daryl Davies, a Black blues musician
25  who has studied these shows, described these minstrel characters in an interview.

It wasn't about trying to look Black, he said, but trying to look Black in a way that
portrays Blacks negatively. Davies has long argued that context is key when judging
the use of blackface; in the 1900s, for example, White artists such as Al Jolson painted
their faces as they performed ragtime and blues music pioneered by African Ameri-
30  cans. Davies credits Jolson with spreading Black music to white audiences and advocating for Black artists.

In the internet age, social media has fueled furors over blackface. "You get in trouble if you are a White person who puts on blackface for Halloween or a Black person
who puts on whiteface for Halloween, like … when I was a kid, that was okay as long
35  as you were dressing up as a character."

Last year, talk show host Megyn Kelly defended blackface on the air. Though Kelly
was already struggling with poor ratings, the episode and the resulting fury led to her
ouster.

"Breaking news about another high-ranking state-wide official who finds himself
40  embroiled in a blackface photo controversy." Now here the country is again, talking
about blackface, about minstrel shows, about Jim Crow.

*based on: https://www.washingtonpost.com/history/2019/02/02/northams-ugly-yearbook-photo-racist-origins-blackface/*

The text is spoken very fast, so knowledge of American history and society is useful for you to be able to find the solutions. Before listening, also highlight signal words which may give you a hint as to where you can find the answers to the questions. These signal words are marked in bold below – in the tips the words and phrases they refer to are underlined.

1 "Jim Crow [...] stood for hate [...] the Jim Crow laws, that made racial segregation in the South legal" (ll. 1/2); "symbol of inequality" (l. 9)

2 The signal words "[n]ow", "re-emerged" and "recent" can guide you here: "Now that ugly name has re-emerged [...] thanks to the recent political scandals [...] where both the governor and attorney general have admitted to wearing blackface in their past" (ll. 3–6).

3 Here the signal word for "impersonations" can be "fictional character" (l. 9): "He was a fictional character [...] who, to entertain his audiences, [...]" (ll. 9/10).

4 There are several aspects you can mention: "He [...] danced like a buffoon and spoke with an exaggerated imitation of Black slave vernacular. [...] White actors [...] wore tattered clothing and used shoe polish to blacken their faces" (ll. 9–13).

5 "who drew from his observations of Blacks in the South to create an extremely exaggerated and stereotypical Black buffoon" (ll. 20/21)

6 "as a result the character of Jim Crow spread, becoming a common stage persona" (ll. 22/23)

7 "Davies has long argued that context is key when judging the use of blackface" (ll. 27/28)

8 "White artists such as Al Jolson painted their faces as they performed ragtime and blues music pioneered by African Americans. Davies credits Jolson with spreading Black music to white audiences and advocating for Black artists." (ll. 28–31)

9 "talk show host Megyn Kelly defended blackface on the air" (l. 36)

| | |
|---|---|
| 1 According to the speaker, what did the **Jim Crow laws** **embody**? | • **hate**<br>• (legal racial) segregation / (symbol of) racial inequality |
| 2 What has **recently** led to a **new** public discussion about Jim Crow? | two high-ranking politicians admitted to wearing blackface in the past / scandal in Virginia about White politicians having worn blackface |
| 3 What was the purpose of the Jim Crow **impersonations** in the past? | to ridicule / to denigrate Black[1] people for entertainment / entertain the audience / a White audience |

1 The words "Black" and "White" are capitalised to signal that they are not natural categories but social ones (for more background information on this topic see, for example https://www.theatlantic.com/ideas/archive/2020/06/time-to-capitalize-blackand-white/613159/).

| | | |
|---|---|---|
| **4** What was **typical** of the Jim Crow stage performance? *(Name two aspects.)* | *zwei aus:* <br> • danced like a buffoon <br> • spoke with an exaggerated Black accent <br> • wore tattered clothes <br> • White people used black shoe polish to appear Black | |
| **5** Where did Thomas D. Rice get his **inspiration** for the Jim Crow character from? | from his observations of Black people (in the South) | |
| **6** What was the **consequence** of Rice's performance? | popularised the Jim Crow character / made Jim Crow a common stage persona | |
| **7** According to Daryl Davies, what does the **perception** of blackface depend on? | on the context / on the time / on the person's intention for wearing blackface | |
| **8** Which **positive example** of the use of blackface does Daryl Davies mention? | (White artists tried) to advocate Black musicians and their music | |
| **9** Which incident led to TV host **Megyn Kelly** losing her job? | she defended the use of blackface | |

## Transcript 3   *The Mindful Chef*

1 **Host:** If you're self-employed, you're in good company. The number of people in self-employment has been rising steadily since 2001. Natalie Donovan visited *The Mindful Chef.* It's an online recipe box delivery service and it's almost five years old and it's just been named "London & South East Start-up of the Year" in the
5 Great British Entrepreneur Awards. Co-founder Giles Humphries, now at the ripe old age of 33, told Natalie how it's been.

**Humphries:** Here's myself and two friends and we were working in different industries, we always had ideas and throwing ideas round to each other, but basically, I think we all enjoyed our jobs, but we realised that you can, a lot easier than before, start
10 your own business. Actually, the biggest thought was "What's the worst that could happen?"

**Donovan:** Did you feel like your, the jobs that you were doing, weren't going in the direction that you wanted to go, and that was why you decided to set back, or was it more that you had a passion about cooking and recipe boxes?

15 **Humphries:** I think it was twofold really. One, we'd always had a bit of a passion to start something ourselves and we'd chat about a load of ideas over the years. And two, just looking at other friends, who had taken the plunge, taken their skills they'd honed over a few years in bigger businesses and using them to grow and develop their own businesses and I thought, hm, that's interesting cause you've got a lot
20 more control over your lifestyle and your working hours. So, that's kind of what

formed the initial ideas. And then we've, we've all got a real interest in health and wellness, all of us are sportsmen and we all, actually it was kind of a personal pain point, was coming home late, working long hours in a big company and then getting home and just being a bit too tired to think or plan and shop for the right stuff, even
25 though we knew what we should eat.

**Donovan:** And how lang did it take you to come from the idea to actually quitting your job and setting up on your own?

**Humphries:** Probably about six months. We moved pretty quickly. It was in the summer of 2014, we were on a fishing boat, just helping out a friend actually, it was in the
30 summer holidays, we had a week back down in Devon – we all grew up in Devon together. We saw the fish they were landing, and they were bringing it back in and they'd text the local villagers and they said, "We've got, you know, codling etc." and the villagers'd come down and get this fresh fish. And we, the three of us, were just chatting and said: "This is amazing, this is how the food chain should be". So
35 this, that was one kind of lightbulb moment. And then the discussions developed from there and it was, I quit my job pretty quickly, I was the first to go and it was December 2014.

**Donovan:** The business is UK-wide now. Did you know that when you started that that's what you were aiming for or did you start small?

40 **Humphries:** Best piece of advice I always say is "always start small". We had a hunch that maybe *Citygoers* would be keen on the product, but we purely did that because we were driving our own little Del Boy trotter van round …

**Donovan:** So, you were delivering the boxes …

**Humphries:** So we were delivering, yeah, we were going to the warehouse at 7 a.m.,
45 pack them till about 5 p.m. and then deliver. We'd be stuck in traffic coming back through London, Myles would be on the Instagram …

**Donovan:** … hoping you were getting a good review and a like.

**Humphries:** Yeah, yeah, yeah, going on review sites, seeing if we got any reviews, posting pictures. We started small but then we really quickly realised, once you've
50 nailed that, you got it right, you've ironed out problems – and there were plenty of them – then you can grow slightly bigger, and when we got to that level, you know, we're now doing about, just shy of half a million ingredients through our warehouse every week, but at the same time you have targets to hit and you are, you're trying to grow this business focusing on reaching quite large numbers of customers now,
55 so, you definitely have more of a life, you know, we're not doing the packing every weekend, there's a huge team who do a phenomenal job, but the challenge is in different areas.

*http://www.bbc.co.uk/sounds/play/p07xl6h5*

1 "it's just been named 'London & South East Start-up of the Year' in the Great British Entrepreneur Awards" (ll. 4/5)
   The name of the prize and also the word "Awards" give you hints here.
2 "we always had ideas and throwing ideas round to each other" (l. 8)
   "[T]hrowing ideas round to each other" is like "playing with ideas" and leads you to "toying with the idea" (**c**). Even if you do not know those expressions, you can find the similarity here.
3 "more control over your lifestyle and your working hours" (l. 20)
   Don't get confused by buzzwords such as "more satisfied in their job" (**c**) but listen closely to what the new job would enable them to do.
4 "kind of a personal pain point, was <u>coming home late, working long hours</u> in a big company and then getting home and just being <u>a bit too tired to</u> think or plan and <u>shop</u> for the right stuff, <u>even though we knew what we should eat</u>" (ll. 22–25)
   "Coming home late" is also mentioned in the audio, which gives you a hint that you should now listen closely.
5 "fish […] they were bringing it back in and <u>they'd text the local villagers</u>" (ll. 31/32)
   The signal word "fish" should make you listen closely here; the expression "text the local villagers" indicates that the fishermen use modern media.
6 "we were going to the warehouse at 7 a.m., <u>pack</u> them till about 5 p.m. and then deliver" (ll. 44/45)
   Listen closely – the word "pack" will give you a hint regarding the correct solution. Don't be distracted by buzzwords such as "traffic".
7 "going on review sites, seeing if we got any reviews, <u>posting pictures</u>" (ll. 48/49)
   The phrase "posting pictures" indicates the correct solution. The mentioning of "Instagram" (l. 46) and getting reviews and likes (cf. l. 47) also points towards social media rather than other forms of advertising.
8 "We started small but then we really quickly realised, once <u>you've nailed that</u>, you <u>got it right</u>, you've <u>ironed out problems</u> – and there were plenty of them – then you can grow slightly bigger" (ll. 49–51)
   The repetition of phrases that are used in the context of "tackling something" should be of help here.

1 *The Mindful Chef* is an online recipe box delivery service that has …
   c ☑ received a prestigious prize.

2 When the partners started their business, they …
   c ☑ had been toying with the idea for a while.

3 According to Giles Humphries, this new start would allow them to …
   d ☑ use their working time more flexibly.

**4** Looking back, Humphries says that coming home late from work they …

   **c** ☑ were too exhausted to go shopping.

**5** In the summer of 2014, Humphries observed Devon fishermen …

   **d** ☑ using modern media to sell their fish.

**6** At the beginning of their business, Humphries and his co-founders …

   **a** ☑ did the packing themselves.

**7** In their marketing strategy, they relied on …

   **b** ☑ pictures shown on social media.

**8** Success came after Humphries and his co-founders …

   **d** ☑ tackled initial problems successfully.

| Teil III: Analysis

1 **TIPP**

The analysis task is twofold. In a first step, you must explain what "bridging" means in the context of the article and in a second step, you need to apply the concept to the character of Sue in *Gran Torino*. Then analyse what personal qualities she has that enable her to "bridge".

In the article, "bridging" is defined in contrast to what the author calls "Othering". Thus, it should be explained along those lines.

When you apply the concept of bridging to Sue, you should mention what enables her to bridge – her background, her knowledge and her character – and connect these aspects to examples from the film, in which she reaches out to Walt and builds a relationship (across ethnic lines) with him.

End your analysis with a conclusion in which you briefly sum up your points. You could also point out how Sue is the driving force behind Walt's and Thao's friendship, which forms the basis of the film's plot.

You could include the following points in your answer:

**Part I: "bridging" in the article**
- "bridging" in contrast to "Othering"
- important aspects of bridging: reaching out to others, being aware of differences but welcoming them, being open to change, finding a common basis in "shared humanity"

**Part II: Sue's "bridging" in *Gran Torino***
- "bridging": Sue's contact with Walt who is her opposite in many ways: elderly White American male vs. young Hmong female
- description of Sue's background, knowledge and skills
  - "at home" in two cultures, bilingual, well-educated, close to her family, but also has friendships outside Hmong culture (boyfriend Trey)
  - exemplary scenes: Sue explaining Hmong culture and history to Walt, Sue inviting Walt to family celebration and making him feel at home there
- description of Sue's character: self-confidence, intelligence, humour, empathy, openness

**Conclusion:** Sue's behaviour as a perfect example of "bridging"

John A. Powell's article "Us vs Them: the Sinister Techniques of 'Othering' – and How to Avoid Them", published in *The Guardian* in November 2017, talks about how societies react to sudden changes and to the anxieties these changes cause. With a special focus on American society, Powell juxtaposes what he calls "Othering" – the rhetorical technique of dehumanising certain groups (cf. l. 23) and depicting them as a threat to the already established "ingroup" (cf. ll. 13/14) – and the contrary approach of "bridging".

Part 1: "bridging" in the article
contrast: "Othering"

Unlike "Othering", which is what populist politicians do to divide society in order to secure their own leadership, "bridging" is the attempt to overcome divisions in order to build a more inclusive society. "Bridging" is based on the idea that, besides their differences, all human beings have some fundamental things in common, something the quote calls an "inherent, shared humanity" (l. 59). In other words, people who "bridge" initiate contacts with people of different cultural and ethnic origins and try to overcome the trenches drawn by right-wing populists (cf. ll. 58/59). According to Powell, "bridging" does not mean "saming" (cf. l. 68). People who "bridge" are aware of the differences between groups, but they acknowledge them and see them as something positive, as an enrichment (cf. ll. 10/11, 69/70). They are open to change and cooperate in creating a society in which everyone can develop a sense of belonging (cf. ll. 66–68).

definition of "bridging"

In Clint Eastwood's *Gran Torino*, Sue is the character that builds bridges between herself and her family and their neighbour Walt, who in so many ways is her opposite: she is of Hmong origin, he is Polish-American; she is a young open-minded female, he is an old, narrow-minded male who, at the beginning of the film, seems to be hardened in his chauvinism and his contempt of everything Asian. That he turns into a friend of the Hmong family next door and a hero of the Hmong neighbourhood is mainly due to Sue's ability to overcome the initially deep gap between them. What enables her to do so?

Part 2: Sue's "bridging" in *Gran Torino*
Sue's contact with Walt, her "opposite"

Sue is a second-generation immigrant who has grown up with the American culture, goes to college and has a White American boyfriend. Still, she lives the Hmong culture at home and knows about their traditions and history. She speaks both languages, English and Hmong, which is why she can interpret the conversations when Walt meets her older family members, thus providing a communicative basis. In short, one can say that she has the best of both worlds and navigates between them more or less seamlessly. After the initial contact with Walt is established, her knowledge of Hmong and American culture enables her to explain the Hmong traditions to him while also taking into account and understanding his needs. One scene in which this becomes clear is the family celebration to which she invites Walt. She is not put off by his rude behaviour which is

Sue's background, knowledge and skills

partly due to his ignorance and insecurity in such a foreign environment, but patiently manages to make him feel welcome and even gradually change his mind, for instance towards the shaman, whose words he truly takes to heart.

Apart from the knowledge she acquired growing up in two cultures which are both native to her, it is also her character that makes her Walt's perfect counterpart. She is self-confident, persistent and witty. So, she is not intimidated by Walt's initial rudeness but stands her ground. Her charm and her sense of humour draw him into conversations full of irony on both sides. She challenges his wit and banters with him in a way that he only knows from his male White friends. Furthermore, she also recognises Walt's loneliness. She includes him in her family and also lays the ground for the friendship between Thao and Walt by explaining to Walt why Thao behaves in such a seemingly disrespectful way. Finally, her openness breaks through Walt's armour and promotes his willingness to support Thao's attempts to become a respected member of American society. Sue's character

To sum up, it is Sue's background of two cultures as well as her personality that enable her to "bridge". It is her initiative that finally brings about a mutual understanding between Walt and his Hmong neighbours. More specifically, it is Sue who helps Walt and Thao to develop trust in each other and a deep sense of belonging, cumulating in Walt's self-sacrifice and Thao's finding a home in American society. Conclusion

*(745 words)*

## Teil III: Composition

**2a** **TIPP**

For your assessment, you must consider several aspects. The task talks about "different kinds of loss", which means that you are to name several categories where Silas loses something. Illustrate these with examples from the novel. In a second step, you should describe in which way these losses affect Silas and how he deals with them. Finally, you are asked to assess his behaviour. It makes sense to consider his behaviour from a psychological as well as a moral point of view, because Silas's experiences have a negative effect on his psyche as well as on the way he treats the people around him. It seems reasonable to combine all three steps, a description of the kind of loss Silas experiences, his resulting behaviour and the assessment thereof, for each kind of loss in a separate paragraph.

In your conclusion, you can sum up your findings. You could also use the open ending of the novel to give an outlook on how Silas seems to finally overcome his immaturity and find a better way of dealing with the losses he experienced.

You could structure your text in the following way:

**Introduction:** the experience of losses in Silas's youth has had an impact on his personality

**Main part:** the different kinds of losses in Silas's life, how he deals with them and how his behaviour can be assessed
- loss of home and security: Silas must leave Chicago where he felt he belonged
  - reaction: Silas's desperation and humiliation culminate in him running away, conflict with his mother
  - assessment: loss of security traumatising for an adolescent, could explain his later troubles with stable relationships
- loss of friendship: forced fight between Larry and Silas and "nigger" insult end the boys' friendship
  - reaction: Silas breaks with Larry, overcompensation with his popularity due to baseball talent
  - assessment: Silas's fury understandable because of widespread racism and the hurt connected with it, however, Silas's refusal to mend things with Larry hurting both boys/men
- loss of honesty: Silas does not own up to having been with Cindy the night she disappears, destroying Larry's life
  - reaction: running away from his guilt, even Silas himself seems to realise at some point that he has acted irresponsibly and selfishly
  - assessment:
    - Silas's initial reaction understandable (feeling of being owed his baseball career and fear of being attacked for his mixed-race relationship)
    - but morally wrong and an immature reaction for an adult to keep his silence

**Conclusion:** outlook on Silas's character development

Silas, one of the two protagonists in *Crooked Letter, Crooked Letter*, has to deal with loss in different forms from a very early age. These experiences in his childhood and adolescence have a deep impact on his development, and in a way, even form his character as an adult. While many of his initial reactions to the losses he experiences might be understandable, the ending of the novel makes it clear that his way of dealing with the past needs to improve. **Introduction**

The first possibly traumatising loss for Silas is the loss of his childhood home in Chicago. He used to live in an all-Black neighbourhood where he felt he belonged. The sudden arrest of his mother's **Main part: loss of home and security** boyfriend Oliver and their journey to the South, which almost seems like an escape, end this phase of relative security in Silas's life.

Silas is too young to really understand what is going on and is even more disturbed by the lack of a reasonable explanation from his mother for this decision to go to a place completely foreign to him. On the journey, Silas even suspects that because of their desperate situation, his mother might have to prostitute herself simply to get them a lift, and he snaps: he tries to run away, hiding in a dark corner, only to be robbed by two youths. On top of everything else, this also leaves a crack in Silas's relationship with his mother, who goes so far as to ask her son to sit in another booth in the restaurant because she is so disappointed in him. reaction

Naturally, this loss of his home, their possessions and the security of a hitherto unquestioned bond between mother and son traumatises him. Maybe his later tendency to avoid any really intimate relationships is a result of that experience. assessment

In Chabot, the first friend Silas makes is Larry, who helps him to regain some sense of belonging by roaming the wilderness with him, teaching Silas how to use a gun and a fishing tackle. Even though their friendship is rather unbalanced, because Larry is far more interested in it than Silas, it comes as another deeply felt loss for Silas when Carl Ott forces the two boys to fight for his gun and puts their friendship to an end. Again, this loss is combined with a psychological injury and humiliation: during their fight, Larry, who is physically inferior and sees no chance to defend himself, insults Silas with the "n-word", which provokes Silas to hit him even harder. loss of friendship

After the fight, Silas breaks with Larry completely. His focus on his blossoming baseball career and the friends he makes in that environment can be seen as on overcompensation for his earlier losses and as a desperate attempt to belong. reaction

On the one hand, Silas's fury is completely understandable. As an African American boy, who has grown up in poverty, he must feel like he is always at the receiving end of racism and injustice. Consequently, he thinks that the privileged "mummy's boy" Larry does not deserve his friendship any longer. However, in the further course of the novel, Silas's refusal to mend things with Larry has catastrophic consequences and deeply hurts both of them. assessment

These catastrophic consequences become apparent when Silas decides not to tell the truth about the night Cindy disappears. He does not exonerate Larry and thereby factually destroys Larry's and his family's life. Furthermore, he obstructs the police investigation and the true murderer can never be brought to justice. Even later on, when he is back in Chabot, he keeps his silence and only breaks it reluctantly when another girl is missing and Larry is again the main suspect. loss of honesty

Silas's immediate reaction shows that he himself seems to realise that he has now crossed a line and has lost something very important, namely his integrity: he leaves Chabot for university and returns as seldom as possible. In other words, he is running away from his guilt. reaction

For some time, Silas's feeling of being owed his baseball career and his not wanting to risk his one chance at success might seem understandable. The way he would probably be attacked for his mixed-race relationship with Cindy would be outrageous, which is why he can certainly be seen as a victim of a racist system rather than the guilty party for not telling the truth. Yet, while his silence over all those years might not make him guilty in a legal sense, his complete disregard for Larry's undeserved ostracism can certainly be described as an utter moral failure. What could be excused as an instinctive reaction in a child shunning punishment must be seen as irresponsible and morally wrong in an adult. assessment

Silas experiences different kinds of loss – the loss of his childhood home, the loss of a friend and finally the loss of his honesty. As a child and adolescent, he fails to find an adequate way of dealing with these experiences. He tries to run away and represses his feelings of bereavement and shame. He also ignores the fact that he might share a part of the responsibility in some of his losses. Silas ends up as quite a sociable and likeable person and as the respected constable of Chabot, but he remains a somewhat immature character. Only in the end, when he tells the police that Larry had nothing to do with Cindy's disappearance and when he tries to make amends for what he did, does he seem to have found a more mature way of dealing with the complex feelings of loss and mortification that have built up over the course of his life. *(939 words)* **Conclusion**

**2b** **TIPP**

In a first step, you must explain Ramos's statement. So, have a close look at each of the terms he uses and say what they mean or what they refer to.

In a second step, you are to discuss whether Ramos's definition can be applied to the US. If you are to discuss a thesis, it is important to name arguments for as well as against it and to come to a convincing conclusion.

The following structure and arguments have been used in this solution:

**Introduction:** explanation of quote

**Main part 1:** different definitions of greatness
– greatness as power
– greatness from a "moral" perspective

"The greatest nations are defined by how they treat their weakest inhabitants." This statement by the Mexican-American journalist Jorge Ramos, which he made in 2010, questions traditional concepts of a "great nation" by putting the emphasis on solidarity and not on superiority.

**Introduction**

Ideas of "greatness" in a nation will always vary because they depend on personal opinions and political attitudes. However, people who talk about great nations more often than not think of power. The greatest nations are those who have considerable military strength or are admired for their economic potency.

**Main part 1:** different definitions of "greatness"

From another viewpoint, however, a nation could also be called "great" because it has a fair political system, or it is exemplary and honourable in respect to the values it endorses. It is within this framework that Ramos seems to define "greatness". For him, it is important that those people that are weak in a socio-economic, political or legal sense, for instance unemployed people, members of minorities, people with disability, or also children, are treated in a fair way. Interestingly, Ramos does not speak of the weakest citizens, but of the weakest inhabitants, which means that he also includes people like undocumented immigrants among the groups who need solidarity and support from a nation that wants to be considered as great.

Is the USA a great nation in this sense? Since the American Revolution, the country has seen itself as a nation that is superior to others because its founding was based on ideas like liberty and equality before the law as well as equal opportunities for everyone. The US traditionally welcomed every immigrant, granting a free pursuit of happiness to those who came to its shore. For example, the engraving on the Statue of Liberty reads, "Give me your tired, your poor", thereby explicitly addressing the poorest and weakest people and promising them hope.

**Main part 2:** discussion of whether the USA is a "great nation"

In the course of its history, however, the political reality in the US has not always lived up to these ideals of the Founding Fathers and the promises of the American Dream, and it is a legitimate question to ask if the US is still a great nation as Ramos defined it. Particularly in the light of Donald Trump's presidency, who claimed to "make America great again", it has become obvious that there are conflicting ideas as to what makes a nation truly great. Does the US still practise solidarity with the weak and support those that cannot help themselves?

The US has a long history of philanthropists and benefactors whose donations helped many poor Americans to attend good schools through scholarships or to cover their basic needs. In order to give people who belong to a minority group better chances of getting a good education or a living, the US has furthermore introduced the principle of "affirmative action".

Besides these forms of legal and financial support, many political movements have arisen in the USA that fought for equality and civil rights for everyone, especially for those whose voices are too weak to be heard. The latest example of such a movement is "Black Lives Matter", which condemns police violence against African Americans and has developed into a worldwide phenomenon. In a way, the US is a great nation, because it has always been the birthplace of political movements that have become the model for other nations around the world.

However, the kind of greatness that Trump tried to reinstall seems to go in the opposite direction. Despite generous donations, the US does not provide sufficient social security for its citizens: Particularly among conservative political groups, the belief is widespread that a governmentally organised health care system or unemployment benefits contradict ideas of freedom and self-determination. Coupled with very high fees for universities, this results in only the rich being able to afford the luxury of a good education, thereby securing the best jobs and becoming even richer, whereas others are caught in a vicious circle of poverty from which it is almost impossible to break free.

There is still a lot of financial, legal and political inequality, especially along ethnic lines. Programmes, such as "affirmative action", often seem like nothing more than lip service and the mere necessity of a movement like "Black Lives Matter" highlights the above-mentioned imbalances. Furthermore, Trump and other conservative politicians have always tried to reverse or block measures, such as DACA, which offer support to one of the weakest groups in society that is especially worthy of protection, namely the children of illegal immigrant families. In this light, the US cannot be described as ranking among the greatest nations as Ramos defines them.

A final verdict can only be an ambivalent one. The US has a tradition
of welcoming and supporting the weakest as well as a tradition of
treating them badly. With Joe Biden's new administration, it seems
as if the support of the weakest has become more popular again.
Maybe Biden and those forces in American society that support him
will make America great again – in Jorge Ramos's sense.

*(833 words)*

TEIL I: LISTENING COMPREHENSION

You will hear each recording twice. After each listening, you will have time to complete your answers.

| Task 1: Book reviews | (5) |
|---|---|

Preparation time: 40 seconds
You will hear the beginnings of five book reviews.
Choose from the list (A–G) which description best applies to which book review (1–5).
For each book review there is only one correct answer. There are two more descriptions than you need.

| | Description |
|---|---|
| A | Dealing with characters' secrets |
| B | Describing a character's dreams |
| C | Tracing a character's self-exploration |
| D | Inspired by very different historical events |
| E | Presenting the lives of prominent individuals |
| F | Telling the story of formerly overlooked people |
| G | Based on historical events and connected to current issues |

| Book review | 1 | 2 | 3 | 4 | 5 |
|---|---|---|---|---|---|
| Description | | | | | |

Preparation time: 1:30 minutes

You will hear a radio report about Lady Jean Trumpington (born Jean Campbell-Harris, 1922–2018, a British politician).

While listening, fill in the missing information. You need not write complete sentences. Unless otherwise specified, name one aspect.

| 1 | Why did Lady Trumpington's departure from politics attract so much attention? | |
|---|---|---|
| 2 | Why does the host of a TV show mention the invention of television? | |
| 3 | Which incident made Lady Trumpington widely known? | |
| 4 | What is said about her education? | |
| 5 | In which two different fields of work was she active during World War II? | • <br> • |
| 6 | Why did she return to Great Britain? | |
| 7 | What did she change in her life during her time in Cambridge? | |
| 8 | Why did she choose the title "Baroness Trumpington"? | |
| 9 | What was special about her holding her governmental position at the end of the 1980s? | |
| 10 | What did she do in Downing Street that helped her keep her position? | |
| 11 | What was her duty as Baroness in Waiting? | |

| 12 Which interest will she continue to pursue after retiring? | |
| --- | --- |

Now think of the text as a whole. Tick (✓) the correct answer (a, b or c). There is only one correct answer.

13 In the radio report, Lady Trumpington's personality is presented as being …

a ☐ charitable and caring.

b ☐ cautious and level-headed.

c ☐ self-confident and unconventional.

## Task 3: Sea otters (6)

Preparation time: 1:30 minutes
You will hear a radio report about research on sea otters in Canada.
While listening, tick (✓) the correct answer (a, b or c). There is only one correct answer.

1 The research focusses on the …

a ☐ effects of sea otter populations on the local economy.

b ☐ behavioural patterns of sea otters living close to humans.

c ☐ consequences of climate change for sea otter populations.

2 There was more seafood in the area after the Europeans had arrived because …

a ☐ sea otters were exterminated.

b ☐ Europeans relied mainly on farming.

c ☐ the native population was moved inland.

3 The scientists have chosen Vancouver Island for their research project because …

a ☐ university facilities are readily available.

b ☐ a particular species of sea otters lives there.

c ☐ the place is suitable for comparative field studies.

**4** The sea otters affect the ecosystem because …

   **a** ☐ they tend to destroy habitats of other species.

   **b** ☐ their feeding behaviour fosters the growth of fish.

   **c** ☐ they help to reduce the impact of invasive species.

**5** Ecologist Edward Gregr addresses the issue that …

   **a** ☐ visits to the area need to be regulated.

   **b** ☐ not everyone in the area profits in the same way.

   **c** ☐ too many sea otters threaten the fragile ecosystem.

**6** Native Canadians living in isolated communities perceive the growing population of sea otters as …

   **a** ☐ a potential threat.

   **b** ☐ a minor nuisance.

   **c** ☐ a welcome source of income.

*\* Der Prüfungsteil „Reading Comprehension" wird in Ihrem Abitur nicht abgeprüft und wurde deshalb hier weggelassen.*

| Text | Neighborhood

1   In Seattle, the neighbors don't want apartments for formerly homeless seniors nearby. In Los Angeles, they don't want more high-rises. In San Jose, Calif., they don't want tiny homes. In Phoenix, they don't want design that's not midcentury modern.

  Homeowners in each of these places share a common conviction: that owning a
5 parcel of land gives them a right to shape the world beyond its boundaries. The roots of this idea are as old as nuisance laws that have tried to limit how one property owner can harm another. Over the decades, though, homeowners have expanded their claim on the world beyond their lot lines. This means they look out for schools and streets in ways that are vital to American communities. But increasingly it also means the senior
10 affordable housing, the high-rises and the tiny homes – also arguably vital to the larger community – are never built.

  "One of the reasons why we always justified the mortgage interest deduction was we wanted people to be rooted in their communities," said Vicki Been, the faculty director of New York University's Furman Center and a former commissioner of
15 Housing Preservation and Development in New York City. The idea was for people to be invested in the quality of nearby schools, the safety of neighborhood parks and the outcomes of local elections. In one sense, the triumph of this idea should be celebrated, she said. But the danger of it is becoming more apparent, too. "Communities always need to be changing," she said, "and we can't have a process that gives every individual
20 sort of a veto over change."

  The new tax law has raised the possibility that homeownership may be losing some of its privileged status in American society, as the benefits of the mortgage interest and property tax deductions shrink. Those changes could dampen how attractive housing looks as an asset. But it would take much more to alter the belief that owning a home
25 in America today means that you effectively own a neighborhood, too.

  That notion didn't make much sense when most Americans lived on farms, where the neighbors were remote and the value of property came primarily from what happened on it. The boom in city living changed both of these things. "As people are increasingly living in urban areas really close to each other, it starts to be the case that
30 so much of the value of your property is bound up in things that are happening outside of your parcel," said Lee Fennell, a law professor at the University of Chicago who has written about what she calls the "unbounded" nature of our homes. In denser living, a trash dump or a park next door affects the value of your parcel. So does the access to jobs, the ease of transportation and the amenities nearby.

35   The story of how Americans came to peer beyond their own properties is also, inescapably, about race. As urbanization brought blacks and whites closer together,

white communities reacted with racially restrictive covenants, aiming to keep blacks and their perceived threat to property values out of white neighborhoods. The Supreme Court ruled such covenants unenforceable in 1948, but they had long-lasting effects on
40 how homeowners looked at the world around them, and the need to control it. "One of them was to make white people think that the value of their homes depended on living in a segregated community," said Carol Rose, a law professor at Yale. "That outlived racially restrictive covenants."

Another shift came with the advent of citywide zoning in New York City in 1916.
45 Nuisance laws had targeted problems like noxious odors or chemical spills that crept across property lines. Zoning, rather than punishing people for proven harms that came from their property, told people what they could do on their property in the first place. And it prohibited many things – like buildings of a certain height – that had never been considered nuisances before. Zoning effectively invited homeowners to look beyond
50 their properties in ways they hadn't. And it helped create the expectation that communities would change little over time – or that homeowners would have a say if they did. "Prior to zoning, you didn't ask yourself if you were buying a piece of property, 'What's the use of the land next to me, or down the block, or half a mile away?'" said William Fischel, an economist at Dartmouth. "Zoning becomes an opportunity for you
55 to think outside the box of the lot lines of your own property. And people definitely start doing it." […]

These forces amount to a powerful brew: Our homes have become our wealth. Racial fears linger even if they've become encoded in other language. Change invariably looks like a threat. And the universe of threats has broadened from the toxic spill to
60 the garden shadow, from the property next door to the potential development five blocks over. "We ask home equity to do so much more for us in terms of providing retirement, providing a bridge during drought years, allowing us to have collateral for other kinds of loans," said Nathan Connolly, a historian at Johns Hopkins University. "Then you add schools and crime into the mix." "To the extent that people can control
65 anything," he said of property values, "they try to control for that."

No wonder it has become so hard to untangle the benefits of community "ownership" from the rising harms. We want people to be invested in their neighborhoods, but not to the exclusion of anyone else who might live there, too. We want to empower neighbors to fight a trash dump, but not to halt every housing project the region needs.
70 "Who speaks for the community as a whole?" Ms. Been said. "I worry about that."

*958 words*

*Emily Badger, "How 'Not in My Backyard' Became 'Not in My Neighborhood'"*
New York Times, *January 3, 2018, accessed on October 15, 2021*

**Annotations**
line 12: mortgage interest deduction: *Zinsermäßigung auf einen Kredit für eine Immobilie*
line 24: asset: (here) sth of financial value, like property
line 46: zoning: the practice of defining areas of land to be used for a particular purpose
line 61: home equity: *(hier) Immobilienbesitz*

**1**   The author of the article mentions "the belief that owning a home in America today means that you effectively own a neighborhood, too." (ll. 24/25)

Briefly explain the quote in the context of the article and examine to what extent Walt Kowalski in *Gran Torino* can be said to embody this idea.

Choose *one* of the following:

**2a**  "Alienation is a form of living death."

© *Martin Luther King Jr.*

Assess to what extent this quote applies to Larry Ott in *Crooked Letter, Crooked Letter*.

**or**

**2b**  Interpret the cartoon and comment on its message.

Biden's big job

© *Theo Moudakis, https://www.thestar.com/opinion/editorial_cartoon/2021/01/21/ theo-moudakis-bidens-big-job.html*

## Lösungsvorschlag

 **TEIL I: LISTENING COMPREHENSION**

| **Transcript 1** | **Book reviews** |

1 **1** Welcome to Book Club and a novel that's set in the aftermath of the First World War but crackles with contemporary relevance. James Meek's novel *The People's Act of Love* is set in the wastes of Siberia in 1919. And in a way, it is a Russian novel, because its action springs from the turmoil of that country in its dark history.

5 **2** Hello and welcome to Book Club from Swansea. Sheers's book is a psychological thriller that mixes suspense – Michael, the central character, tries to conceal an awful event out of fear – with a story of the relationship between two men who both have something to hide.

**3** Hello. If you look at *The New York Times* for October 4th, 1951, you will see two
10 headlines jostling together on the front page, one reporting that "Giants win over the Brooklyn Dodgers in a famous baseball game", the other saying, "Soviets explode atomic bomb". Well, when Don DeLillo looked at those headlines in the early nineties, 40 years on, the prickle of excitement started him on a journey of the imagination that led to *Underworld*.

15 **4** Hello and welcome to Book Club and a biographical feast. We're talking this month about the story of two interlocked families, and at the head of them, the two most glamorous figures of the late Victorian stage, Sir Henry Irving and Ellen Terry. They're the joint subjects of one of our most admired literary biographers, Michael Holroyd, now in his eighties, who's our guest today.

20 **5** Hello and welcome to Book Club. This month's book is funny and breezy, but don't be misled by that. *Rachel's Holiday* is also a journey into darkness with Rachel discovering the depths of her drug addiction and its threat to her whole life. Her holiday is, in fact, a trip into rehab, away from the high life she's been enjoying in New York to a clinic in Dublin, the Cloisters, where she imagines that she'll get away from it all,
25 but instead discovers more about herself than she expected.

*based on: bbc.co.uk/sounds/play/m000dxtp; bbc.co.uk/sounds/play/m0007b4t;*
*bbc.co.uk/sounds/play/b07sxttn; bbc.co.uk/sounds/play/b072htqw; bbc.co.uk/sounds/play/m000fw1j*

> **TIPP**
>
> You do not have a lot of time to read through the task, so concentrate on high-lighting the keywords which sum up the main idea of each description. Also mark words you think are essential for comprehension. You will have a very short break before and in between sets to look them up, but do not overestimate the time frame. The listening comprehension in your exam takes its complexity not only

from the level of sophistication of the audio files, but also from the speed with which you have to solve the tasks.

- **1 – G:** The key phrases in the description are "historical events" as well as "connected to current issues" (= "contemporary relevance", l. 2), which is the main difference when compared to description **D**, which only speaks of "historical events". It also differs from **D** in that it does not deal with "very different historical events" but rather focuses on a specific historical period of a specific country.
- **2 – A:** The key word here is "secret", which is indirectly mentioned several times: The review talks about the protagonist "tr[ying]" to conceal" (l. 6) something and about two men "hav[ing] something to hide" (ll. 7/8).
- **3 – D:** The fact that the review talks about "headlines jostling" (l. 10) points towards "very different historical events", as mentioned in **D**. If you do not know the word "jostling", the headlines give you an even stronger clue: One is about a baseball game (cf. ll. 10/11), the other about the explosion of an atomic bomb (cf. ll. 11/12), which do not have anything in common.
- **4 – E:** Finding the correct solution can be tricky here, because you might mistake the word "interlocked" (l. 16) for "overlooked". In this case, you might be tempted to choose **F** ("story of [...] overlooked people") as an answer. It is, however, stated that the book deals with "the two most glamorous figures of the late Victorian stage" (ll. 16/17), which then leaves **E** ("prominent individuals") as the correct solution.
- **5 – C:** This review hints at the correct description quite often. It is about "self-exploration", which is expressed in phrases like "journey into darkness" (l. 21), with the protagonist "discovering the depths of her drug addiction" (ll. 21/22) and "discover[ing] more about herself than she expected" (l. 25).

| Book review | 1 | 2 | 3 | 4 | 5 |
|---|---|---|---|---|---|
| Description | G | A | D | E | C |

## Transcript 2    Baroness Trumpington

1  **Edward Stourton:** It should surely not come as a shock when a nonagenarian decides to retire. But Lady Trumpington's decision to leave the House of Lords when she reaches 95 this month made a splash. Perhaps that's because she's been part of the place for so long no one can quite imagine the scene without her.

5  **TV host:** It would be ungallant of me to tell you Her Ladyship's age. So let's just say she was born before this programme started. And before BBC One started. And before television started. Please welcome Baroness Trumpington.

**Stourton:** She began among pearls and ermine, and she's ending her long career in similar territory. On the way, she's lived our history and known most of the people who made it. But she only really became famous in her late eighties when she was caught by the cameras making a V-sign at one of her fellow peers, as the comedian Jack Whitehall reminded her on "Have I Got News for You?".

**Jack Whitehall:** Did you regret swearing at him or …?

**Baroness Trumpington:** No, because I regretted what he said, which was that people of my age were starting to look very, very, very old. Well, wouldn't you do that if you …?

**Jack Whitehall:** Yeah, I can see …

**Stourton:** Jean Campbell-Harris was born in 1922. Her father was a former major in the Bengal Lancers with the right connections. Her mother was the heir to a Chicago paint fortune. Her formal education was limited, as was often the way for women then. And she says she's never taken an exam. But finishing school in Paris gave her good French and German. The war began when she was 16.

**Old news report:** Down on the farm, the land girls are doing their bit and a bit more.

**Stourton:** Like thousands of other young women, Jean Campbell-Harris was sent to work as a land girl, filling the gap left when the countryside's young men went to fight. In 1940, she took her language skills to the secret codebreaking centre of Bletchley Park. She was a cipher clerk. Jean worked on Madison Avenue in the post-war Mad Men days, and it was in the United States that she met her very English husband, Alan Barker, a historian, then working at the Ivy League University, Yale. His career brought him back to a teaching post at Eton and then to the headmaster's job at the Leys, a private school in Cambridge. *[excerpt from song]* And it was during her years as a headmaster's wife that Jean Barker, as she then was, really turned her attention to politics.

**Georgina Morley:** She became a councillor in Cambridge and then ultimately mayor of Cambridge, and I think she rather loved being mayor.

**Stourton:** Cambridge local politics was a long way from life in Mayfair and Manhattan, and her early political career was hard graft. She tried and failed to become an MP. The political scene was dominated by another powerful woman, Margaret Thatcher. In 1980, Jean Barker was given a peerage by the new Tory government. She already had contacts in the House of Lords, including the Tory peer, Viscount Astor, whose mother had been Jean's friend and fellow clerk at Bletchley.

**Viscount Astor:** Jean took to the House of Lords like a duck to water, as it were, because she could actually kind of deflate someone who was being pompous, for example.

**Stourton:** There remained the little matter of deciding on a title. Her reputation for a robust speaking style was already established, so she rejected Baroness Barker. She explained her final decision to the prominent eighties Tory John Gummer, now Lord Deben.

**Lord Deben:** So, she said, "I had to choose the village nearest to me". And there were two possibilities. One was Trumpington and the other was Six Mile Bottom. She thought that was not a good idea. So, Trumpington it was.

**Stourton:** Lady Trumpington's husband Alan died after a stroke in 1988, leaving her a widow in her mid-sixties. She was serving as a minister of Agriculture at the time, the first ever woman minister there, and threw herself into her work. She survived at the ministry when John Major succeeded Margaret Thatcher until ...

55 **Georgina Morley:** At one point she was called into Downing Street. And John Major, it turned out, had decided that the time had come for her to retire from the front bench, and she was not expecting this. And she told me afterwards, shamelessly, that she cried. Whereupon the Prime Minister patted her on the shoulder and said, "There, there, all right then, well, never mind, we'll leave you as you are." So, she stayed

60 on.

**Stourton:** By 1992, she was the oldest ever serving woman minister, and during John Major's second term, she became a Baroness in Waiting, representing the Queen on formal occasions until the Tories lost power in 1997. Lady Trumpington isn't giving up all her passions. Her enthusiasm for horse racing, for example, is as fierce as

65 ever. But her son, Adam, says that by giving up the Lords, she's giving up more than a job.

**Adam Barker:** The Lords became her family.

*based on: bbc.co.uk/sounds/play/b098bqr1*

---

**TIPP**

This task requires an in-depth knowledge of vocabulary, the ability to distinguish between several native speakers talking, and the skill to understand various accents of British English. You also have to cope with inferior sound quality in bits of historic audio documents. However, do not worry too much, as you can rely on the order of the questions following the chronology of the recording and you mostly need to note down only one aspect out of several mentioned.

1 There are several reasons why "Lady Trumpington's decision to leave the House of Lords" (l. 2), or in other words "politics", attracted attention or "made a splash" (l. 3): "she's been part of the place for so long" (ll. 3/4), "no one can quite imagine the scene without her" (l. 4), and also "she reaches 95 this month" (ll. 2/3).

2 By mentioning the invention of television the host reveals Lady Trumpington's age in an indirect and humorous way ("It would be ungallant of me to tell you Her Ladyship's age." l. 5): "So let's just say she was born before this programme started. And before BBC One started. And before television started." (ll. 5–7)

3 You do not need to know that the "V-sign" is a rude gesture (when the palm is facing towards the person making the sign) – it is enough to recognise the host mentioning that "she only really became famous in her late eighties when she was caught by the cameras making a V-sign at one of her fellow peers" (ll. 10/11). In the next sentence it becomes clear that she was swearing at him (cf. l. 13).

4   The show continues with milestones in Baroness Trumpington's life. Be careful, however, because this task only asks for Trumpington's education. You only need to note down one aspect from lines 20 to 22: "formal education was limited [...] she's never taken an exam [...] finishing school in Paris [...] good French and German."

5   Listen closely here: The short clipping from a wartime news report serves as a distractor and the term "land girl(s)" (ll. 23, 25) is mentioned quite fast, meaning that she worked on a farm during the war. Her second job as a "cipher clerk" (l. 27) is not only hard to understand, but also no longer common and you need to know "clerk" as another word for "secretary" or "office worker". Bletchley Park was a facility of the British Intelligence Service to decode secret German messages in World War II. If you know that, you can also give "intelligence work" or "code breaking" as an answer.

6   Here, you need to deduct the answer from what is said about Trumpington's husband, whom she met in the United States (cf. ll. 28/29) and who was "a historian, then working at [...] Yale. His career brought him back to [...] Eton and then to [...] a private school in Cambridge" (ll. 29–31), so Jean Barker, as she was now called, became "a headmaster's wife" (l. 32) in England.

7   In order to answer this question correctly, you must not lose track of the audio. It ends with the story of Trumpington's husband who got a job in Cambridge. And here, the Baroness "turned her attention to politics" (l. 33) by becoming councillor and mayor (cf. l. 34) there.

8   Listen particularly closely after the key word "title" (l. 44). As Trumpington "rejected [the title of] Baroness Barker" (l. 45), she then "had to choose the village nearest to [her]" (l. 48) and as she refused to be called "Six Mile Bottom", she chose the other village called "Trumpington" (cf. ll. 49/50).

9   Pay attention when the year 1988 is mentioned (cf. l. 51), which points towards the question of "her governmental position at the end of the 1980s". The audio says that "[s]he was serving as a minister of Agriculture at the time, the first ever woman minister there" (ll. 52/53) and that she still was "at the ministry when John Major succeeded Margaret Thatcher" (l. 54).

10  Here, "Downing Street" is the key word. Pay attention to what Lady Trumpington did when she was asked to resign by John Major, then Prime Minister: "she cried" (ll. 57/58), which led to "the Prime Minister patt[ing] her on the shoulder" and leaving her in office (cf. ll. 58–60).

11  The moment the audio mentions "Baroness in Waiting" (l. 62), it is explained that she was "representing the Queen on formal occasions" (ll. 62/63).

12  This information is also given very fast and rather at the end of the audio when your concentration might be decreasing. It is stated that the Baroness has a passion for horse racing (cf. l. 64), so you can deduce that this is what she will continue to follow after retiring.

13  Here you need to understand the general character of Baroness Trumpington. By having a look at your answers in tasks 1 to 12, there is nothing that hints

towards "charitable and caring" (**a**). If that were the case, the audio would have given some examples. The same goes for "cautious and level-headed" (**b**). A person who became a politician without formal education (cf. ll. 20−22, 32−35), went to the United States on her own (cf. ll. 27/28), gave inappropriate hand signs towards a colleague (cf. ll. 10−16), and was still active in her 90s (cf. ll. 1−4) can be nothing other than "self-confident and unconventional" (**c**).

| 1 | Why did Lady Trumpington's departure from politics attract so much attention? | she had been there for so long / she retired at the age of 95 / hard to imagine House of Lords without her |
|---|---|---|
| 2 | Why does the host of a TV show mention the invention of television? | to show / allude to Lady Trumpington's (advanced) age / because Lady Trumpington had been born before TV was invented / to introduce a guest in a humorous way |
| 3 | Which incident made Lady Trumpington widely known? | making V-sign / swearing (at a fellow peer) / making a rude gesture |
| 4 | What is said about her education? | limited formal education / has never taken an exam / (went to) finishing school (in Paris) / (fairly) typical of women's education at the time / good command of German and French |
| 5 | In which two different fields of work was she active during World War II? | • farming / agriculture / (work as) land girl<br>• code breaking / intelligence / office-work / (work as) cipher clerk |
| 6 | Why did she return to Great Britain? | followed her (English) husband / because of her husband's job |
| 7 | What did she change in her life during her time in Cambridge? | started her political career / turned her attention to politics / became councillor / mayor |
| 8 | Why did she choose the title "Baroness Trumpington"? | (name of / refers to) nearest village / did not like other options (Barker / Six Mile Bottom) |
| 9 | What was special about her holding her governmental position at the end of the 1980s? | first (ever) female Minister at Agriculture / first (ever) woman holding that position / stayed in office when the Prime Minister changed |
| 10 | What did she do in Downing Street that helped her keep her position? | she cried / she made the Prime Minister feel sorry for her |

| | |
|---|---|
| **11** What was her duty as Baroness in Waiting? | representing the Queen on formal occasions |
| **12** Which interest will she continue to pursue after retiring? | horse racing |

**13** In the radio report, Lady Trumpington's personality is presented as being …

c ✓ self-confident and unconventional.

---

## Transcript 3   Sea otters

1 **Ari Shapiro** *(host)*: Let's talk about sea otters. They float on the water, cuddle their little babies. Same time, they're voracious eaters that gobble up shellfish. And that has brought them into conflict with people who rely on shellfish for their livelihoods. NPR's Nell Greenfieldboyce reports that scientists have now assessed the economic 5 impact of restoring sea otters to their historic homes.

**Nell Greenfieldboyce** *(byline)*: Sea otters are pretty big. They can weigh 60 pounds or more. To survive in the cold waters of the Northern Pacific, they need to eat a lot.

**Jane Watson:** And so a sea otter is going to eat about a quarter of its body mass, its body weight, in food each day.

10 **Greenfieldboyce:** Jane Watson is a researcher with Vancouver Island University in Canada. She says historically sea otters coexisted with Indigenous people. But when the Europeans arrived, hunters with the fur trade wiped the otters out.

**Watson:** All of a sudden, all of the prey that otters eat no longer had their principal predator eating them anymore.

15 **Greenfieldboyce:** Clams, crabs, sea urchins – their populations took off, and people got used to the abundance. Well, a few decades ago, sea otters were reintroduced to the west coast of Vancouver Island. Edward Gregr is an ecologist at the University of British Columbia. He says further down the coast from where the otters now live, there's another spot where the otters haven't yet moved in.

20 **Edward Gregr:** And so we thought, this is, you know, this is a perfect natural experiment to compare what the ecosystem looks like with and without sea otters.

**Greenfieldboyce:** In the journal *Science*, they say otters do eat up clams and crabs worth millions of dollars. They also devour sea urchins, and that allows kelp to flourish. The kelp supports fish species that are worth a lot of money. What's more, tourists 25 will pay to watch the otters frolic. Gregr says, all in all, the financial benefits of otters are more than seven times greater than the losses. But, he says...

**Gregr:** We want to make sure we don't lose sight of the caveats around that, mainly the fact that, you know, these costs and benefits are not going to be distributed equally across fisheries or communities.

30 **Greenfieldboyce:** Tourism, for example, isn't necessarily a realistic or attractive option for people who live in remote areas where access to food is a real issue. Barbara Wilson is a member of the Haida Nation who's studied Indigenous people's feelings about the sea otters.

**Barbara Wilson:** The impact for us is fairly critical.

35 **Greenfieldboyce:** She says Canadian law currently protects the otters. The otters have a right to eat, but so do people. Nell Greenfieldboyce, NPR News.

**TIPP**

This task can be difficult insofar as the vocabulary is rather sophisticated or technical and the correct answer is often hidden behind complex expressions. Take your time before the first listening round to look up keywords to which you should pay attention while listening to the text.

1 The scientists are doing research on the impact sea otters have on the local economy (cf. **a**): in lines 2 and 3 the host mentions "gobbl[ing] up shellfish [...] brought [the otters] into conflict with people who rely on shellfish for their livelihoods" and in lines 4 and 5 he says that "scientists have now assessed the economic impact of restoring sea otters to their historic homes".

2 The audio mentions that otters were "wiped out" (another word for being "exterminated", cf. **a**) by the Europeans (cf. l. 12). Next, the podcast explains that "all of the prey that otters eat no longer had their principal predator eating them anymore" (ll. 13/14), which eventually led to an "abundance" (l. 16) of seafood in the area.

3 A scientist explains why Vancouver Island is the perfect place for a "natural experiment to compare what the ecosystem looks like with and without sea otters" (ll. 20/21). A key word which helps you find the correct answer is "comparative" (cf. **c**), which is the adjective of the verb "compare" that is mentioned in the audio.

4 Here you need to find out that in places where there are sea otters the fish population increases. The following sentence explains why: "[The otters] also devour sea urchins, and that allows kelp to flourish. The kelp supports fish species that are worth a lot of money" (ll. 23/24), which means that "their feeding behaviour fosters the growth of fish" (**b**). The other options ("destroy habitats", **a**, and "help to reduce the impact of invasive species", **c**) are not mentioned in the text.

5 The solution can be found in lines 28 and 29: "these costs and benefits are not going to be distributed equally across fisheries or communities." A potential threat to the ecosystem (cf. **c**) is not mentioned in the audio and although one

might be tempted to tick **a** because of tourists visiting the area (cf. l. 25), this is not called an issue at all.

6 The correct solution lies in the quote by Barbara Wilson, who is a representative of the Haida and expresses "Indigenous people's feelings about the sea otters" (ll. 32/33). She explicitly states that "The impact [of the growing population of sea otters] for us is fairly critical" (l. 34). This is too severe a way of talking about that issue to call it "a minor nuisance" (**b**), while "a welcome source of income" (**c**) is not mentioned at all.

1 The research focusses on the …

  **a** ☑ effects of sea otter populations on the local economy.

2 There was more seafood in the area after the Europeans had arrived because …

  **a** ☑ sea otters were exterminated.

3 The scientists have chosen Vancouver Island for their research project because …

  **c** ☑ the place is suitable for comparative field studies.

4 The sea otters affect the ecosystem because …

  **b** ☑ their feeding behaviour fosters the growth of fish.

5 Ecologist Edward Gregr addresses the issue that …

  **b** ☑ not everyone in the area profits in the same way.

6 Native Canadians living in isolated communities perceive the growing population of sea otters as …

  **a** ☑ a potential threat.

| Teil III: Analysis

1

**TIPP**

Follow the task instructions when you structure your text. Start with an explanation of what the author means by "own[ing] a neighborhood". You should focus on both positive and negative consequences of this attitude, especially because in the second part of your answer, which will probably also be longer, you have to compare the article's definition of "own[ing] a neighborhood" with Walt's behaviour. Here, you could show how Walt develops from a xenophobic houseowner, who in some aspects perfectly embodies the negative attitude described in Badger's text, into the open-minded, responsible and ideal neighbour referred to at the end of the article. You need to give examples from the film to illustrate this development.

Structuring your text according to the steps mentioned above should make it easy for the reader to follow your line of thought. So, start new paragraphs whenever you introduce new aspects and end your answer with a conclusion that sums up your ideas.

You could include the following points in your answer:

**Part I:** explanation of the quote with regard to the article
- positive aspects of "own[ing] a neighborhood": feeling responsible for their neighbourhood can make homeowners invest in their local area (cf. ll. 12–17)
- negative aspects of "own[ing] a neighborhood": racism, exclusion of certain "unwanted" groups (cf. ll. 9–11, 35–43)

**Part II:** Walt's development in *Gran Torino*
- initially, embodiment of the negative attitude described in the article because of his ideal of a safe, clean neighbourhood and his xenophobic behaviour towards his Hmong neighbours
- Walt learns to appreciate his neighbours; his behaviour changes and he accepts the new diversity

**Conclusion:** Walt has left his negative attitude behind and has become the embodiment of the open-minded neighbour mentioned at the end of the article

In her article "How 'Not in My Backyard' Became 'Not in My Neighborhood'", published in *The New York Times* in January 2018, Emily Badger describes the fact that American homeowners feel increasingly entitled to have a say in how their neighbourhoods develop. She calls that attitude "the belief that owning a home in America

Part I: explanation of the quote with regard to the article

today means that you effectively own a neighborhood, too" (ll. 24/25).

Becoming truly a part of a neighbourhood can come with a certain feeling of responsibility for its wellbeing, which, according to Badger's article, is primarily a good thing. Responsible citizens want "their" neighbourhoods to be clean, safe and prosperous and so they will do their part to safeguard this development (cf. ll. 12–17).

positive aspects of "own[ing] a neighborhood"

However, the majority of Badger's article focuses on potential problems that can arise if this investment is too strong. She illustrates these by describing both the building projects, which meet with resistance from "dedicated" citizens (cf. ll. 9–11), and the resident groups who are not welcomed with open arms because they could reduce the value of an area. This is especially relevant when it comes to race because an exclusively White neighbourhood is often still associated with higher prestige than one that is ethnically diverse (cf. ll. 35–43). All in all, when diversity and change are seen as threatening while order and homogeneity are perceived as desirable, "community ownership" is bound to lead to behaviour marked by racism, exclusion and oppressive conformity.

negative aspects of "own[ing] a neighborhood"

This is also partly true for Walt Kowalski in *Gran Torino*. He lives in a Detroit neighbourhood that used to be homogenous, populated with White Americans who often worked in the car industry and spent their free time on their porches or in the backyards of their family homes, exactly like Walt himself. With the decline of the automotive industry, the social structure of his neighbourhood has changed. The houses have lost their value and many people from ethnic minorities have moved in while Walt's former neighbours have died or moved away. In a way, the situation in which Walt finds himself is one that is still only a potential threat for the White homeowners mentioned in Badger's article.

**Part II:** Walt's development in *Gran Torino*

At the beginning of the film, Walt obviously regrets this development. He dislikes his Asian neighbours and feels threatened by them. One reason for this is that they remind him of the enemy he fought against in the Korean war, but it is probably also true that Walt is simply bitter about the change. He mutters racial slurs whenever he sees one of his new neighbours and attributes the condition his formerly clean and tidy neighbourhood has fallen into to their alleged sloppiness. He also perceives the very real threat of youth gangs making the area an unsafe place. At the beginning of the film, his answer to this danger is to withdraw even further into his own property, which he is ready to protect at gunpoint if necessary. So, in a way, he could be seen as the perfect embodiment of the negative attitude Badger depicts in her article. Walt's ideal is an all-White, clean, safe neighbourhood. As he, unlike the White residents Badger

initially, Walt as an embodiment of the negative attitude described in the article describes, feels helpless to influence the ethnic make-up of his area, his racism and bitterness become all the more pronounced.

Nevertheless, Walt does not remain in a state of passive aggression. While his violent confrontations with the youth gang at first seem like vain attempts to restore order and to protect his own property against the hated Asians, his chauvinism turns into a much more positive sense of responsibility for his neighbours as soon as he gets to know them better. He slowly learns to accept the new diversity around him, enjoys the Hmong food when invited to the party at the Lors' house and starts to appreciate both Sue for her toughness and sense of humour and Thao for his often doomed efforts to find direction in life. So, when he protects Sue and her boyfriend from a gang assault and especially when he sacrifices himself for both siblings at the end of the film, this can be regarded as a real desire to make his neighbourhood a better and safer place instead of just an act of resistance against anything foreign. A very good symbol of this real desire for positive change is the way he deals with Thao. The tasks he sets him as punishment for the boy's attempt to steal his car turn from rather stupid menial work into necessary repairs to the houses around them. So, the initial grudge that Walt bears against his new neighbours just for being different turns into an attempt to teach them his ideals of honest, hard work, while at the same time also learning from them about opening up or accepting help from others, for instance.

Walt learns to appreciate his neighbours and his behaviour changes

The sense of owning your neighbourhood when you own a home has mainly negative connotations in Emily Badger's article. This matches Walt's initial attitude, especially in its racial undertones. However, in his development throughout the film, Walt turns into a more open-minded and responsible person who embodies the beneficial aspects of "community ownership". The way he "owns" his neighbourhood is no longer by selfishly protecting his own property. Instead, it is characterised by his supportive behaviour towards his neighbours and by their communal efforts to make their area a better place. Therefore, the end of the film shows that it is not homogeneity which makes a neighbourhood close and cohesive but rather a shared set of goals. *(924 words)*

Conclusion

2a **TIPP**

---

As the first step, you need to explain the quote, referring to both "alienation" and "living death". As this is a quote by Martin Luther King Jr., it could be a clever idea for a fitting introduction to allude briefly to the context of the Civil Rights Movement, which will probably provide the historical backdrop to the experience that the quote refers to so drastically. However, as you are to apply the quote to the fictional character of Larry Ott, you do not necessarily need the historical context. You could also just use a dictionary definition of "alienation" to explain its meaning and then show how the paradoxical formulation of "living death" expresses how bad life can be when you feel alienated: it is a life not worth living, a life in which you can feel like a zombie.

This could lead you to Larry's state, which is often compared to that of a monster or zombie. You can start by referring to the different areas in which Larry experiences alienation: he is rejected by his father as well as his peers and finally by the whole community in his home town. Here, you should give apt examples from the novel that illustrate Larry's experiences and show to what degree he is finally excluded from any kind of social life.

As the next step, you can describe why Larry's experience can be compared to the life of a zombie. He becomes resigned to complete solitude, and the only sign that he is still alive consists of his desperate need for human contact that even makes him crave the company of the sociopath Wallace Stringfellow. The zombie mask that plays a role at different points in the novel symbolises his state.

The word "assess" in the assignment also means that you do not have to agree wholeheartedly with the quote in that specific context. You could also take a more balanced view as to its applicability. For instance, you could use the end of the novel as evidence of the fact that the word "living" in the quote is very relevant too, because it provides some hopeful indication that Larry could overcome his isolation. That does not make the quote untrue, but shows its complexity. In contrast to real death, which Larry only thinks he suffers at Wallace's hands, the "living death" of alienation is not a point of no return.

One possible structure for your composition could be as follows:

**Introduction:** explanation of the quote

**Main part:** assessment of the applicability of the quote to Larry Ott's situation
- areas in which Larry experiences alienation:
  - his family
  - his peers, including his only friend Silas
  - the community of Chabot

- why Larry's experience can be compared to a "living death":
  - Larry is alive, but suffers immensely from his loneliness
  - the zombie mask as a symbol of Larry's form of "living death"
- **Conclusion:** optimistic outlook at the end of the novel

"Alienation is a form of living death." This quote by Martin Luther King Jr. inevitably evokes the context of the Civil Rights Movement and its activists' attempts to gain equal rights for everyone by law. What they fought against was widespread discrimination against Black Americans, one aspect of which was alienation. The dictionary defines "alienation" as the feeling of not being part of a society or group. Against the backdrop of the bitter experiences of African Americans who were excluded from many of the benefits of society, it becomes clear why Martin Luther King describes alienation so drastically as a form of living death. "Living death" is paradoxical – a contradiction in itself. The metaphor expresses that a life in alienation is not really worth living, but is instead a joyless and dark "half-life".

**Introduction:** explanation of the quote

Interestingly enough, it is the White character Larry Ott and not his Black counterpart Silas Jones who suffers most from alienation in the novel *Crooked Letter, Crooked Letter*. He is not discriminated against racially, at least not in a straightforward way. Instead, he is not accepted by others simply because he is different.

**Main part:** applicability of the quote to Larry Ott's situation

As a shy and physically weak child, he is exposed to his father's contempt, to whose ideal of a son he can never live up. What Carl Ott expects is a strong, healthy boy who is popular with his peers and interested in sports. His father's rejection makes Larry even more withdrawn and drives him into the arms of his overprotective mother. This, again, seems to confirm his father's picture of him as an effeminate weakling. He does not support Larry when he is growing up and excludes him from the male world around his garage.

areas in which Larry experiences alienation: Larry's family

Neither can Larry connect with his peers at school because he is shy and does not share their main interests. He withdraws into the books he reads and cannot keep up with his classmates physically, especially in sports. As a result, he is bullied from an early age, even though he desperately tries to belong. On one occasion, he insults a Black girl just to please his White classmates and ends up being excluded by everyone, White and Black children alike. The only relationship to a peer that could have developed into a friendship is thwarted by his own father, who forces Larry into a fight with Silas. This results in the end of the boys' friendship, a loss from which Larry will suffer for the rest of his life.

Larry's peers

His timidity and lack of support also make Larry the perfect victim for being falsely accused after Cindy Walker's disappearance. Everyone in the community believes that Larry has killed her and even though he is never formally charged, he is rejected by the whole village. When he returns to Chabot after his time in the military, hardly any customers come to the garage Larry has taken over from his father. In his private life, he is also completely isolated: he lives alone in his parents' house on the outskirts of the town with only his books and his mother's chickens for company. As people in the community nickname him "Scary Larry" and readily suspect him of whatever crime is happening in the area, he even stops going to church and avoids contact with the townspeople as much as possible. On a superficial level, Larry is of course still alive, with a job, a house and not too many financial worries. Yet he is socially dead. Due to the many rejections he has already suffered in his young life, he also seems to have lost the will to make any more fruitless efforts at connecting with others, and mutely accepts his loneliness. Nevertheless, he suffers immensely from his isolation. This becomes obvious in his desperate craving for a friend, which makes him fall quite easily for the sociopath Wallace Stringfellow without recognising the perverted nature of the younger man's interest in him. Only when it is almost too late does Larry finally admit to himself that Wallace is dangerous. However, even after being almost fatally attacked by Wallace, Larry seems rather relived to die and thus escape his utter loneliness.

> the community of Chabot

> why Larry's experience can be compared to a "living death": Larry suffers immensely from his loneliness

The kind of "social hibernation" Larry goes into after Cindy's disappearance and the ensuing ostracisation he experiences are perfectly symbolised by the zombie mask that plays an important role in the novel. Larry once wore it to a Halloween party in his youth and he still keeps it in his house as an adult. This can be attributed to the fact that that Halloween party was Larry's one brief experience of being admired and deemed cool by his peers, only to be rejected again afterwards. No wonder then that Larry's life in the zombie universe of his novels and his mask is almost more real to him than his actual existence.

> the zombie mask as a symbol of Larry's form of "living death"

Yet, ironically, it is also the mask (or rather Wallace Stringfellow who attacks Larry wearing it) which finally opens a passage to Larry's redemption from his "living death". When it becomes clear that it was Stringfellow who attacked Larry and murdered Tina Rutherford, Larry is finally vindicated. As a result, he manages to re-establish contact with Silas and there are small hopeful signs of them rekindling their friendship. So, in contrast to a real death, which the "zombie-like" Larry might even have considered a relief, his "living death" of alienation is not a point of no return. *(899 words)*

> **Conclusion:** optimistic outlook at the end of the novel

When you have to interpret a cartoon, you should always start with a description of its most important elements. However, as the description should not be overly long, leave out details that you do not want to refer to in your analysis afterwards. In this case, you could point out what the Statue of Liberty looks like and the way Joe Biden is depicted. You should also refer to the caption as well as to the thought bubble. The date of the cartoon's publication is also quite relevant, because in January 2021, Biden was inaugurated and was about to start the "big job" that is referred to in the caption.

In your analysis of the cartoon, you should further elaborate on the historical background: Biden took over the presidency from his predecessor Donald Trump, who had systematically tried to attack the political order. This is shown by the condition of the Statue of Liberty, which has been destroyed, but whose elements are still recognisable. You can give examples of how Trump attacked values that are symbolised by the statue, such as the welcoming attitude towards immigrants as well as basic civil rights for every citizen. This description helps to explain why it is such a "big job" for Biden to re-establish the former order. The cartoon makes it quite clear that this is an almost impossible task by depicting Biden as a rather small figure with a small bucket beside the huge debris of the monument.

You should then move on to a comment on the cartoon's message. In the solution suggested here, the sceptical stance of the cartoonist is repeated. Reference should be made to examples of how Biden tries to mend the broken pieces of the American political system. Point out his willingness, but also his realism ("This won't be easy"). Consequently, you can also mention how difficult or almost impossible it is to overcome the deep division in American society that is the main reason for the current mess it is in. A summary of your own opinion could also serve as a conclusion.

Your composition could consist of the following parts:

**Introduction:** short description of the cartoon and its main elements

**Analysis:** what the destruction of the Statue of Liberty and the figure of Joe Biden express
- Trump's attacks on the political system and traditional American values
- Biden's willingness when taking over his office from Trump, but also his realism as to his limited capacities

**Comment:** agreement with the cartoon's message
- Biden's willingness for change: examples of some of the first measures he took after coming into office
- difficulty of the task: the deep division of American society as the reason for its current flawed state

**Conclusion**

The cartoon from January 2021 – published around Joe Biden's inauguration as President of the United States – is captioned "Biden's big job". It shows the Statue of Liberty cut into pieces that are lying on the ground. Beside it, in the bottom left-hand corner of the cartoon, you can see Joe Biden with a bucket full of ready-mix cement in his right hand and a small trowel in his left. He seems to have taken on the task of trying to rebuild the statue. His thought bubble reveals his opinion that this will not prove easy.

**Introduction:** short description of the cartoon

Published at the beginning of 2021, the cartoon's reference is clear: Biden's predecessor Donald Trump has systematically attacked the values symbolised by the Statue of Liberty. Lady Liberty has always stood for the welcoming attitude of the USA towards immigrants, as expressed in the poem by Emma Lazarus engraved on its pedestal, which addresses the "tired, poor huddled masses yearning to be free". Trump's immigration restrictions for people from both Central America and Muslim countries clearly broke with this ideal. Furthermore, his attacks on the Black Lives Matter movement, his attempts to infringe on Black voting rights and his disrespect for the result of the presidential elections of 2020, which culminated in the attack on the Capitol in January 2021, all undermined the constitutional foundations and – as shown symbolically by the cartoon – seriously damaged the democratic institutions of the US.

**Analysis:** Trump's attacks on traditional American values

The traditional values of the constitution – life, liberty and the pursuit of happiness – still hold their appeal – Liberty's torch and her tablet are still recognisable – but they need to be re-integrated into a functioning political system. This is "Biden's big job". But how frail he looks in his suit beside the broken monument! The cartoonist seems to be wondering if this job is not in fact too big for Joe Biden. The small bucket in his hand does not contain enough cement to rebuild the statue, and he is obviously not strong enough to put all the broken pieces back in their original place. While Biden seems willing to take on the task, he also quite realistically admits to himself, as the thought bubble shows, that it will not be easy.

Biden's willingness, but also his realism regarding his limited capacities

I agree with the cartoon's message. Despite Biden's promises during his presidential campaign and at his inauguration, he does not have the power to re-unite the American people and be a president for all of them. He certainly tries hard, by addressing the concerns of those who are afraid of losing their position in society or their economic status, for instance. Biden's infrastructural package, for which he even got the support of some Republicans, might help create more jobs and win him back the support of some disappointed workers who previously voted for Trump. Furthermore, Biden tried to re-establish traditional American values, such as a welcoming attitude to immigrants, when he released a comprehensive immigration reform

**Comment:** agreement with the cartoon's message: Biden's willingness for change

plan and enabled the reunions of families that had been separated by Trump's executive orders.

However, as I see it, it will be impossible for him to win back those who are simply not interested in the re-establishment of a functional political system that gives a fair and equal chance to all members of society. While different people might have had different reasons for voting for Trump, they all put up with or even supported the ex-president's open disdain for the political institutions and traditional American values. They got used to or even applauded a discourse and rhetoric that was completely dominated by partisan politics and aimed more or less openly at dividing society into opposing groups. Balancing the interests of different groups and giving everyone the chance to share in what American society has to offer no longer seems to be a goal on some political agendas. Instead, the right to life, liberty and the pursuit of happiness is only conceded to those who are on the "right" side of the political spectrum. People in whose consciousness this attitude is deeply ingrained have no interest in rebuilding Lady Liberty, and they are the ones who will make it impossible for Biden to fulfil the task he has imposed on himself.

difficulty of the task: deep division of American society

As the cartoonist points out, despite all the goodwill of the new president and his administration, the deep division within American society and the increasing radicalisation of the American right in particular make it impossible to fix the political system. Even Trump was only a symptom and not the reason for this unstable situation. It needs more than one just president willing for reconciliation to make the United States of America deserve its reputation as a country in which Lady Liberty and what she stands for are truly honoured.

Conclusion

*(782 words)*

Um Ihnen die Prüfung 2023 schnellstmöglich zur Verfügung stellen zu können, bringen wir sie in digitaler Form heraus.

Sobald die Original-Hörverstehensaufgaben 2023 freigegeben sind, können Sie über die Plattform **MyStark** darauf zugreifen. Ihren persönlichen Zugangscode finden Sie auf der Umschlaginnenseite, vorne im Buch.

# Aktuelle Prüfung

**www.stark-verlag.de/mystark**